THE HISTORY
Volume One

GROWING UP THE HARD WAY
IN THE 1930's

Edited by
HAROLD GAUER

977.595
H693

Precision Process/Urge Press

This Volume Of The History
Is Dedicated To:

SYLVESTER W. SKADIETNDAPMN

Special Thanks is given to;

Dr. Arnoldi, Captain Applejack, Molly Bloom, Count Bruga, Philip Carey, Lady
Contance Chatterly, Stephen Dedalus, Duc Jean des Esseintes, Friederich
Freuhlighausen, Titus Groan, Frederic Havercamp, Jules Jerphanion, Felix Kennas-
ton, Daniel Morley, Dr. Ocatilla Nork, Winston Smith, Aimee Thanatogenos, George
Webber, and Finnley Wren

This Book Was Designed and Produced by
Tom Maurina

Copyright (c), 1989 by Harold Gauer
6040 North Apple Blossom Lane
Glendale, WI 53217
(414) 964 2716

This First Edition is published by
Precision Process In Cooperation with the Urge Press
In The United States of America

Library of Congress Catalog in Publication Data.

Gauer, Harold
The History, Volume One
Growing Up the Hard Way in the 1930s
165 Illustrations
I. Title
973.971 1989 89-61921
ISBN 1-877831-01-8

AUTHOR'S PRELIMINARY
And
First Person Foreword
To
VOLUME ONE

BRADY STREET

Ordinarily a History, even so informal a one as this, is set forth in the third person. In this context, actually, I am the third person, after William H. Williams and Robert A. Bloch. Between the three of us a long time ago we started *The History*, which was a third person narrative concerning our (to us) remarkable experiences in our post-high school days of the middle and late 1930s.

To set the scene, so to speak, I must take to the first person to account for my presence on Brady Street, to examine the pre-History years and get the flavor of the times, and to wallow in a nostalgic fit of yearning and remembering.

You can't go home again. Thomas Wolfe nailed that down back in 1934, using about 300,000 words to do it, as I recall. Everyone knows you can't. And in the case of BRADY STREET, the old stamping ground is in worse shape now, after all these years, than the Roman Pantheon.

The gutter strips of dirt between the sidewalks and curbs are now filled with concrete. That's where I found most of the butts for my cigar-band collection. The towering elm trees are gone, probably cut down years ago as a threat to the trollywires, and the backyards are all paved over with asphalt. Brady Street is now a dry gulch of shops, a cement arroyo lined with a facade of shabby store-fronts, most of them still with living quarters in back or on the second floor. There are no kids to be seen.

Time has destroyed many things, but it has not taken away the old building that housed the candy store and The Lab. It still stands. Although Schowalter's Drug Store, a block away at Humboldt burned down in a big fire a long time ago, it is still possible to view the building across the street where Tommy Dawson's School Store used to be. That was where I bought all my crayons and watercolor paints for school. My Vireo tablets and ruled note paper, my mucilage and gumballs.

Tommy Dawson, an Englishman with the heavy body and simple features of Babe Ruth, catered to the every need of young innocents. He stocked just about everything necessary to life; penny candy, pea-shooters, mesh bags of mibs, petsy tops, sun pictures, skin decals, dime novels in the Frank and Dick Merriwell series at two for a quarter (and sexy magazines like Pep Stories and Spicy Western).

He had firecrackers in season, punk, invisible ink, cap pistols and strips of caps, Indian beads, baseball gum with picture cards, any kind of rubber ball, diabolos and yoyos, balsa wood aircraft, flying tin propellors, pen knives, kite makings including sticks, tissue paper and balls of string, pressed pulp novelties for all holidays, and every trick, puzzle and novelty known to man.

The place is now occupied as a shoe repair shop and katy corner across the street is St. Hedwig's Church, in the steeple of which bells sounded the quarter hours of my life, with a special bonging for funerals, holy days and Sundays. The massive iron fence that protected its skirt of grass is gone and the lawn strips are covered with a deposit of concrete left behind by a departed glacier.

From that corner, at Humboldt, Brady Street dips modestly for a block down to Franklin Place. The old firehouse, minus its tower in which hoses hung to dry remains, though the firemen don't sit out on the ramp any more in captain's chairs whistling at the girls.

The enormous horse chestnut tree that towered over Baumann's Grocery Store just off Brady Street at Franklin Place isn't there now, and just as old man Baumann is gone, so is the gutter strip in which we juveniles pitched horseshoes - with shoes of different sizes and shapes from actual horses. The tin smith's on the northeast corner is vacated in favor of an army-navy surplus mart filled with olive drab dry goods and rubber boots.

Further along eastward is the old candy store locale on the north side of the street and next to it is a tavern in a sturdy brick and stone structure (Frankie Parker, the famous tennis player, used to live upstairs). Then a narrow lot and Suminski's Funeral Parlor, a shoe store - you went up four stone steps to get into that one - Mazurek's Drug Store and soda fountain, the Great Atlantic & Pacific Tea Store, and Ross's hardware store with two wrought-iron steps in front. They even sold separate roller skate wheels there at 15 cents each, and those very useful little cans of red enamel paint. Window putty came out of a barrel and you took a gob of it home in a fold of newspaper. The buildings all seem to be there today, just the contents are different.

The south side of the same block started with Jazdjewski's Savings & Loan at Franklin Place, then a brick commercial building, supplanting a wooden one once occupied by Reiselbach's Dry Goods Emporium. Almost exactly across the street from Vernie's Home Made Candy shop was a yard and private residence with a front porch and further east, Lerner's Fruit Market with the stuff in crates all over and the spoiled stuff in cans at the curb. There are more residences between there and what was another grocery store on the corner at Arlington (formerly Sobieski street).

North of there and around behind Brady Street, Pulaski Street slanted off of Arlington in a northwesterly direction. The Milwaukee River was not far away and it was only three blocks from Arlington & Brady to the bluffs of the Lake Michigan shoreline.

Many of the Brady Street area settlers were of Polish origin and came from the "old country". They were called "Kaszubas" and were from Putsigk, a fishing village on the island of Anova in the Baltic Sea. Some of the residences were "A" addresses, that is, a house behind a house on the same lot, renting for $25 or $30 a month. Along the back of the first house were usually garbage cans, tilting in the mud, and an ashbox half-full of a damp brown ash from a coke stove. A withered old lady in a black babushka might come off the back stoop into what I remember as a Monday-dark, gloomy, laundry-soapy, naphtha-ish cold rain with a newspaper full of coffee grounds and moldy breadcrusts. She would leave it among the battered tin cans and broken catsup bottles stinking against the wet, splitting boards. There would be matted gobs of paper and string in there with a broken broom with blackened straws, a twisted umbrella frame and a smashed shopping basket. A broken coaster wagon with rusted and tireless wheels foundered in the ashes.

In the house behind the house - maybe the areaway and approach to the wooden stoop at the side were paved with old cream city brick and flanked by unpainted fence boards - a man might be sitting at an oilcloth covered kitchen table, suspenders over white underwear, drinking coffee or smoking his pipe, staring out the streaked window. In any weather there always seemed to be an odor of cooking cabbage in the air, mingled with the nutty smell of urine-soaked baby diapers, laced with an acrid, sulphurous over-smell of burning soft coal and rotted pine kindling.

Similar living accomodations lined Humboldt Avenue north of Brady street as it went downhill across the river valley of bridges and railroad crossings and uphill toward North Avenue. The latter half-circled Reservoir Park - there was actually a big pond of emergency-storage water in the scooped-out crater of the big earthen mound - came down past Humboldt eastward and ended up at the old water tower mounted on the bluff overlooking the lakeshore.

A child has the time to examine his intimate surroundings without value judgements, and I think I viewed basement windows with a neutral naivete, and stored the impressions that now come back to me on my mental computer as a calm acceptance of mediocrity.

The basement window remembered has a crushed newspaper stuffed into a triangle where the glass was broken out. Next to it, rain water gushed out of rusted holes in a drainpipe and into the window well, which was filled with wind-blown trash. It was set part-way below ground level, but allowing light to come into the basement, a clammy redoubt filled with wooden boxes packed with broken toys, worn shoe brushes, discarded work trousers, bottles, jars, lids, pipes, iron parts and blue - rusted copper fittings.

Since there was no upstairs toilet there was a board privy enclosing a messy, stained bowl with a tank and pullchain from which water trickled constantly.

The odor of decayed wood, mildew and sour earth had settled over the rickety wooden steps lined with scrub pails, black, shriveled gobs of rag, slivers of brown fels-naphtha soap caked with soot, a sour mop stuffed in the jaws of a metal squeezer. Mop strands caught under the nail heads of the stair. A single 25-watt bulb, naked near the coal bin, supplied a death cell glimmer. The cat desposited its excrement in the coal pile, and men-folk probably peed right

there as well, adding to the miasma. Spider webs dangled and the water meter ticked dolorously.

It was not quite like that when the Gauer family lived on Franklin Place and Papa was working and Brady Street was only three blocks away and the wonderful drug store at Franklin and Ogden Avenue only a block away, Bobby Burns statue and Dog's Park with its great, high-squirting water fountain and Juneau Park overlooking the lake only two and three blocks further on. The streets were spread with hot tar and scattered with sand. That incredibly evocative stench allows only the most ecstatic sensation of joy to filter through and I therefore have no pity or sorrow or despair to contribute to the memory of childhood.

I could lay under the front stoop watching ants, sit in the doorway during a summer rain whittling on a broom handle, throw snowballs with sopping wet mittens, and go on long six - block hikes for "thornies" and horse chestnuts. It wasn't until I learned to read and to use value judgements that childhood fled.

I saw the kid on the billboard holding a candle, with a tire over his shoulder and accepted it as part of the scenery until I realized it said ITS TIME TO RETIRE and that it was an advertisement for Fisk Tires - and I got the pun - by that time it was all over and I could never go back ...

THE CANDY STORE

Papa was Roundhouse Foreman of the C&NW Railroad at the Chase Avenue yards. The soot-blackened brick buildings were filled with roaring cast-iron monsters spread-eagled over pits where men banged with hammers, let go with jets of steam, made an inferno of flying sparks, hot grease, and sizzling metal. They hauled boilers overhead on chain hoists and fitted steel rims heated white hot to drive wheels of locomotives.

It was a magical place to experience the terrifying thrill of being taken into the cab of a chuffing switch engine for a rumble out onto the turntable, with probably some extra whistling clouds of steam courtesy of the wonderful man in the striped engineer's jacket with matching beaky cap.

Railroading was the life and it would be tragic to lose the prestige and the free passes for travel and all that, but Papa wanted to quit. His gall bladder was killing him. And Mama was talking about starting a Mom & Pop store on Brady Street. There was the example of our uncle, Gus Crongluski, a "fathead" according to Papa, who got rich simply by sitting in a candy store on Third Street. If we all pitched in, Norman and me included, Mama declared, we could be rich also.

A machinist's strike was called. There was union trouble. Papa set up an office in a caboose in the yards. Mama came with potted flowers to plant in its window boxes. I sniffed the odor of cedarwood shavings from the hand-sharpened pencils on Papa's oaken rolltop desk, yellow with old varnish.

There was some violence. Papa got beaned by one of the strikers. When he came home with a cross-patch of tape on his brow, Mama screamed and made the kind of frightful fuss that convinced me, and my brother, Norman, too, that the end of life as we had known it was at hand.

Why it didn't start Norman and me on a lifetime career of bed-wetting, I don't know.

Maybe family life hadn't turned out to be all that Papa expected of it. Maybe he wanted to quit the whole game, not just railroading, and abandon us! Maybe. But if he did, he lacked the resolve - or the conscience, perhaps - to break his bonds and so he was trapped ...

I was about eight years old and Norman was six. Warren G. Harding was elected President, to Papa's dismay. We waited to see if the Republicans would lead us straight to hell before going ahead with plans for a candy store on Brady Street. But go ahead we did.

Uncle Gus provided some financing, Papa quit the railroad, and we rented part of a vacant building owned by Jazdjewski's Savings & Loan Association. (To my ear, the name was pronounced "Yah-jesky".) Ours, like most of the commercial stores on Brady Street, was a converted residence, and was entered, like most of them by three wooden steps. The display window was hewn from what was formerly the bay window of the living room.

**Vernie and John Gauer with their sons, Harold and Norman
on the bluff overlooking Juneau Park in 1917**

Mama (Vernie), who had spent years, off and on, helping her brother, Gus, in his store on Third Street, knew all about dressing the display window, setting out fancy candy boxes and glass-stoppered hard candy jars. Uncle Gus was on hand a lot to provide hints about suppliers and middlemen and to provide technical assistence in setting up the candy kitchen.

Mama soon became known as Mrs. Vernie, the Candy Lady. Unfortunately, Papa was kind of out of it, working behind the scenes more or less under Mama's direction, and he was pretty unhappy with that. He was a skilled mechanic and held managerial sway over an important industrial segment of the economy, and now he was rowing, so to speak, with his oars out of the water. We lived in the flat upstairs, with the store directly below. We could hear burglars better that way, Mama said, with the kind of tortured logic that, I think, tended to drive Papa out of his skull.

Mr. Jazdjewski came from across the street and signed up Papa to be a member of the Brady Street Advancement Association. On Sundays Papa could take Norman and me in our Graham Paige touring car to a public park to watch our baseball team play class AAA in the muny league. I was an admirer of one Luke Warzala, home run hitting idol of the Brady Street gang, and now I would be attending as one of the sponsors!

The marble slab came, a stupendously heavy table top of polished stone, which was set on trestles in the back room. There was a huge double boiler vat made of copper for melting chocolate, big, round-bottomed cauldrons set over gas burners for boiling up batches of ingredients, and a commercial, bakery size oven.

We began to use the room as a combination dining, living and working area. The stout wooden boxes in which slab chocolate came became stacked shelving, decently screened with a hanging dish towel, to contain pots, pans and housekeeping necessities. Indeed, up-ended wooden packing crates were just right as chairs around the slab when we were busy and had our meals there.

In the back hall next to a barrel of corn syrup (religiously kept covered on pain of a severe bawling out) lay Norman's and my recreational gear - several baseball bats, a number of hairless and black tennis balls, an indoor baseball pounded soft and podgy with its outseam re-stiched with sewing thread, a regulation baseball with a winding of black electrician's tape replacing the knocked-off horsehide cover, hard as flint, and three fielder's gloves of leather with all the padding pushed into the fingers and none in the palms...

Plus two sets of roller skates, two hockey sticks for sidewalk hockey, and in the winter, galoshes and rubbers, clamp-to-the-foot ice skates with supplementary straps, and, I believe, for a good long while there was also a doughy pancake of a catcher's mitt, whitely mildewed, when we were small enough to use the narrow areaway between the buildings for fast-pitch practice.

Sugar, the principal ingredient in candy making in addition to the corn syrup, came in 100-pound bags from the A&P store, lugged by sled or coaster wagon and stored in a bright galvanized ash can under the backroom counter.

We were in business, Papa abandoned his ironic pretense that he would have to get a pushcart and sell vegetables on the street.. To him it was irony. To me it was an appalling possibility. Sarcasm went right over my head. I am sure we had a reasonably good relationship because we went to the Washington Park Zoo and watched fireworks from the lakefront and visited Soldier's Home and heard the band play Tango Tzigane in the Lake Park pavilion and we went blueberry picking by taking the train to Wyeville and Papa brought chocolate eclairs and creampuffs home from Weber's... but I can not remember any specific one-on-one encounter with Papa that involved warm emotion. Maybe none was called for.

We were open for business from nine in the morning (although hardly anyone came in before noon) until eleven at night. Mama was back and forth with Uncle Gus with this problem and that, and he was around a lot in an advisory capacity. He and Papa didn't get along very well, but Gus Crongluski's contributions to our welfare were considerable in time and money and Mama would not hear a word against him.

After a few indecisive store-keeping years, Papa died. Norman and I were with Papa upstairs in the flat, gathered around the dining room table. We had a one-tube radio tuned to station KDKA in Pittsburgh, listening to the Dempsey-Sharkey fight. Each of us had a set of earphones, all connected to the primitive tuner in a clutter of wires, Burgess dry batteries and clamps.

The first round was just starting when Papa ran out of cigarets. His complexion varied from yellowish to a high pink and he was beginning to have black-outs, but he kept right on smoking with a grim distaste.

He dug a quarter out of his shiny serge vest and gave it to me. "Run quick down to the drugstore, Harold, and get me two packs of 'humps'." Camel cigarets. I didn't know why he always had it in for me and favored Norman. I respected him, even liked him. But he didn't know everything. I had seen him in a lot of mistakes. Even the way he got mad all the time showed he had problems.

"Hurry up!" he cried, "nothing's going to happen for a while yet!"
How did he know that Dempsey wouldn't clout this guy a good one early in the second round? The tears started, judgement fled and my resentment flamed. I wrenched away from the table, forgetting to take my earphones off first.

Before I knew it, I had dragged the radio and batteries to the floor, the pointed tip of our tube broke off, everything went dead and the future turned black.

Papa's reaction was immediate. He turned purple with rage and I must have been stricken by the disaster to a sniveling white mess. He did not glare at me directly, nor look at Norman either, for his eyes stared unseeing as he evidently became conscious of an even greater outrage taking place within.

His hands clenched and unclenched with the effort to squeeze down a volcanic eruption of temper, but I believe something had already broken inside him. His face crumpled with a sob of defeat and despair and he pitched sideways, stiffly, and hit the floor head first. He lay there inert, helpless, with the wrecked radio set around him.

* * *

There was an extra paper hawked on the streets that evening, but I did not see it. I had to look it up later. Dempsey kayoed Sharkey in seven, Yankee Stadium, July 21st, 1927.

After that I watched the store. The alarm clock kept ticking on a shelf in the back room. Almost every night I stayed there alone, sitting on an up-ended chocolate crate, my elbows on the cool of the marble slab, staring at nothing, listening to the alarmed beating of my heart and the frightfully loud ticking of the alarm clock.

John N. Gauer
In His Masonic Parade Uniform

Mama was at the hospital and would bring back no hopeful sign or omen, saying only that the medical bills would finish us. After two weeks, Papa died.

I had killed my own father.

The aching dread of the bad news, the days of agonized anticipation of death made it almost anticlimactic. I actually felt a sense of relief, clouded, of course, with a numbing doubt about the next day's dawning.

Uncle Gus did not become a surrogate father or anything, but we saw a lot more of him after that and life played the first of its many dirty tricks on me by making me a little too young to drive his Franklin. He gave me a couple of lessons with the old automobile, but I just

10

didn't have it. The gear shift was not like that on other cars. First gear was lower right, second was upper left and high was lower left. Reverse was upper right. There was some struggle and a few grinding clanks involved but most importantly you had to race the motor to proper speed or it would stall.

A few jolting stalls proved I was hopeless and the lessons ceased. Otherwise I might have qualified as one of the youngest rum-runners on the east side. Uncle Gus fell - or was pushed - into moonshining, no doubt by economic necessity. He got there by way of the potato chip business, an off-shoot of candy-making. It looked like a dangerous game to me, although I guessed it was popular enough. Scarface Al Capone, for instance, was temporarily in prison in Philadelphia for carrying a pistol, but he'd soon beat that rap, and besides, much closer, in Chicago, his gang of hoodlums was running illegal beer in trucks with tarpaulins flapping and federal agents were splitting the kegs with axes and shooting holes in them with bullets. I knew, I had seen it all on Pathe Newsreel at the Astor Theatre, the beer squirting all over.

From what I could make of our moral code, it was not the punishment for wrong-doing that was so bad, it was the shame and disgrace of getting caught. Snitching something was one thing, getting nailed for it, quite another. It was the same thing with girls, I was beginning to suspect.

Like that Mary Cadjadge around the corner on Arlington Place, the one that had the baby, the crying and running to church and all, whether she died or not I never heard ...

The potato chip factory was out on Clinton Street in part of what once was an endless row of buildings constructed of cream city brick on the near south side housing the Allis Chalmers Manufacturing plant. There was no light in the cavernous interiors except that which came through the sooty floor to ceiling windows. Uncle Gus had four dark-skinned youths working there and two white truck drivers. I got a small weekly wage, which, I guess, was charity from Uncle Gus to Mama. Norman and I also went up north with him in a borrowed truck to buy potatos grown in the sandy soil of Waupaca County.

There were other factories all around us blasting industrial dirt into the air, which tended to overwhelm the stench of fermenting potato mash and the distilling of ethyl alcohol, but there was no sense teasing the sniffers of blue noses and federal agents with telltale wafts of moonshine stink, and for a while Uncle Gus had some guys ... there were a lot of rough looking characters moving in and out as the bootlegging became more widespread ... some guys digging a trench and laying ventilator pipe right into the stack of a smelting and drop forge operation between us and the Menomonee River. They quick took it out again one dark and stormy night. I don't know why.

I don't know why we heard rumors either, that some entrepreneurial chaps in the hardware store had been tunneling under Brady Street to a gas main and were using free gas obtained by that unlikely black and midnite stealth. I think Uncle Gus pulled my leg a lot, but then, that's how legends get established and history gets corrupted.

We drifted on the bosom of the years into a kind of double jeopardy represented by both the Prohibition Era and the Great Depression. The potato chip business-turned-bootlegging soon folded under its own weight and Uncle Gus's dilatory sales and distribution system. The candy store survived. Until beer came back, Mama and Mr. Jazdjewski from across the street made near-beer in the kitchen sink, there was accordion music and polka dancing in the basement on Saturday nights, Norman and I had the run of the building from attic to basement. We snitched nickels and dimes from the penny candy till for anything we wanted and were envied throughout the neighborhood for living in a candy store.

* * *

THE ELEMENTARY SCHOOL ON CASS STREET

It would be nice to exist as a juvenile forever, free to do anything, go anywhere, with a vision of life that had no forward movement in time nor any end in sight . . .

One could anticipate a care-free day at McKinley Beach, or a pick-up game of rock-bowling in the street on Franklin Place, or maybe some games in the dirt yard along side of and behind the funeral parlor. Perhaps a roller skating hike to the edge of town at Capitol Drive. Or a long walk downtown to the public museum and a stop at Hampel's Bookstore to buy a 10 cent packet of assorted stamps for my collection. Norman and I could drag our coaster wagon, which was fitted with four upright sticks and a sheet of burlap over them to resemble a conestoga wagon, to the East Side Public Library for a load of books about the Bob's Hill Boys in Vermont, boy scouts in the Dismal Swamp, Poppy Ott and the Perigreen Pickles, or the Tin Woodman of Oz.

School would start, of course. Something as natural and recurring as the seasons, part of an ordered universe without anxiety, surprise. or crisis. I would not want to be late for school any more than I would want to kill myself. Nobody ever skipped school altogether that I knew of. My ambition was to arrive on time and keep out of dirt until after the clean-hands inspection. I had little trouble with the English language, elementary arithmetic and history were easily handled, and it was a cinch to loaf over an art pad copying a sprig of lilac stuck in a jar on the teacher's desk, using a black tin box of water color and a little brass pan for water.

Problems of filth or insurgency were those that the Principal, Mr. Boyce, dealt with. He comes back to me as a tall, black-haired hulk featuring a teardrop sculpturing of the belly with enormous feet and bony knees. Yet his face, with silver rimmed eyeglasses and a thin slice of nose over flat, thin lips, was almost saintly with its delicately tormented smile.

He thrashed recalcitrants with hands like canoe paddles and he also dished out discipline by grasping his victim from behind by the collar. Then he propelled him along the hall with a kneeing action to the cloakroom for a few swats on the behind and some loud instruction in proper deportment. He would occasionally dart into the lavatory, pluck out an evil-doer and knee-kick him into the detention ward for processing.

Offenses were of two kinds - masturbation and heating the wall thermometer with a match flame until it popped. Retribution for either was of about the same severity.

Cass Street School, Thos. Boyce, Principal
Carolyn Gardner, Teacher
(H. Gauer 3rd to Miss Gardner's left)

Cass Street School lay on an ethnic frontier between the Polish neighborhood and the Italian one west and south of Brady Street. Most of the kids of Polish extraction went to St. Hedwig's School and Cass Street School was heavily patronized by Italian kids. The latter, if Italian was spoken at home, often had to translate their learning from English to Italian before they could properly absorb it. That gave kids like myself an advantage in the teacher's pet department, and if our clothes were a little better and our temperaments a little less fiery, as in the eraser-throwing game, we moved easily to the heads of our classes.

RAINY DAYS IN THE BASEMENT

The hours out of school were easily filled with roller skating, petsy top contests, mibs-playing around a circle drawn in the dirt, ball games in the street, and if nothing else just hopping up and down and yelling. If the weather turned bad, one could always go down into the basement and pound on a work bench, "making things". It was a place to go and sulk after a severe reprimand. It was a natural retreat on a rainy day in which to make something useful from an apple crate or to take apart something that was no good anyhow.

I liked to experiment making electromagnets with old dry cell batteries salvaged from the smoking dump and landfill on the lakefront. I found some great test tubes at the dump. I threw away the pledgets of stained cotton in the necks and washed out the nasty stuff in them, and added the lot to my Chemcraft Set of fine chemicals. I still have a nifty glass graduate with markings etched on the side that my friend, Elmer Anderson found there. We used it all through the candy making years ...

There were never any tools in the basement worth a damn. Usually a rusted crosscut saw with some teeth missing and the remaining ones not very sharp. An ancient hatchet, used as a hammer, with a dull, chipped cutting edge, its handle held in with innumerable pounded-over nails. There was the inevitable hand drill with gears that slipped when the going got tough, and an all-purpose bit permanently clenched in its jaws.

The boy scout knife was O.K. cutting wood away from your hand, but it took a lot of bleeding to learn not to strain the blade toward you. When your hand slipped and gave a cut to your very dirty fingers the brownish syrup would well out, but it was worth the risk in order to dominate the obdurate wood.
    A screwdriver, twisted too desperately, slid from its slot and plunged into fresh young skin. A nail, struck awry, collapsed, letting a thumb take the hammer blow. Almost any tool could make a blood blister and usually did. A saw, taking its last bite from a board, not infrequently also took a bite of pants fabric in the thigh area.

Screws were simply the wrong size for the job. The head of a used screw was always damaged to start with, could be screwed into the job only about halfway, maximum, and there it stuck, refusing to go further or to screw out either. Finally, it twisted off in the hole and that was that!

To pound a nail into wood was to split the wood and nails driven into the edge of wood always followed the cockeyed grain and came out the side. Applecrate wood never split straight down - it split crooked. Nails never went in cleanly all the way, they bent over on the second to last hammer hit.

No amount of pounding would make the bent over part really flat, and no amount of digging would get it out again, either.

The workshop supply shelves consisted of the gifts of ancestors who saved things. They bequeathed to the dim place a Prince Albert tobacco can full of bolts, some with nuts, some without, all the wrong size for anything.

Here was a cardboard Quaker Oats box (with the bottom coming unglued) of assorted only mildly bent nails and tacks, and a metal box full of washers and cotterkeys. Surely there was some bright vision of the day this stuff would be used to build or fix something. Now, with the dream unrealized, it was still here with other hoardings of the past, such as ...

Half-pint paint and enamel cans slobbered on the outside with dried-out stuff inside, cigar boxes full of dirt, sawdust and roodled screws. Wooden cheese boxes storing sink faucets, pipe couplings, radio tubes, broken pocket-knife blades, flashlight cases. Old wheels, curtain rods, broom handles. An ancient stone grinding wheel, lopsided and grooved. Electrical outlet boxes, coils of wire with rotting insulation, copper toilet bowl floats with green patina. Unlabeled bottles of mystery fluid.

This would be the place to make a sidewalk scooter. A length of two-by-four was brought in along with a fruit crate salvaged from the corner grocery, and a single roller skate.

The idea was to nail the crate to the end of the two-by-four. Two of the largest nails would be selected from the Prince Albert Memorial Collection and the hammer applied briskly, using the basement floor as an anvil. If the crate wood did not split, the two-by-four wouldn't and the deed was done.

The roller skate could be disassembled, front trucks from back, and nailed to the bottom ends of the two-by-four with spikes. The skate heel socket could not be removed, so it had to lap the back end. A fabulous number of nails of all varieties studded the result.

A tin can from the ashbox made a "headlight". (Sure, with a lighted candle in it for night driving!) And a couple of sticks made handlebars.

The vehicle was propelled by standing on the floorboard with one foot and prodding the sidewalk with the other, with an upward jerk of the entire contraption at each division in the sidewalk, since the small wheels would catch on anything and send you flying. Fleets of such unmuffled boomers were dragged up out of basements all over the east side I knew, and the noise was something to hear as herds of drivers gimped down sidewalks or thundered with both feet aboard down hills like the one past St. Hedwig's toward the firehouse, all of them transfixed with the joy of making that much racket.

If there was anything the youth of the day liked better than making a racket it was making a stink. My inspiration came from my Chemcraft #5 chemistry set. I augmented the innocuous salts and reagents that were in the little round boxes and tiny bottles of the chemistry set. Sterner stuff was available at Drake's Drug Supply on North Water Street and by mail from Eimer & Amend in New York City. One essential was sulphuric acid, with which to make the good old rotten egg smell, and Potassium Chlorate, with which to make things that exploded.

At the public library I found that by mixing ordinary household ammonia with a water solution of iodine I could filter out a brownish precipitate of nitrogen oxide - a compound so unstable (after it dried) that it would explode in a purple smoke if a bug crawled on it. I would carry these and other secrets into the attic laboratory in later years, which became the hub for our fabled "History".

One thing I cannot understand, after all these years, is how, with the fantastic number of nails of all sizes hammered around and through the half-roller skate into the two-by-four, it still fell off the back of the scooter! You would think that would be impossible!

The kid designed and built his own vehicle.

BESIDE LAKE MICHIGAN'S WATERS

The lake beaches in summertime, when the livin' was easy, attracted foot travelers of all ages, who came by the hundreds every day to run and scream on the sandy shores. "Decoration Day" was when the bathhouse opened, when school was out, and when the season started.

On the east side of town a ritual hike began toward McKinley Beach and on the south side they trended to South Shore Beach and to the parks on the bluffs overlooking the expanse of blue water.

It was really the only game in town, since bathing in the Milwaukee River above the dam near Humboldt Avenue was no longer very attractive by the late 1930s. For one thing, the river water was too tepid, which only emphasized the dirtiness of it. There was no bottom or at best a squashy mud, and no place to sit except on wet planking. At Bechstein's there was always somebody shouting not to get too near the current going over the dam. One could not be in the water or standing around in the shade all the time and have any fun.

They came in great tribes to the lakefront, across the Holton Street viaduct, from the Italian enclave of the "third ward", from a broad section of the area around Brady Street within hailing distance of the water. They funneled down Ogden Avenue, down Brady Street, down Kane and LaFayette Places, the younger ones barefoot, some of the older girls carrying baskets.

The great hegira was joined by others who came by way of the number 15 Oakland/ Delaware streetcar line and the number 10 Wells Street line - and in parental automobiles with all the religious fervor of a children's crusade.

The lake bluffs were aromatic with blossoming bridal wreath where pilgrims might pause to drink in the grand panorama of the lake's bright pageantry of sailboats and the two beaches swarming with people.

Bradford Beach, the lesser of the two, had no facilities but was close enough to be reached by walking from the McKinley Beach bathhouse. If there was any problem in this recreational program it was frequently the chilling temperature of the water. It was always colder on the Bradford Beach side because it was not protected by the government pier. It was, however, cleaner, for the same reason, and featured speckled black and white stones, like bird eggs, smoothly rounded, and flotillas of shore birds bobbing on the swells just before they crested and broke. . .

A towel with a bathing suit wrapped in it was all the gear necessary. Life could be sustained with two hot dogs flooded with yellow mustard and one bottle of grape pop. Once in the cool shelter of the public bathhouse with its wet cement floor streaked with sand and reeking of perspiration, clothing could be almost furtively stripped off in full view of one's

**The Morgan sisters with the Gauer brothers
sporting the latest in swimwear at McKinley Beach
circa 1920**

peers and a one-piece woolen suit jerked on. A wire basket with rolled-up belongings was given to an attendant and a brass disc with a number stamped in it, with a safety pin through the hole, was one's identification tag. The checking was free.

Bathing suits could be rented at the McKinley bath-house, but no one could ever understand how anyone poor enough to be without a suit could afford the extravagance of renting one. They were a hideous washed-out navy blue with white numerals on front

Sunbathers arriving at the beach in their disc-wheel Jewett Touring Car The lady in the rear is Mammy Gauer. 1926

and back and they hung to the shoulders by skinny straps, like baggy summer underwear.

In order to get out, one had to dash through a stinging icewater shower squirting horizontally from both sides across the exit, thence onto burning sand, over which the customers hot footed like fakirs over coals, to the wet velvet of a wave swabbed, gently sloping strand edged with a suds-like foam.

The water was pellucid enough. One could see minnows swimming there in casually attended schools, colored stones and snails, even an occasional crayfish scooting backward across the bottom, wavering refractively in a dappled sundance.

The first few feet out were deceptively warm. Beyond that it was numbing cold. It was a long way though the knee deep ice water to belly depth. Then came a gasp making insane flop, full length, for total immersion! It was O.K. to splash any of the hang-backs whose suits were still dry. An

Cousin Dorothy Koch with the Gauer Bros. at the South Shore Yacht Club just after World War I.

irresistible urge to urinate followed - a secret sin lost in the immensity of water, noise and people, discharged with a most casual guilt.

After a thoroughly chilling romp in the frigid liquid and a few accidental gulps of the raw stuff it was time to charge out and sit shivering grimly on the beach. Some youths seemed to turn a bright blue at that stage. Damp bottoms were ground into the abrasive sand and the celebrants sat with jaws firmly set against chattering, their eyes glazed in stupor until the chill passed. Then they would race back into the water again!

Only the little kids, probably guided by mommie and daddie, used water wings, which were white cloth bladders blown up like balloons. An inflated inner tube was an even dumber idea, but not so·sissy as waterwings. Coming by automobile offered several advantages not the least of which was the good old picnic basket, extra towels, play equipment, and a bypass of the bathhouse routine. The change in and out of bathing suits could be made in the back seat in transit. It was, however, thought to be somehow immoral, and executed with furtive haste.

Few hardy souls passed up the ritual barefoot ramble out to the end of the U.S. Government breakwater at McKinley Beach.

A sandy road led from the bathing area close by the Milwaukee Yacht Club slip to the foot of the concrete pier. An odor of dead fish was pungent there, site of the little store that sold minnows for bait, lines, sinkers and hooks, and rented buckets and bamboo poles. Fishermen did not like to spoil the fishing by dumping their minnows in the water, so they saved them until they got to shore and gave them the heave-ho there, giving rise to the ever-present stench.

The south side of the cement wall, lined with people jiggling poles over the swell, was a sheer drop to a ledge almost at water level. It was the calmer side. The north side slanted to a similar ledge taking the brunt of dashing waves that sent droplets spattering to the top. Even on calm days the dark water bulged up and down ominously and a kid with slippery bottom sandals could easily slide down the incline to his death. So it was best to go barefoot.

The closer one got to the end of the pier the more dangerous the idea became. The waves were more vigorous, the wind blew harder. Big yachts and tugs came through the gap where the water looked frighteningly, endlessly deep. At that point it seemed like an awfully good time to start the long walk back.

It wasn't quite the same at South Shore Beach because the breakwater there consisted of a long pile of heaped stones that you couldn't walk on. People in the Bay View area behind it tended to be older, more mature folk who came by car, sat on the sand on blankets with baskets of plums and bananas under parasols and watched the goings on at the South Shore Yacht Club. It was a place more for swimmers and divers than for kickers and splashers since the bottom shelved off quickly into deep water.

The net effect of a visit to the shore was a pretty fierce sunburn, particularly among the young fry. Little white blisters speckling the untouchable crimson skin were evidently caused by droplets of water acting as tiny lenses. Burns to the top of one's feet made the wearing of shoes an excruciation, and sand in the shoes was blister-making, even for those effete ones who affected socks.

20

It was back to the bathhouse again to dry off with a sandy towel, thrust blue, clammy buttocks into street clothes and return to base, starting with a scramble across the C&NW railroad tracks and up through the bushes to the top of the bluff at the foot of LaFayette Place. Then it was down the elm arched splendor of Prospect Avenue to Brady Street.

The late afternoon sun was a bright orange torch blazing straight into one's eyes with headache-making intensity. The Homeward Bounders finally realized how tired they were. Norman and I would throw our wet suits in the bathtub, responded to cries from Mama and revised that so they were hung on an attic clothesline, and we took a new lease on life when we sniffed the aroma of frying potatoes and round steak down there in the candy kitchen.

We were careful to put some Benetol on the cuts on our feet because we remembered it was "lockjaw" that killed President Coolidge's son - we read about it in the Hearst newspaper Sunday supplement pages. Supper was fetched by Mama on the marble slab. We had brought lilacs swiped from the park for a center piece and to convince Mama that her dutiful and devoted sons did think of her from time to time. She might bring out an enormous angel food cake thickly frosted with caramel icing and an extra cupful of frosting for smearing on the sides of each slice.

Then we dashed outside again, leaving Mama to do the dishes and keep the store open until bedtime. Thoughtfully, we left by the rear door and not through the candy store, so the odor of cooking would not drift out through the curtained doorway and possibly give a chance customer the wrong idea.

I wonder now, what Mama thought about. Alone in the kitchen, conscious of growing older, surely weary of heart, as the darkness of another day closed in. With so little to show for it. Perhaps she would sniff the flowers and sit, as she so often did, swaying gently back and forth on an upended chocolate crate, hands folded in her lap, waiting.

Did she dream of days gone by?

How quickly one's yearning for the past changes to a desire to change the past - to somehow make amends or to be a different kind of person, armed with all the accumulated hindsight of the years since! But the regret remains. Poignantly.

* * *

THE SIDEWALKS WERE STAINED BLOOD RED

The gutters of Brady Street, on the Fourth of July, looked like a ticker-tape parade had passed through, for they were inches deep in a confetti of exploded paper bits, the remnants of firecrackers that began booming early in the morning and continued to go off until well after dark.

Garbage cans hung blown open at the seams after five inch salutes had blasted their lids onto the house tops. Animals were in hiding. The sidewalks were stained blood red. Muck was blownout of the sewers. Windows were broken, property damaged and commerce disrupted. Norman and I were out on the street shortly after dawn letting off bombs in an hysteria of delight.

Our crimes were many: we had not only shattered Mr. Jazdjewski's store window, but had rent the canvas of his awning with lesser fireworks, burst his ashcans with bombs split his downspouts, crazed the glass of the basement windows in the house we rented from him, and shattered the tile street numbers attached to the front of our building - known crimes - and had perpetrated other outrages he never got to know about.

One of the latter was the rocket-in-the-attic caper, which was Norman's idea. It used solid fuel - an idea they picked up later in the space program - namely firecracker powder stuffed into the barrel of a fountain pen, mounted on a toy fire-truck. The attic, a great tent-like structure of bare boards stretching the length of the building, was the testing ground. We wanted to see that little vehicle scoot!

Ignition and blast-off were faultless. It squirted fire and accelerated rapidly, belching smoke behind. But then, guided by the maladroit hand of a mixed-up fire god (who saw to it that we did not ever burn the house down) it swerved in several directions and then shot smash-damn through the lower panes of seven storm windows stacked against the far wall! There it exploded, knocking out three upper panes ...

When the smoke and horrid sound of broken glass abated I searched Norman's forehead for shards of Bakelite or window glass sticking out of it, but the fire god had spared us once again. Mama came running from downstairs. To keep Mr. Jazdjewski from finding out she had to pay for reglazing the storms with money from our slender hoard in the candy store.

Tommy Dawson laid in a special section of fireworks in the rear of his store near the delicatessen department. Their packets of brilliant red and yellow glossy paper bore attractive pictures of dragons, coiled snakes and Chinese idols, a feast for the eye and smelling heavily of gunpowder, glue, and boiled ham.

Norman, ready to shoot up Brady Street on a glorious Fourth of July.

Sample packs, torn open, revealed neat rows of firecrackers in splendid array, their fuses lined up and joined in a center pleat. In the basement our friend and mentor usually laid in a secret cache of illegal 5-inch salutes at three for a quarter. Unlike the flashcracker's many-layered roll of thin colored paper with the ends crimped, the Giant Cracker was a hard, thick tube of heavy cardboard, solid as stone, bearing a formidable, erect, wrapped-powder fuse.

Norman and I were privy to this subterranean treasure and allowed to descend the dark stairway at will on exhibiting our "two-bitses". We considered it a fair arrangement to buy three and steal three -- fifty-fifty.

In possession of these during the several days before the actual Fourth of July, it was our good fortune to discover, behind our landlord's Savings & Loan establishment, a wooden boat containing freshly-mixed lime plaster for use in rehabing a storeroom.

Three five inchers blew almost half the boatload of plaster all over the brick courtyard, over the firehouse adjacent and onto our clothing and skin. Dr. Hardy had to be called to treat us for lime burns, but it was nothing compared to the frightening rage exhibited by our long-suffering landlord when he rushed out to collar us and fell down in the stuff!

If we had a problem it was with the tale of Idzy Rutkowski, an immigrant youth on the south side who set dynamite bombs against the post office and the police station. While the desperate search for him was at its height he blew himself and the garage in which he made the bombs into unrecognizable bits.

We could not abide anyone who would corrupt gunpowder and dynamite to such non-fun purposes.

While girls, dogs, cops and parents went into hiding, we tried to keep the explosions going. It made sense to slip the bangers down rain gutters, behind bills posted on telephone poles, into drains, pipe openings, and every slot and crevice. Firecrackers into the sewer did not work because water extinguished the fuse. For sewer work the thing was the 2-incher.

These went off with a fine deep-in-the-bowels grunt and a fine "schtoomp!" from the dank hole in the street. The group kneeling in the gutter could easily catch a faceful of gelid charcoal-colored goosh from a well-timed drop.

It was Norman's idea to throw a half-can of calcium carbide down there. Carbide, mostly for fueling bicycle lamps, could be purchased at Ross' hardware store for a quarter. After a good long wait for the acetylene gas to accumulate, Norman threw in ignition. We got an earthquake that probably set the seismographs in Tokyo to flailing at their drums. We hopped up and down and ran stooped over with the rapture of it!

The sidewalk in front of Suminski's Funeral Parlor turned red all over because the Suminski kids had a son-of-a-gun fixation and were whirling like dervishes out there all day. Son-of-a-guns were red phosphorus patties that snapped, crackled and banged when scratched on a hard surface. They gave off a rich, if poisonous smoke: they left behind an indelible red stain when ground under heel on the sidewalk, delivering gratifying waves of shock all the way to the grinder's jawbone.

The pavement remained stained for weeks afterward, a happy reminder of 1776. Barney and I assisted in this worthy enterprise, but our scientists discovered that the best way to achieve maximum benefits was to set them on the streetcar track. There was a terrific report and blazing bits and pieces went blasting and scattering all over.

They also researched the silvery magnesium powder of flashcrackers and released a finding saying it could be detonated by percussion - by hitting it. (This was an important break-through that made our "Big One" possible.) It likewise led to experimentation in the manufacture of Giant Crackers. If a little powder made a big bang, we reasoned, a lot of powder ought to deliver an enormous wallop, so we rolled a lot of powder into big tubes of cardboard in the hope of creating ordnance that would split off a piece of the earth's crust. The idea was a complete failure, all flash and no bang and I believe we were lucky there was a limit to that kind of thinking.

Others, less prudent, stuffed flashcracker powder into sections of lead pipe, getting no doubt a few grains in the threads and when they screwed the cap on they blew their heads off. It was a simple law of physics, you just don't scrape a percussive substance with metal.

By midday of the fourth, all of the kids and the adults of juvenile mentality were out shooting fireworks, among the latter the much-envied Georgie Bucholtz, the Brady Street butcher. He appeared in front of his shop with a kitchen chair and a huge carton of explosives. His swarthy, genial muzzle was fitted with a shredding cigar smoked down to sub-butt size. He held it in his teeth by drawing back his lips in a gargoyle like grimace and lit firecrackers with it. He accumulated a huge spit that way, which he aimed in the general direction of the gutter.

Georgie did not dispense much of his hoard to the kids because they would have taken the packets apart and shot them off one by one, whereas Georgie wanted to see them hurled into the street as a unit for Chinese-style lickety-split and we could not deny the splendor of the act. The resulting smoke was like an aromatic fog risen from a magic bog in broad daylight when it rolled westward toward the old firehouse on the corner.

Toward day's end Georgie was about through splitting the ambience and the younger kids were already scavenging his duds, which they broke open and lit as "squibblers". Norman and I retired to the attic to get ready for our "Big One" as night came on.

The mason jar - a quart size - contained all the red phosphorus and Chlorate of Potassium we could afford to buy at a downtown wholesale drug outlet and it was nearly full. It had been mixed wet with rubbing alcohol, to prevent premature detonation, and was by then perfectly dry as it hung reeled out the attic window on the end of a fishpole. Three stories below, it would land on the cement-paved areaway between the candy store and blank brick wall of the tavern next door, just a few feet in from the street.

Norman hung out the front attic window with a pea whistle. When he saw that the vicinity was clear of people and cars, more or less, he was to blow the whistle and I was to cut the string for the Big Drop.

Georgie had gone back into his shop and locked up. Most of the populace was gathering in Juneau Park for the public display of aerial works. The street was fairly deserted except for an excited clot of kids across the street and more than a half block away, who stood expectantly with hands clapped to their ears. This was a well if furtively advertised event in the juvenile community. The whistle blew. The bomb dropped.

It was more than we had any right to expect, a blooie of unimagined proportions. In volume alone the sound exceeded anything we had ever heard, a great, intimate, blossoming boom, like Krakatoa blowing its stack in 1883, followed by echoing reverberations. Something like a seven point five on the Richter scale. Later, we found only specks of glass, so finely was the container atomized.

Even more awesome was the bloom of light that rekindled the bright of day, and then in the suddenly pale glimmer of the street lights there emerged a rolling, bulging cloud of poisonous smoke floating horizontally, as in the atrocity at Ypres in World War One.

Subsequent phenomena were the brittle sounds of plate glass sliding and breaking on cement. Evidently the areaway served as a kind of sounding board to concentrate the shockwaves. Our landlord's store window had caved in. So had the one in the tavern next door and a number of smaller stained glass ones in the funeral parlor!

Our gratification at having achieved the greatest and most gorgeous ba-room in all history quickly soured to a kind of nausea up there in the dark of the attic. A big piece of glass hung suspended in Mr. Jazdejewski's window and did so until all other sounds had ceased. Then it let go with a crash and an obbligato of tinkles.

We got the distinct impression that the neighborhood had collapsed inward on itself. I joined Norman in deep apprehension, trembling, my tender years having held no experience to defend against this moment, this criminal disaster, and I knew I was going to bawl. It was too much for Norman also. He threw up.

There was a visit from the juvenile authorities, who were utterly unable to devise a rationale from what they could see and what they were told. There was an interview with Mr. Jazdjewski and maternal sobs from Mama followed by due process. It would never happen again.

The city fathers would see to that. It was the last fireworks Fourth. An ordinance appeared on the books that same year, banning everything but sparklers and punk.

It was the last Big One. We had killed a national holiday!

The small family-operated retail establishment was an important part of neighborhood living and family life in the days that used to be. Life moved at a predictable pace even without the supermarket, the self-service gasoline station or the shopping mall.

The price of most things was widely known or could be easily determined. Anyone who thought they knew how to buy at wholesale and sell at retail could be a local merchant. Bank interest stood at 3%, compounded semi-annually. Reliable clerks could be hired simply by putting a help wanted sign in the store window. Faithful and loyal service was insured by a pervading work ethic.

In their formative years the chain store had women behind counters fetching groceries for the customers, cutting fresh butter out of tubs into paper boats, and weighing out a pound of something just like in the small family stores.

They put your Eight O'Clock or your Bokar or your Red Circle coffee beans in the electric grinder - the Eight O'Clock brand at the National Tea Store was the cheapest, at three pounds for a dollar - and tied a string around the packages just like in any other retail store.

Baumann's Grocery Store was typical. Mr. Baumann had a stalk of bananas hanging in the rear in a cloud of fruit flies, slowly turning from a light green to a speckled purple. A huge boiled ham lay on a greasy cutting board with a slicing knife next to it, waiting for an errand-running child to present some coins so old George could try his none too steady hand at cutting off some.

He maintained a bank of glassine-topped cookie boxes in a slanted rack with such favorites as Almond Shorts, Twilight Desserts, fig bars and pfeffernuesse visible within. Breakfast cereal boxes were on the topmost shelves, hooked down, sometimes onto his noggin, with a tongs on a long handle. Baumann's was open by seven in the morning and hardly ever closed before nine at night.

The neighborhood butcher shop had a fresh supply of sawdust on the floor every day, strings of kielbasa hanging in the window with matching strips of spiraling brown paper coated with fly tanglefoot and the bodies of dead flies. In the fall there might be rows of wooden barrels out front, hung with the unskinned carcasses of rabbits. During the hunting season a deer corpse was hanging by its hind legs from a hook in front of the shop - a trophy to be displayed for a few days before being taken inside for butchering.

Pickled pigsfeet and sulze were dispensed from jars. Brains and sweetbreads lay on open trays, and lovers of fine home made chile could get all the tripes they needed there. Free liver for the cat was unstintingly available to regular customers, as was suet for those who would render their own lard.

One could buy a goose for its enlarged liver and a regular one for, among other things, the lard, which, salted and spread on rye bread was considered something of a delicacy. Live ducks were in demand for holiday season blood-letting in local basements.

A Polish favorite, Charnina, was made of duck soup with a lot of duck blood added, plenty of duck meat, vinegar, prunes, and a special dumpling for each bowlful, made separately. The vinegar was to keep the blood from clotting ...

Vernie's Home Made Candy Store was Mom & Pop all the way, and we paid cash for our ingredients. Filberts came at 36 cents a pound came from the jobber, Rahtjen, Truss & Heider, pecan halves were 43 cents. A 50-pound burlap bag of shelled peanuts billed out at $7.50, less 2% for cash. A 100-pound sack of cane sugar from the A&P was $2.25 in 1939.

Two quarts of regular cream from the Blochowiak Dairy were required for caramel-making. The bill for that was 50 cents. Five thousand crinkle-paper bonbon cups cost $1.50 from the H.C. Schrank Company. The fancy heart shaped Valentine's Day candy boxes cost 45 cents wholesale. Local swains often not only paid $5 for the box full of assorted chocolates, but supplied engagement rings or other specials to be tucked among the nested bon bons, maple nut cremes and salted raisin clusters.

We used Eline chocolate and switched to Ambrosia later, but during the time of the Volstead Act when breweries were beerless, the Schlitz Brewing Company, operated by the Uihlein people, used the name Eline on the milk chocolate they manufactured meanwhile, at from $11 to $15 a hundredweight.

The corner drug store, with its soda fountain, was perhaps less Mom & Pop in character but it offered personal service on a face-to-face, proprietor-to-customer basis. I have intimate memories of Schowalters on Brady and Humboldt, Mazurek's at Brady and Arlington, Smith & Webers at Brady and Farwell, the Sanders Brothers one on Franklin and Ogden, and the Bellview Pharmacy at Bellview and Downer Avenue.

They had what we needed - besides the swoon-making chocolate malted milks - Nujol and Benetol and Tonsilene (our preferred laxative, antiseptic and cough medicine, respectively) and more old-fashioned places sold Dr. Robert's Udder Balm (with soothing lanolin) and No-Kik teat salve. For personal daintiness in the cow department, a gallon of Genito-Wash was a popular selling item. The drug store was the only place to buy boxed pink or blue writing paper with fancy envelopes, a bottle of india ink, pure ethyl alcohol without a prescription, a Wellsbach mantle for a gaslight fixture, a rubber bathing cap, a hairnet, or a pair of water wings. I had my first taste of a beverage called Green River in one of those places.

The odor of a drug store was unique, inescapable and remains stored in memory forever. When a little leaks out, the old days come wafting back. You brought your best girl in for a strawberry ice cream soda served in a special glass that inserted into a pewter holder and to consume those you sat very ceremonially at one of the round iron-legged tables set out between the pharmaceuticals and the hot water bottle display.

A tear moistens the eye.

Before the refrigerator, there was the ice box, which was okay, but someone had to keep re-stocking it with ice. That was supplied from a horse-drawn wagon going past on the street. The driver would know when another chunk was needed when he saw a sign in the living room window with "25" on one end and "50" on the other.

The average household ice box held a 50-pound block of ice on a corrugated zinc tray in one of the compartments. Three other doors opened on modest cooling areas. The clop of hooves on cobblestones slowed and ceased when the iceman cast an iron weight on a tether to curbside - a "horse anchor" - and hopped out. With tongs he seized a big block of ice and dragged it from under the protective canvas in back. It was clearly divided into four 25-pound sections slightly melted together. He hacked it apart with a murderous-looking ice pick drawn from a holster, slivers flying.

Hoisting a piece to his shoulder where he had a little pad, he trudged up the stairs and into the back hall, or onto the rear vestibule to deliver his burden. He might have to remove a small remaining glacier of old ice and perhaps a jar of pickalilly relish snuggled next to it, which was replaced after he put the new ice in.

On the floor underneath was a dishpan to catch the melt. Heaven help the kid who forgot his ironclad assignment to empty it when he was supposed to.

Meanwhile the youths outside on the street were climbing up in the wagon to steal shards of sucking ice. It was potable enough, having been sawn out of a clear inland lake and preserved by the Random Lake Ice & Coal Company. Parents cautioned against the practice - the horse might get fractious and they might get hurt - but the kids never paid any attention to that.

The taverns usually needed several hundred pounds of ice, for truly Olympian ice boxes full of bottled beer.

The other end of the ice business was the coal business. Soot begrimed, gnome-like men lugged canvas baskets of coal over lawns and into areaways to basement windows into which they poked metal chutes. The coal thundered into the basement coal pile. It was shoveled from there by the householder into the furnace by muscle power unless he had a hopper with a worm gear arrangement that fed pea coal into it.

Kindling was boxcar bracing and the remains of shipping crates or some otherwise useless wood, and was stored under the basement stairs. A brick ashpit was nearby where hot clinkers were doused with water, giving off the doleful smell of a crematorium. A hatchet and chopping block were handy, but hardly equal to the task of breaking up the twisted and terribly hard scraps. If you wanted to heat the house, first you had to start a fire with newspaper and kindling and then skillfully add coal in a way that would not douse the fire again.

The Horse Trough was provided as a public service around town, along with a "bubbler" from which kids could drink

Youths assigned to the task had to understand the art of grate shaking as well. There was a lever on the furnace one jerked back and forth to dislodge caked ash and keep the blaze going briskly. Ash removal, from a door that opened lower down on furnace than the fire door, was on the back breaking side.

If there wasn't an ashpit in the basement, the assignee had to lug ashcans full of it outside.

All kinds of self-employed tradesmen and colorful vendors were around all the time creating a ruckus and yelling in the backyards and alleys. Tattered fellows with burlap sacks came along to enter into lively deals with those who sold their worn out clothing or newspapers for a potential fifteen cents. Trash men had wagons into which they pitched their booty - maybe a mattress, a bedspring or some pieces of pipe. If not a wagon, a pushcart, maybe with a nifty yellow umbrella over it. How, otherwise, would anybody get rid of things like that? There would be no place to throw it - certainly not out on the sidewalk.

We used to visit a big dump that was always burning, when they were filling in at the lakefront, but that was to bring good things back, not to get rid of anything.

Scissors-sharpeners came along pedalling carts with a clanging bell and a whirling sandstone wheel on which to sharpen knives right there in the street. Old Munta showed up spring and fall with his horse drawn rig. In fall it was to take down window screens, get the storm windows out of the basement, wash and dry them on both sides, lug them up a ladder, and hang them, for I don't remember how much, but surely a most modest fee.

Fruit vendors parked on the side streets with loads of produce from Commision Row down on Broadway and set up an insistent yammer and cries of "waddi-melones". They let down the sideboards on their wagons, loaded them with seasonal merchandise as the hausfraus strolled out with net bags and straw baskets. The fruits and vegetables were weighed on a scale pan hanging from the buckboard. Most customers knew precisely how much the prices undercut Lerner's Fruit Market on Brady Street and bought accordingly.

Hot liquid tar was squirted on the side streets.. It came from a thickly caked, black-clotted horse-drawn tank wagon with a crosspipe full of vent holes across the rear end. Workmen expertly swished shovels full of coarse sand over the pungent black stuff. Kids ran joyfully behind in bare feet.

The same juvenile tribe, with the same ecstatic devotion, followed the city's gutter-watering wagon, running after it through the wet street smell, reveling in the cool squirt that was carrying the horse apples, cigar butts and other detritus into sewer gratings.

As spectacle in the street maintenace game it was the steamroller that got the prize. The front wheel was a big drum filled with water for extra squashing power and two very large rear wheels tracked a path on either side of the front roller. Escaping steam whooshed from the contraption at various points as it rumbled ponderously over fresh-laid "ashfault".

The idea was to lay various objects in its path and then to wonder with juvenile naivete at the impossibility of extracting them again from the pavement. The machines had a large outside fly wheel whirling constantly, for a purpose we didn't question but never figured out and I imagine it had something to do with maintaining the thing's elephantine momentum. Next to burning leaves in the gutter, the aroma of roofing tar or street asphalting will slide me right out of present time as though a hypnotist or magician had cried out a magic word.

When they demolished the remains of the old dry goods store on the corner and started to construct the building for Mr. Jazdjewski's new quarterss they had to dig a new excavation. The steamshovels came. Sidewalk superintendents and lovers of holes in the ground came to stand at the lip of the pit to study the coal-fired scooper as it snorted and flatulated in the orange clay. I had trouble figuring out how it was going to get back out after having dug itself in so deep, but it did, along the same precarious dirt ramp up which the horses toiled, hauling their dumpwagons of earth.

Some of the clay trailed out of the wagons along the street. We needed some of that for throwing. It was like modeling clay and would hit, flatten out, and stick to anything, so we threw it all over, at anything - at the globes of street lights, high enough on the sides of buildings so it couldn't be scraped off again, at passing cars, at each other, or just as far as we could at invisible targets over the rooftops, tirelessly, with the most intense devotion.

In the time of coal-fired, horse-drawn fire fighting equipment there had to be a tower on the firehouse in which to hang hoses to drain and dry. Evidently they don't have to do that any more to keep them from rotting. There also had to be a broad, brick-paved ramp out in front where the hot coals could be scraped from under the boiler after a gallop to a fire.

When they were not keeping the eternal flame going under the fire rig, they tended the horses and cooked their meals, but when the alarm sounded and the annunciator started dinging within the mysterious depths of the firehouse there was a great running and sliding down poles and hitching up the three stallion team.

Bells started to clang on the equipment, the fire was stoked under what looked like a giant coffee urn that began to belch black smoke and all the kids and dogs for blocks around came running. Everything in the barn blasted off over the cobble stones, striking sparks on the streetcar rails in an hysterically noisy cavalcade.

Men clung to side rails with one hand, struggling into oilskins with the other arm. Those with seats desperately tugged on their rubber boots. The chap in charge of the bell kept ringing it with frantic diligence. It was pure spectacle and it surely attracted an appreciative following.

Horse-drawn and gas-driven equipment arriving at a big fire.

The hook-and-ladder was not barned at the Brady Street locale, but if we waited a few minutes it would come banging and wailing down the street. It was a real treat to see the guy on the back end work the steering wheel that guided the rear trucks of that fantastic equippage around corners.

Neither horse-drawn nor steam-driven was a quieter mode epitomized by the electric passenger car. There were a lot of them, usually steered by dignified ladies in black, with two similar ladies in the back seat wearing large hats. It was guided by a stick that could be moved horizontally. The small, buggy-like vehicle had large spoked wheels with narrow rims and what looked like solid rubber tires. It sped silently down lovely arching arcades of elm trees, and on a wet Sunday morning in spring the tires hissed pleasantly on the pavement.

There were sight-seeing, open-sided motor carriages originating at the Northwestern Railroad Depot that carried festive parties of newcomers around to gawk at the breweries and parks and principal streets - and probably the lakefront - and that attracted the attention of the younger set. They pointed and yelled "Rubberneck!" and the passengers would wave airily back.

There was plenty of room, then, for jitney busses, horse drawn vehicles, and steam boilers on wheels too, because there weren't so many of us populating the earth, because there weren't so many duplicates of ourselves to make demands on the environment. We have outlived the whole shebang now.

It seems kind of a pity.

* * *

WHERE THE STEET CAR BENT THE CORNER AROUND

I was born in 1914, and by that time there were hundreds of banging, clanging steel street cars thundering through Milwaukee, and in fact, the Oakland/Delaware (#15) line bashed right past where we lived on Brady Street. Until Henry Ford began turning out flivvers in great numbers almost everybody got around town and into the environs by electric street railway.

Tracks and switches were embedded in the streets everywhere. Live wires were strung over them from utility poles. Whining and panting, the self-propelled contraptions, redolent of ozone, rolling on solid metal wheels, crashed along the tracks with a reverberating roar, day and night. The racket was something people just got used to as a necessary part of urban life.

The great clangor began at the turn of the century and continued through a great war, through Prohibition's driest days, through the aching era of the Great Depression, and through another great war and out again. Streetcars rocketed over trestles, clanked over river bridges, packed through cement canyons of office buildings and shops, went into tunnels and out onto grassy meadows, up hill and down dale, in fair weather and foul.

Even turning a corner was something of an event. The streetcar produced hideous screams of tortured metal doing that and the outcome of such an adventure never seemed certain. At times a man in a red and white striped curve-greaser's tunic was waiting. He responded to that heart-rending cacophony by venturing into the street with a bucket of smear and a stick with a rag on the end. He dipped into his supply of ointment and vigorously applied it to the aching curve of steel so that the next following passage might be to some degree a less hair raising experience.

At some intersections the motorman could operate a switch from inside the car. At others he had to get out and prod the blade in the street with an iron bar until it snapped over with a smart 'clack!'. In either case, in wet weather, that exercise clapped a quart or two of dirty water or icy slush into the air, much to the surprise and dismay of anyone nearby.

The trolley pole was expected to follow the overhead wire in the direction the car was going, but at a branching of the way it sometimes took the wrong route and would be dragged off with a scatter of sparks. It waggled on its tether until the conductor could hop out and guide it, with ominous crackling and flashing, back onto the proper wire. These were not phenomena to improve the disposition of the trainmen, but anyone who remembers riding a streetcar anywhere will recall that it was great entertainment, good transportation, and a dime well spent.

In the northern clime, deep in the iron cold of a Wisconsin winter night, there would be a friendly light glowing at some of the major intersections of deserted thoroughfares. It would be the 'owl car', stoically waiting. Periodically it would give out with a 'tung tung-tung' throbbing sound as it refreshed its airbrake tanks. Men heavily bundled and women in men's clothing, if it was during the war production years of the 1940s would crouch inside over the few seats under which an electric heater afforded a few grudging therms. The motorman sat immobilized on his stool in front, a black shade drawn down behind him hooked to a ring in the floor.

A hardy old geezer, perhaps otherwise a client of the of the rescue mission soup kitchen, might let aboard to sell copies of the bulldog edition of the morning newspaper, letting in a blast of cold air, and then get off again, letting in another. Finally, with everyone numbed and shaking, passengers would come running through the dark from a connecting cross-route, most of them on night shifts in the war effort, and the trolley would at last move on down the line.

In good weather some riders liked to stand up front next to the motorman where the breeze poured in through the open front window. One could watch the cobblestones rush under the car and see how the motorman would roodle his rheostat lever back and forth in sweeping arcs to make the car go, while he kept joggling the brake handle with his right hand to slow it down. He sent the car crashing over switches with a hackle-raising screech at full speed so that the trolley would not stall on a dead spot in the overhead wire. He had to pass that dead spot with the power off, or a circuit-breaker would go out with a deafening report. That could also happen if he accelerated too rapidly. Ka-bang! But he would calmly reach overhead to knock the lever sticking out of the black box up there back to the contact position and the car would have power once more.

The one-man 'safety car' was invented in 1915 by Charles O. Birney and by the 1920s some 4,000 "Birneys" had been manufactured, and ultimately there were probably 6,000 in use, especially in the smaller communities in the country. They were light in weight and built at reasonable cost. One man handled everything. It had only two 25 horsepower motors and was thus seriously underpowered in some situations. After 1930 or so, a larger version with two trucks took its place.

Before the 'safety cars' the motorman at the front was aided and abetted by a conductor at the rear who collected fares, punched transfers and yanked a cord on a totalizer to produce the familiar ding-ding sound.

At peak load periods and on heavily traveled routes, street cars might come double, like dragon flies mating, stuck end to end with an accordion-pleated passageway between them, where passengers paid as they departed either car. Those articulated arrangements seemed to suffer a flat wheel more frequently than the ordinary single cars, which served to even more heavily underscore the din of their passage.

In that more leisurely time, every corner was a street car stop. As automobile parking at curbside became common and traffic grew more congested, the slow-pokey stop and start riding began to get irksome. Automobiles could not pass the streetcar except at 'no-parking-to-corner' areas where passengers boarded. In some places those waiting to board were protected by lines in the street and metal signs on standards like floor lamps.

One or even two autos could maneuver next to the loading zone and when the street car door banged shut they could make a mad dash across the intersection to get out in front. .The rest of the traffic plodded on behind. If a wagon was parked too close to the tracks while men toiled out of a fruit market with barrels of garbage, the street car had to wait, futilely clanging, its passengers stewing in the summer heat and the automobiles radiating shimmering hot air from their black hides, honking.

A winter's snow pushed parked cars closer and closer to the tracks or glued auto tires in the ruts of the rails. Trolleys could not leave the rails to pass, as the trolley busses could that came later, so that the system had its frustrations.

On snowy days the street railway company would send out a special-duty creation resembling a wooden boxcar, strung with naked light bulbs, mounting a huge revolving whisk broom set at an angle in front, which brushed the tracks clean, while somebody inside tooted on a piercing whistle-horn. At other times special cars would come with grinders fixed to their underbellies, which would set up a blazing cascade of sparks as they levelled lumps and welds in the rails.

The first one-man cars did not have the automatic treadle exit at the rear, but that invention was in most of the Birneys by the mid 1920s. It was a convenience for those who liked to perform a public service by letting non-paying passengers in through the unattended rear door. There was an identical set of controls at either end of the trolley. At the end of the line the two set of tracks merged into a single set and switched back to go the other way.

Frozen and abandoned, its power pole still up, this trolley and all the others along the line behind it, waited to be rescued.

There were few turntables such as those needed for cable cars in San Francisco. The motorman drew on his infamous black and greasy motorman's glove and went outside to pull the trolley pole down and hook it. Then he went around to unhook the other one, and if his aim was good he could hit the overhead power line on the first try. If he missed there was an electrical display and the lights in the car flashed on and off until he made the connection.

The controls at the opposite end were thus energized and every thing was all set for the return trip except that the seats were all facing the wrong way. Starting at the front end, the motorman went down the aisle grabbing a seat handle in either hand, pulling them across the shiny, yellow rattan seats, bang, bang, crash, into reverse. They were very nice seats, inflexible but not uncomfortable, and practically indestructible.

The motorman then lifted his levers from the controls at the back and brought them forward for installation in front. He also plucked a toadstool-like pedal out of a hole in the floorboards so he could use it to clang the bell. It was worth the trouble because if, as sometimes happened, a pedal was left sticking out at both front and rear, the dinging on it by juveniles was more than anybody could stand.

Milwaukee's Wells Street line had probably the most spectacular ride anywhere. It went over the Menomonee Valley on a 9O-foot-high trestle and it was a hair-raising experience for some 1,800 passengers who traversed the swaying structure daily. Many of them were on their way to and from work at the Allis-Chalmers industrial plant or headed for an outing in the park at Soldier's Home. Some thought the trolleys passing on the bridge should do so slowly, but when they did that they swayed more, and it was generally agreed that passing at full speed was a better risk. Milwaukee Braves baseball fans were still rocketing out over it to the county stadium as late as the 1957 season, but that was about the end of the\ streetcar era.

They were supplanted by double-trolley electric busses and it no longer seemed necessary to have a cowcatcher in front to drop on the rails to scoop up wayward pedestrians. The trolley busses had as much trouble with their overhead power lines as the streetcars did but they got around things more easily in traffic. They were, in turn, supplanted by gasoline-powered busses, which could follow any desirable route without any power lines or rails to restrict them. It was a great idea until the energy crunch came along, but by then the electric railway system was an anachronism.

Gone is the time, hazy in the golden memory of yesterday, when a motorman called out the street names at every stop ... when he swabbed his window with a hand-operated wiper and never failed to escort blind passengers to and from the curb ... when great crowds of men in dark suitcoats and women in babushkas lugging baskets took up every seat in the conveyances and the fares were a mere 7 cents or a dime ... when families were going to picnics and band concerts or to the ballgame at Borchardt Field, situated on a single city block in the middle of town.

Dorothy Parker said that men were like streetcars and another would be along any minute. It would be nice to have one come down along the street now, just for old time's sake, especially if we could have our youthful Toonerville Trolly days back also, but I know it won't, any more than I'll ever see the "Old Lab" in the attic again, either ...

Boarding a #15 Oakland/Delaware street car at the Farwell, North, Murray, Ivanhoe five-point transfer corner. A trolley bus follows out of the turn-around next to the Murray Theatre a block away. The Oriental Theatre, the East Side Library, the 'Koombacher' bierstube, The Ivanhoe Restaurant, The Pink Pig, Dan's Chicken Pie and Hooligan's Tavern were all clustered here.

A 'safety island' gave boarding passengers some protection from the charging auto traffic on Grand Avenue in downtown Milwaukee.

OF SANDWICHES AND BEER

There were always plenty of neighborhood taverns in Milwaukee, beer capitol of the world. A couple of generations ago the city licensed 2,440 taverns, 6,767 bartenders, 2,630 pinball machines, 7 horse-drawn junk wagons, and 14 handcarts. In some areas of the north and south side there were four, five and six taverns to the block.

Dim lights, flickering neon, peanuts, beer, yelling, a juke box and bar dice were part of the steady patron's idea of comfort to the soul. A light lunch was usually available.

For some good souls it was a confessional. For the depressed it was a pool in which sorrow was drowned, and for boasters, appreciative listeners were always there. The tavern served all the purposes of the classic Greek marketplace, the desert oasis, and the baths of ancient Rome.

Some were so insular that all heads at the bar would turn coldly to regard the Stranger, the tavern-hopping outlander, who might accidently blunder in to disturb the private ambience, whereupon the bartender would prepare rites of excommunication.

Way back, in 1850, a law was passed taxing whisky at $1 a gallon and beer at $1 a barrel. Before that a person could buy bourbon for 15 cents a gallon and could get stoned for less than a nickel. But with the new tax, thrifty burghers began to switch to beer for that whirling in the head feeling and that encouraged the growth of the good old saloon. It developed a generally sinful reputation as a refuge for men only and was redolent of pickled pigs feet, braunschweiger, spilled beer, sawdust and bay rum.

The perception of such places as teeming with loose women, plump frauliens in low-cut dirndls thrashing about with four foaming steins bulging from either hand, of femmes fatale sitting atop player pianos swinging gorgeous gams, singing bawdy lyrics, was one fostered by blue-noses and reformers, later known as "Drys".

In the 1930s, neighborhood taverns were in clapboard buildings with names like Ernie & Mary's, Frank & Sally's, Sophie's Place, Shorty's Doghouse, Ma's, Joe's, Steve's, etc., committed to red and blue neon tubing in the front window buzzing like beehives, and with a card reading "Fish Fry Fridays".

Dirty Helen's Sunflower Inn, on St. Paul Avenue, which originated in 1926, was different. It served no food and provided only hard liquor to clients who had to stand, but they loved it. Dirty Helen closed up in 1959.

In the 1940s Barney and Emmet Fredericks operated a widely known watering place favored by journalists and other hard bitten folk, in the heart of downtown, The Wayside Inn. It was at #1 Northwestern Lane, which was an alley opening on East Wisconsin Avenue between North Water Street and Broadway. Although Emmet was lost when the Japanese overran Aitape in the Pacific in World War II, Barney carried on, hustling plate lunches by day and bourbon by night. Familiars could keep track of their own drinks by making marks on the bottle and could substitute their own classical records in the jukebox.

MARY'S LOG CABIN tavern and restaurant on the near south side, run by Mary Sijan after her husband, Peter, died in 1933, in partnership with her son, Syl and with the part-time assistance of her daughters, including Ange, who has attracted the attention of Bro. Vail

The enterprise was started after World War One at Clinton St and Greenfield Ave. and during the prohibition era it was also a rooming house catering to factory workers at the Illinois Steel Plant.

The place is now frequented by workers from the nearby Allen-Bradley Mfg. Co., marine types from the U.S. Coast Guard and great lakes shipping, and by seekers after the ever-popular Friday Nite Fish Fry and Saturday Nite Deep Fat Chicken Jamboree.

PETER SIJAN RESTAURANT   1930   TO   Aug. 1938   MARY'S LOG CABIN

41

Barney earnestly endeavored to clear himself of engrams by practicing a poor man's version of psychoanalysis propounded by. L. Ron Hubbard, called Dianetics. but it was the hot-footing with meatloaf combination plates down the long bar from the galley that finally did him in and he had to quit because of his arches.

Colla's Five & Ten Tap, at Jackson & Knapp on the near east side was a favorite of the younger set during the late 1930s, where Marcella and Francie ported the mugs of beer and responded to cries for "Texas and shoes" by bringing a splendid hamburger flooded in sauce and fixin's and shoestring potatoes in a napkin-lined basket. The five & ten part was five cent wine, ten cent beer and 25 cent cocktails. A hard-boiled egg was also a nickel.

It would usually be a sandwich with a cut of the delicious ham, basted in beer sauce, a-cling with pineapple rings and studded with cloves, at 10 cents, and "lotsa beers". The average account seldom ran over a half-dollar for the stay.

If it was too far to walk between taverns, although walking was hardly a factor for the youth of the period, a ride in a Checker Zone Cab was 20 cents, and that could be split, say, among four passengers. That made it quite economical to venture as far as Lena's on Hopkins, Ferdl. & Mitzie's Trail's End Lodge on Vliet, or Mary's Log Cabin Tap on Greenfield & South Second, and other such exotic garden spots.

Smalley's Tavern on Vliet Street specialized in wines. Smalley imported them (from Chicago) by the carload. He had barrels of them laid on their sides in tiers and tapped from the barrelhead with spigots. There was a choice of white port, tokay, muscatel, zinfandel, claret and a dozen other varieties, all tasting remarkably like sweet sodapop needled with spirits, at 5 cents the glass, 69 cents the gallon, bring your own jug.

Jordan's Cafe at Plankinton & Wells had a very long mahogany bar, brass fittings in the classic mode, an elegant backbar with high mirrors, a smoke-filled back room, and featured a most toothsome side of roast beef for sandwiches. That was supplemented with a widely appreciated pea soup. One could lay a bet at Jordan's on anything, from the Earl Lillydahl/ Carl Zeidler mayoralty election to the Green Bay Packer/Chicago Bear football game. Odds were posted on a blackboard behind the bar.

At The Big Stein on Plankinton Avenue one stood in snow drifts of peanut shells manfully downing sudsy brew out of stone mugs bottoms up. (Now called chug-a-lugging). The trick was to take quick breaths while double-tonguing.

At Wendelin Kraft's Cocktail Bar on Jefferson Street, milk was a festive beverage kept on hand for activists of the Socialist persuasion, who were often teetotalers and wore high-button shoes, and who came for sandwiches and political talk. It had a capacious back room to accommodate City Hall workers, the Socialist Party faithful, and the likes of Mayor Daniel W. Hoan, Frank P. Zeidler, Paul Gauer, and Stanley Budney, all talking at once.

A certain "Baron Lunchausen" held forth in the Terris Theatrical Grill, favored by show biz types on Wells Street's "cabaret row". The Gayety Burlesque House was only a few blocks away down Wells Street, and the popular Belmont Hotel Coffee Shop, open all night, was even closer. Johnny Doolittle, his trumpet and his orchestra backed up the various "acts"

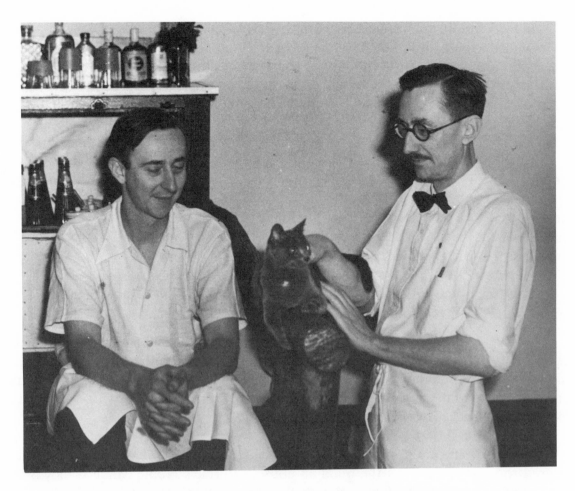

**Emmet and Barney, proprietors of the fabled Wayside Inn
situated in an alley in downtown Milwaukee**

on the stage under the blue lights. "The Baron", drawing on a supply of crush hats he kept in a box under the piano, filled in with comical songs and rib-tickling asides, each in a different hat. On certain nights the attraction was mud wrestling, and the place finally burned down.

There was always a tavern somewhere, to get a package of cigarets when other places were closed, or to take home a pitcher of beer. You could stay and have a bowl of hot chile. It was a place to play pool, or influence the course of a steel marble down the board of a pinball machine by banging it with one's hips. You could take home a turkey if you made a lucky pick on one of the numerous punchboards on the premises.

You could croon Irish melodies around a piano all evening, or sing September Song until the tears came, or sit and hammer playing cards on a table and yell with your friends until all hours at a game of Schafskopf.

Indeed, you could have a couple of 'boilermakers'- a shot of whisky and a beer chaser with maybe a little ketchup in the beer - and smoke a shoepeg cigar before anyone else was awake in the morning if you were on the graveyard shift in a factory or working in a wartime defense plant, because taverns were open and going full blast before cock-crow as The Depression lifted and another Great War broke open and ruined everything.

But that is getting ahead of this version of life in the 1920s and **The History's** account of the 1930s that follows. The idea of keeping a narrative journal occurred to us at the very bottom of the economic down-cycle , in 1934, after we had stayed in school some extra semesters as 'post-graduates'. I caught up on some botany and some European history. 'Shop' - carpentry or metal-working - were supposed to be 'menial', so I avoided those.

It was inevitable then that we had to hop out of the nest and face the world after only 16 or 17 years of life spent avoiding its realities.

We were fortified with the Pythagorean theorem,the Wheatstone bridge, the parsing of verbs, Silas Marner, the principal exports of Venezuela, Boyle's Law, and could ask "A qui est le crayon?" We were also flooded with hormones from another source and suffered the exceedingly weird side-effects thereof as puberty or adolescence or something whacked us lopsided.

It was a time when 'privacy' was a precious commodity. We found that in a plastered room in the attic of the building housing Vernie's Home Made Candy Store on the ground floor and the Gauer flat on the second floor. We claimed that by right of eminent domain as a sanctum sanctorum, pushed aside some flasks, reagent bottles and chemistry apparatus used by the resident boy scientist to make room for typewriters and books. We bought a 3-ring looseleaf binder from Woolworth's and hand-lettered the first page "The History".

What follows is **The History (Volume One)**, word for word, just as it was set down and illustrated, during the period from mid 1934 through the year 1939.

-- Harold Gauer

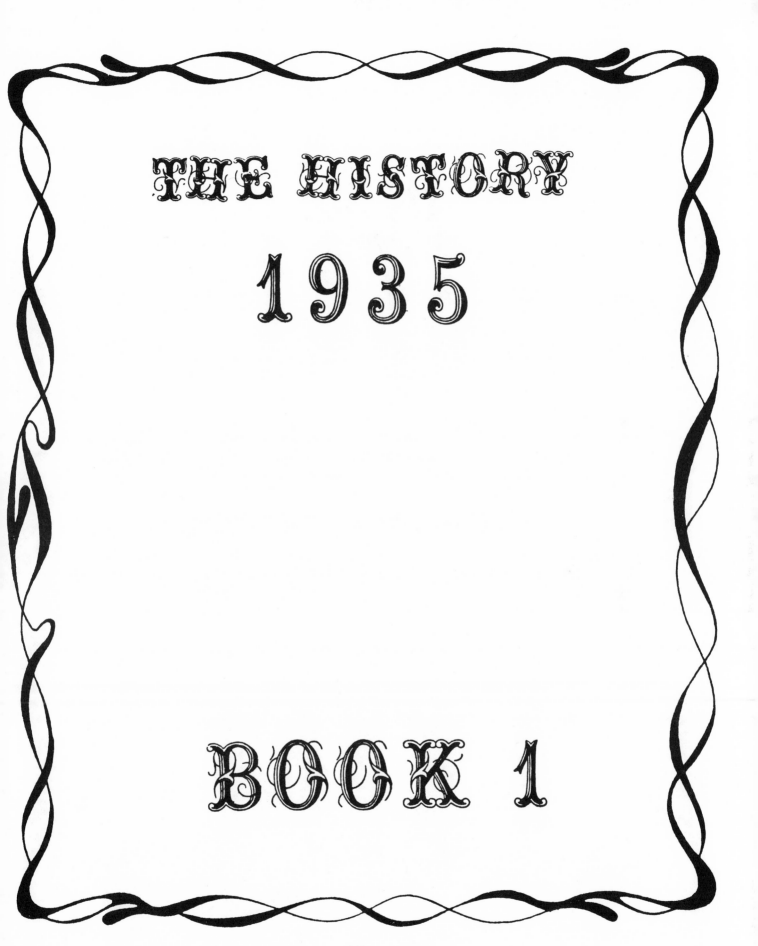

THE HISTORY

1935

BOOK 1

The keeping of this HISTORY actually began in October of 1934 with the formation of *The Federated Arts Council*, which did not deal with "the arts" at all, but with the problem of doing something interesting in the days after high school in the middle of the Great Depression.

A group gathered to organize at the home of *J.C. Lehr*. You got there from Brady Street by going downhill at Humboldt and north across the river and up again toward Reservoir Park to Weil Street. Present were: *Wm. H. Williams, Robert A. Bloch, H. (Mag) Gauer, J. C. Lehr, Margaret Christnacht, Helen Kirsch, Tony Ballistreri*. Others present were: *Loretta Korbel, Art Williams, Frank Klonowski, Carol Davis* and perhaps *Others*.

A topic tried out for discussion was Instinct vs Reason. In spite of a certain amount of screaming, with several talking through the backs of their necks, the total result was pretty good. To set up a formal discussion group a committee was appointed to get some free letterheads printed.

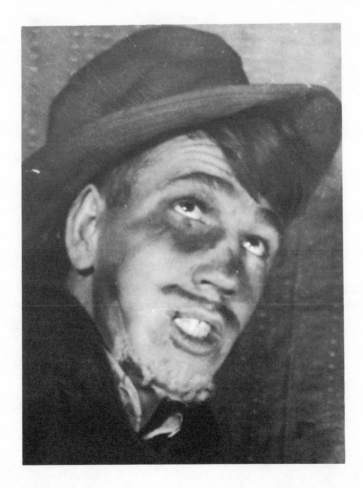

Lehr

FEDERATED ARTS COUNCIL

Room 620, Merchants & Manufacturers Building

More meetings were held at the Lehr household. Membership increased with the addition of *Mike Bonfiglio* and *Alice Bedard*. Helen Kirsch and Art Williams dropped out. It should be known that the names of Loretta Korbel and J. C. Lehr were more or less romantically linked. And also that Miss Korbel's father was Chairman of the Milwaukee County Democratic Committee. There, thanks to Miss Korbel - and Lehr - the FAC meetings were in no time at all being held in the Democratic Committee meeting hall downtown. On Tuesday evenings, already!

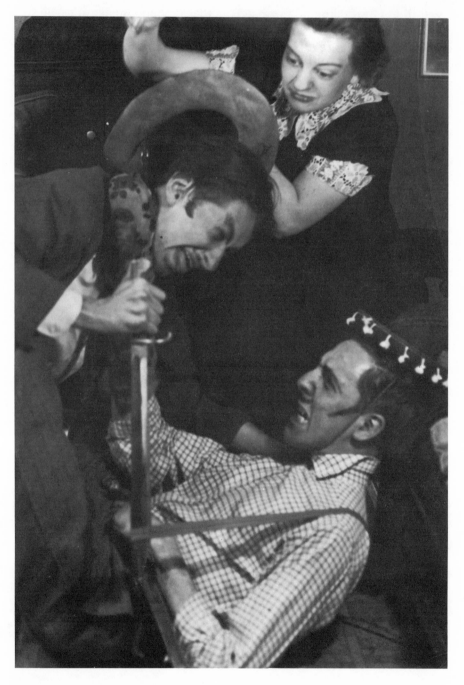

Preparation for the Skit. A discussion period.

The DCC hall had a capacity of several hundred folding chairs, a dozen of which were lined up in front of the chairman's table. The offices of the Democratic Committee and the Democratic News adjoined on the west and the room overlooked the Milwaukee River at the Wells Street bridge.

The sixth floor began to resound to the exploits of a certain legendary character, Sam Lapidus, narrated in dialect by the talented impressionist, Robert Bloch. Although C. Davis and T. Ballistreri got into a fight, things were generally harmonious until the Korbel-Lehr relationship began to go sour.

It was a mild evening in February. The Council met in the usual manner. Chairman Lehr's attitude of brave gaiety deceived no one. Underneath his heart was breaking. Pagliacci.

It was no surprise when he got up and left the room. He went out and stood in the hall. Miss Christnacht reported he was contemplating suicide.

But Lehr returned. He looked reproachfully at his beloved. He spoke briefly with Miss Davis and others of his hopeless existence. He vanished into the hall again to take his fatal plunge down the elevator shaft.

The members sat with bated breath, waiting the imminent disaster. Their ears strained to catch the sound of a watermelon landing on terrazzo. Five minutes passed. No thud. No crash. Then a looming figure appeared in the doorway. It was Lehr. "Hello," he said, brightly.

Crises were like that. They passed. At other meetings a new member, *Frank Klonowski* had a message about Divine Love, which caused eyeballs to roll, Lehr discoursed on Sadism, and Bloch delivered impressions of the weird occult. Gauer outlined briefly a summary of Karl A. Menninger's *The Human Mind* and some impressions on literature dealing with abnormal psychology.

More abnormal psychology came into focus at subsequent meetings chaired by Mr. Lehr, including a paper presented by Gauer of Bernstein's *Suggestive Theraputics*, which in turn suggested the idea of experimenting with hypnotism.

Hypnotic suggestion could apparently duplicate various physical and mental abnormalities.

Lehr tried it and appeared to have placed Miss Korbel in a state bordering on the third degree, but without definite catalepsy or automatic movement.

At a later date Miss Bedard volunteered to be a subject and was placed in an even deeper trance by Gauer. Alice remembered little of what had transpired. Control wasn't very good. When commanded to count to ten and waken at the count of six, Alice counted to five and hesitated. Further counting could not be induced and the patient awakened by herself shortly after. Gauer declined to go any further into hypnotism.

Letterheads were asked from by the corresponding secretary and 20 cents was donated by each member and they were purchased (100 for $2). Five cents in dues was collected thereafter at the suggestion of Mr. Korbel.

Mr. Klonowski continued to talk funny. Miss Kirsch dropped out. An under the counter movement started to oust Mr. Lehr as chairman. At a meeting in March a vote was unanimous. Mr. Lehr was asked to step down and William H. Williams was elected to succeed him.

Lehr, who also belonged to an outfit called The Sons of Syracuse, featuring young people's dramatic acting, and had brought several of its membership into the FAC, namely, *Ruth Botts, Margie Bauer, Alf Jenks, Norbert Lewis* and *Others*. After Lehr's ouster, they left again, and Klonowski departed also. Margie Bauer stayed on a while longer because she was made Secretary. When she did leave, though, she absconded with the minutes.

Messrs. Bloch and Gauer made the acquaintance of a certain Samuel Bollix on the mezzanine of the downtown public library. The talk centered around the psychiatrist McDougall. The fellows were in the philosophy section doing research. They came away with the gentleman's offer to speak to the group. He arrived on a bitterly cold night. A modest group

DEBATE COMMITTEE
Shinners, Bloch, Balestrieri, Gauer

was gathered to hear him talk about philosophy. He touched on Xenophenes and on Zeno and the paradoxes. It later developed Mr. Bollix had encephalitis and was in and out of a sanatorium. He was obviously keen of mind in moments of clarity and his subject was given a brisk going over during the discussion period. Miss Bauer, who was still there, thought his remarks inferred atheism. Mr. Bollix let it be known he did not approve of Marquette University boys.

After that dramatic affair, Williams, Gauer and Bloch got in touch with the Democratic County Committee fellows and agreed to put on a series of debates before ward meetings, the first of which would confound the issue of Voting Machines.

While preparations for the debate were going on, a series of skits was put on before the assembled membership in the meeting hall, the first being on The Fallibility of Witnesses. Williams, Gauer and Bloch talked, saying witnesses had a lot of trouble identifying details in criminal cases. There was the sound of a gunshot in the hall. Norman Gauer, Milt Gelman and

ENTERTAINMENT COMMITTEE

51

Mert Koplin ran in and scuffled. There was another shot and some bananas fell out of a bag and there was yelling and running. The audience was presented with a questionnaire.

Accounts of the activity varied widely, and Bloch mopped up with his summary remarks, pounding home the theme.

New members began to appear at the meetings with the arrival of *Herbert Shinners*. This gentleman joined the ranks and brought in *Milt Gelman, Mert Koplin, Art Gehrman, Adolph Shrager, John Cunningham, and John Heath.* Somewhat later *Helen Mathews and Fannie Grossman* joined the throng. Also Irene Zintz. And a guy named Ray who remained otherwise unidentified:

Came the first debate. The 26th Ward was astounded to see Bloch and Gauer appear for the affirmative and Balestrieri and Shinners for the negative. Everybody first indulged in numerous heavy beers. Somehow, Bloch's humorous antidote about The Maharaja in the Men's Washroom got told, and Gauer had an incident about a voter getting stuck in the machine. Balestrieri and Shinners played it straight. More beer on the way out, leaving things pretty hysterical at the 26th Ward meeting.

The Second Debate ran into a very stodgy audience. It was staged at the 16th Ward Democratic Organization Meeting at Gaynor's Tavern, 27th and Wells St. on Monday, May 14th, 1935, at 8 p.m.

THE PHILOSOPHY GROUP

Despite heroic efforts of the FAC folk, the 16th Ward boys were extremely unreceptive. Bloch and Ballistreri wanted to leave. Shinners and Gauer entertained the same sentiment but prevailed upon the contingent to remain and present the material in order to discharge obligations to the FAC and the Democratic County Committee. This was done. Williams was forced to absent himself on both occasions because of previous engagements at the armory as a National Guardsman.

Miss Korbel resigned as Treasurer on March 4th. Alice Bedard was elected Secretary and has held the position up to the present time, keeping records and handling the club finances.

THE MEMBERSHIP IN ITS PRIME
Gelman, Bloch, Balestrieri, Bedard, Bonfiglio, Schraeger, N. Gauer
Cunningham, Christnacht, Shinners, Williams
Koplin

THE SULLIVAN BOXING CLUB *Organized by Promoters N. Gauer and B. Warren, Dec 1933, Disbanded June 1934. Members: Norman Gauer, George Graham, Gerald Schmidt, Bernard Wahlberg, Bob (Kid) Koers, Miles O'Connor, Joseph Megna, Joseph Boysa, Salvatore Rappa, Charles Peciuini, Fred Zabel, Caspar (Butch) Lutz, William Tippet, Donald Longworthy, Delbert Kent, Vincent Megna, Slominski, Clark, Gardner.*

Federated Arts Council
of Milwaukee County

Mail Address
1212 E. Brady Street
Phone :
Daly 2479

Harol Gauer
Secretary

Wm. H. Williams
Chairman

Robert W. Block
Publicity

Statement by the new chairman:

"It was a calm session. The inimitable Bonfiglio had relaxed completely, a lighted cigarette drooped from his pan dangerously. One of the dizzy cohorts then arises to standing position, gapes unintelligently, and begs permission of the Chair to discourse briefly on a subject of vital importance. The Chair, taking encouragement, is duped into granting said cohort the privilege of the floor. Needless to say the Chair received a nasty jar when the subject was introduced. A rambling discourse on "Why Wear a Truss?"!

Williams Reports on
The Entertainment
For The F.A.C.

The Affair At Lapham Park

Bro. Bloch receives the communication that the hammerheads at the above place would simply love to be entertained during the course of their dance. Thus, a floor show was formulated. Properties were collected. Acts were rehearsed.

The cast for this immortal presentation included Balestrieri, Kirsch, Lehr, Norm Gauer, H. Mag. Gauer, Bloch, and scribe, Williams. Bro. Bloch pulls off the usual gags. Williams is the amiable stooge and takes another of his many beatings when Bloch takes his acting serious and clamps him a mighty blow on the helmet with a hammer. Gauer and Gauer do a goofy shooting scene using hypnotism as the gag. Tony Bal and Kirsch make a scintillating couple who exchange much aimless conversation, and J.C. Lehr was another stooge.

It seems the scrilches like it well enough, but they is anxious to resume their dance. Some of the audience is an unresponsive bunch of hardheads. Nevertheless, the show goes on. Another Federated Arts Council first!

SOME OF THE PEOPLE
Some of the Time

J. Meister

B Warren & G Graham

A. Bedard

F. Schneider

R. Vail

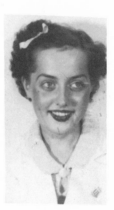

D. Green

J Schmidt

L Schwerm

S Vonier

N. Gauer

H. Shinners

Sea Scouts:

Norman, J. Schmidt, Gib Hough
G. Graham, E. Anderson, A. Galvin

Norman and William (Mim) Powell

Earl Pierce, Jr in **his** lab.

Introduction To Abnormal Psychology

Alice Bedard gave the concept of abnormal psychology to the peer group. From Alice came Karl A. Menninger's *The Human Mind*. It was originally outlined for study by H. Mag. Gauer. The first 12 pages of the volume, a Literary Guild selection, were slightly stained in an explosion in the Precision Process laboratory but is otherwise in excellent condition and reposes in the Precision Process library of good stuff.

With that as impetus a comprehensive bibliography was subsequently compiled, including the titles: *Mechanisms of Adjustment, Introduction to Abnormal Psychology, Nervous and Mental Disease Monographs, The Psychological Approach*, Berheim's *Suggestive Theraputics* (a gift from Dr. Hardy), *The Hypnotic State* and *Psychoanalysis*.

Bloch, Williams and Gauer Carefully Consider The Material

The Big Fight Card

Some of the splendor of the Gauer attic on Brady Street can be seen in this mass photo, taken on the occasion of a monster boxing card presented in a home-made ring by Norman Gauer.

In the back row (3rd from left) is Milt Gelman. The girl with dark hair is Franklin Street neighbor Margie Kedrovich, and the dark-haired girl at her left is Frances Warren. Edith Gelman, Miltie's sister, is smack in front of the chimney. Gib Hough is second from the end in the upper right corner. Seated in the front row (left) is Margie Christnacht and Ruth Caupert. Jimmy Christensen is between the fighters, neither of whom are known. At far right in that row is Jerry Schmidt. Many more spectators were on hand and other gladiators were in the basement getting ready for a thunderous performance on the attic boards.

IN THE BASEMENT
Getting ready, Rivett, Lutz, Graham,
Hough, Whalen, Medea, Warren
and Boxers Megna & Boysa

IN THE ATTIC
Bro. Gnormie sweeps up
the post-fight debris

Monster Debate

In Walter B. Pitkin's **A Short Introduction to the History of Human Stupidity,** and in Karl Menninger's **The Human Mind**, the phases of hypophrenia were discovered in all their discouraging reality. The two works gave rise to several non-violent demonstrations. Among them was a Monster Abnormal Debate at Lincoln High School.

Doom Bye Gauer old pal_ you lousy bum
Herb Williams

WILLIAMS was unquestioned boss of this outfit in high school. Also seen in this album photo are Art Williams, Tony Balestrieri, Helen Kirsch, Alice Bedard, William Shinners. With an original autograph by Wms.

At the urgent request of Laura Boyle, (At Williasms' right in the photo), speech instructor at Lincoln High School, a debate was presented before the Philomelia. It was delivered postage prepaid by A. Balestrieri, R. Bloch, H. Gauer and J.C. Lehr. H. Williams held down the chair.

The question, "**Resolved: Everyone is Abnormal**". Lehr and Balestrieri took the Negative, whilst H. Mag and Bro Blo tended the Affirmative. A large audience attended, including stooges who could be relied on to laugh on cue.

The Negative, goaded, put out with ridicule, rhetoric, somewhat foul personal allusions, and filled the air with misquoted poetry and Pollyanna philosophy.

With frenzied rodomontade the Affirmative demonstrated its points with a dazzling array of information that numbed the senses of pseudo-intellectuals present considerably more than somewhat

J. Harris, C. Scarvaci, B. Kleeman, H. Burns, F. Clark, M. Cutrufelli, J. Thomas, R. Humphreys,

R. Fallon, H. Pritchard, L. Mericle, N. Zeppos, T. Balistreri, J. Spasaro, A. Conte,

...fer, L. Schreiber, P. Cook, R. Bellinghausen, T. Minorik, Capt. J. Fallon, H. Schroeder, R. Lynch.

...Lehman, G. Brusturus, E. Berry, P. Berchuren, J. Vlasis, T. Curro, J. Zingale, B. Schocknecht, P. Corraggio.

FOOTBALL TEAM OF LINCOLN HIGH SCHOOL FOR 1930

WILLIAMS   GAUER

An Excursion to Thiensville

Narration by Wms.

On a Sunday in late August three couples embarked on an excursion to an obscure village. The weather, fair. An important item, grub, was not overlooked on this occasion. The girls came thru nobly.

We left a little before noon on account we didn't have no Kirsch to wait on. Carol Davis, the Duchess, was escorted by R.B. Sister Alice was brung by you know what. Gracie Carpenter was in the company of Wms. And a grand take off affected. After some distance we became aware that all was not well ... while Gauer and me struggles with the tire, the gals imitate papa Pithecanthropus by climbing into apple trees and making a spectacle outa themselves.

We progresses furder with Wms hanging out the car watching the tire which is fast becoming an object of disgust. On account of I bought it. I am taking a terrific beating.

We arrives at our objective. Park along the river and immediately inaugurate a ball game. Wms and Gauer opposing teams - Wms had Grace and Bob; Gauer has Alice and Carol, and we hand the latter an awful beating. After that we looks dopey like for a place to go swimming. It seems Grace don't get enthusiastic when I ducks her a couple of times.

The gals at this point get a bit considerate and crack open the grub. Then there is a local ball game going. We take a romp over there and annoy the home team. Then we hops on the visitors and have much glad roaring at these small time bums. Gracie will never go to a ball game with me on account of I have too much gusto. After this Gauer and me decides to put on a little demonstration of how baseball should be played. Then we find time to satisfy complaining guts with a little food. A search for firewood. Wieners were roasted and consumed while the sun set. Marshmallows met the same fate. The combined party draped themselves on all available blankets and engaged in small talk until time for departure arrived.

After pushing the car half-way back to Milwaukee in the dark, it finally started back to life and gratified us with roaring a bellylaff. In fact we were almost home when the last mishap occurred. On the lousy Capitol Drive we suffered another flat. Gauer tried like hell to make it an all-night party by ripping open the inner tube. But we fixed it and succeeded in distributing the women to their various domiciles.

Capering

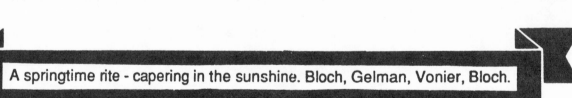

A springtime rite - capering in the sunshine. Bloch, Gelman, Vonier, Bloch.

HISTORY OF THE CAR

Part One

Narration by Wms.

When Williams returned from the woods in July 1934, and was accosted by friend Gauer, it was decided that the purchase of a car, cheap, would result in much fun. So it was a deal. They pooled their meagre resources and looked for something to get sucked in on. This resulted in the purchase of one Model T Ford Touring car of the vintage 1925. Upon concluding this purchase Gauer tried like hell to run it into a streetcar.

Said car had a somewhat mild history, viz: the year of our Lord 1934 saw the questionably painted vehicle introduced to the population of Milwaukee as a Gauer-Williams proposition. Outside of tearing around with a lot of babes of doubtful species, and going to football games, the most outstanding work of the season was the trip to Grafton for a little shooting. The old crate performed nicely (Mr. Gauer had previously made a trip to Madison, thus coming to the logical conclusion that the car wasn't too bad.) The hectic day of shooting was most fittingly ended by cracking a jug of cider.

After having kept the car for short periods in Warren's backyard and in Mrs. Lehr's incomparable garage, a lodging was finally found for Lizabeth in an open parking lot at the expense of $1 per month, phooey. About the only defect the old boat had was it encouraged muscular development. The damned thing had to be pushed if you didn't feel like hitchhiking. It seems that the starting motor is missing. And she can't be cranked when cold. Only one thing left, only one ungodly alternative, cripes !@#$#$% P U S H !

The main objective in purchasing the car was to go on a camping trip. Due to unpredictable difficulties the Goons were unable to absent themselves from this fair city. Incidently, the purchase price was some $17. Horsecollar.

Upon the arrival of downright frigid weather the can was fondly tucked away in Warren's backyard. There, with great ceremony, she was made bare of all valuable accessories. Tires were removed, and rims placed on boards, the battery taken out, hood wired down, side curtains tied up. A sad sight to behold . . . Lizzy which had fluttered so gaily throughout the summer hidder wit tidder wit yon was left to a lonely solitude through a bitter winter.

A Williams/Gauer Proposition

CAME SPRING. Several visits were made to see how Lizzy had stood up under the wear and tear of winter. Reconditioning was started, but procurement of the license would be delayed until July, when it would be cheaper.

THE MONSTER CAMPING TRIP was to begin in mid-summer. Much of the winter had been given over to speculation on the project. Then it seemed that a new but enthusiastic partner in the enterprise was acquired in the ungodly form of Bro. Bloch! Young Gnormie also determined to join in the mightly effort to go camping. The middle of June saw much progress in the car's rebirth.

H. Mag. Gauer's mechanical genius was for the most part indispensable. Lizzy again became recognizable. Then came the first test. We pushed her back and forth, sweated, swore, grunted and moaned. Nothing. Not even a wheeze from her long inactive cylinders. Up and down the yard again. Gauer tinkered and made adjustments and shouted words of encouragement. Finally, a feeble pop. More pushing.

Then a joyous roar! - ear-splitting, from Lizzy's guts. The old iron bowels sang a merry tune and a fine cloud of smoke shot out of her rear!

Lizzie In Her Prime

The most hideous paint job ever applied to any vehicle was started. Bloch worked himself up into a veritable frenzy. Gauer calmly but diabolically considered the most eye-jarring combinations and applied them deliberately. Result: the car looked like hell.

Then came Lizzie's history-making departure from Warren's fabulous backyard. Permission had been secured to dock the car in a vacant stall of Peirce's garage. It received infrequent workouts, as it was intended to preserve its delicate constitution until the mammoth trip was under way. Aside from the journey to Thiensville, its activity was confined to tennis, golf and business trips.

Came August 2nd, which historic date marked the departure of the Fourth Gauer-Williams Expedition and the consummation of the objective for which the jalopy was purchased.

Williams wishes to record here that the car behaved way beyond the highest expectations. All were mightily pleased. This excellent equipage will henceforth be referred to as The Honey Waggon and will be so described in the Second Edition of the Goon Dictionary.

Although the vehicle had neither a starting motor nor a rear bumper, it now had new bands in the transmission, and a new cylinder-head gasket, installed after carbon had been scraped off the valve heads and seats. The spark coils had been gone over and cleaned, and the rear seat was removed in order to accommodate a bunch of tools and the camping gear. The guys in the back could settle down on that. It was voted also, to take the good old horse-anchor along, but one day on Brady Street, somebody swiped it.

ELEVEN DOLLARS each had been deposited in the Precision Process treasury in The

The Monster Camping Trip

Lab by Gauer, Williams, Bloch and young Gauer, Wms was flush with 2-week's pay after maneuvers at Camp Douglass. It was departure time. A few days earlier, Bro. Gnormie got hold of an old canoe. It went on top of the car.

Came time for scramming. Williams collected and worked on what camping equipment he could salvage out of the chaos of moving. Noon arrived, Wms breezes down Brady Street with duffle in tow. It is tucked away along with the Gauer Bros' stuff. A visit to Knapp Street to pick up Bro. Bloch and his stuff and then to Warren's backyard where the canoe is dragged forth and lashed firmly to the

Williams - fresh from Guard camp

70

top of the car with the paddles tucked tenderly underneath. All is set for the momentous takeoff - Gauer bedecked with a girlscout hat (to which he clung tenaciously throughout the trip), Williams and Bloch clapping pith helmets to their craniums. Young Gauer is content with a dilapidated service hat battered beyond recognition. Final farewells are uttered to Ma Gauer and the expedition was off...

Approximately five miles outside the city limits the first mishap was had in a countless series of flats. A genial cop stopped to pass the time of day while repairs were being made, much amused by the scene. Especially by a red dress hanging limply at the end of the canoe as a warning flag.

Our first objective was reached late in the evening and an improvised shelter was set up on the shores of Lake Winnebago midway between Fond du Lac and Oshkosh. Bloch was initiated into the art of sleeping on the ground. Fishing and canoeing were indulged in the following day before departing. Shooting was also in order - so was shooting down eats. Approx. three hours before sundown departure was made from old Winnebago, familiar to Gauer-Williams enterprises of the past, for points North. Objective — High Falls Reservoir on the Peshtigo River. The operation of lashing the canoe was repeated. Equipment again strewed the rear seat. Barracks bags were made snug on the fenders.

A flat occurred this side of Fond du Lac. However united efforts fixed it in due time and it was off again, passing thru the above-named city like gravel thru a duck. Lizzie was pounding valiantly into Neenah when a repetition of the above stated mishap occurred. Without further comment, it should be mentioned that in this stage of the journey there was a succession of mishaps. All tire trouble.

To be sure, after three or four of such occurrences the particular tire that was causing most of the difficulties gave up the ghost. Such was the plight of the expedition that it became necessary to purchase a new tire (used). It was the second day out. It was dark. Williams was sent off on the difficult mission of bargaining for a tire. Omitting all rank details, Williams finally returned with what he was inclined to think was a good buy. By lamp-light the thing was affixed to the wheel and with the moon high it was off again. Immediate objective indefinite. (It was thought Berry Lake might be made with favorable weather.)

The weary quartet chugged along slowly but surely in the direction of Shawano. It was becoming cool and the brisk northern air made it apparent that this was the life. Liz liked to travel at night. She didn't boil over or run a temperature with the same degree of aptitude as she did under the glaring sun. About eleven o'clock p.m., Gauer drove onto the shoulder of the road (somewhere in Wisconsin) for a rest.

Camping Trip Narration by Williams (continued)

After eating a few improvised sandwiches under the moonlit and starlit skies of the North, vigor returned. Gauer yelled contact, Williams spun the prop and Lizzie staggered into the black and mysterious abyss of the woods.

Shawano was achieved after a long grind, Williams acting as chief navigator by checking the course periodically. But instead of pitching camp there, the expedition got involved in a maze of unmarked town roads groggily searching for Berry Lake. For an undetermined reason the lights were growing dimmer. On and on the search went, lights now almost entirely ineffective. Williams and the younger Gauer took turns holding a powerful spotlight on the road enabling Gauer to navigate the craft safely, the lights now of no use whatever. After hours of aimless wandering, Lizzie poked her nose onto a blessed highway. Orientation was made on the nearest town. On entering Surring, no camping spot was found, so an empty lot was located and the group slept. J.J. hovered over the scene.

The third day saw a dilapidated car parked on the edge of a vacant lot in a small town. Four of the most ungodly specimens of humanity wakened slowly from a dead sleep provoked by exhaustion. Unwashed and unshaven and needless to say unkempt in appearance.

Shelter halves on some straw in a ditch provide a night's bedrest for Bro. Gnormie and Bro. Bloch. Morning sun casts a shadow of the canoe on top of the car over the scene.

By noon of that Sunday, High Falls Reservoir was reached and a site selected. Preparations were made to pitch camp. A shelter was erected with a roof of canvas attached to the car at one end and staked to uprights at the other. Beneath this blankets were laid. Most of the day was spent fixing up camp.

The next day dawned cloudy with rain threatening. In the afternoon it began to rain. All ducked for cover to take advantage of the dry recess. But not for long. After the evening repast the shelter began to show signs of weakening. The damned thing began to leak, at first slowly at scattered points. When the rain refused to let up there was hell to pay. Soon there was no living under the damned thing. In order to sleep, a retreat was beat to the car. Much rain. To make the situation more complete, the car roof began to leak, but not seriously. The aforementioned rain soon lulled everyone to sleep. Bloch and young Gauer in the front seat. Gauer laid out in the bottom of the tonneau, and Williams on the equipment where the seat would have been. (One happy family)

Another disturbance of the nocturnal bliss. A twister had risen during the night. With Bloch comfortably snoozing in the front seat the two Gauers and Williams braved the rain and hurricane to cover cans of grub and ditch around the shelter. In trench coats, all got generally soaked. Bloch snoozed thru the storm and racket as if nothing happened. (A sneaking hunch was had he was playing possum). Along about daybreak the wind abated. Leaving the car, Williams found a wet bench and laid himself out and was snoozing when a drizzle came up.

Afloat on the Peshtigo Flowage

When day broke for keeps, the ruins were surveyed with chagrin and sprayed with invective. A pup tent was erected in place of the rent canvas and the campsite policed up. Bloch thereafter preferred to sleep in the car whereas the Gauer Bros. and Wms. slept comfortably in the tent.

The principal source of grub was a farm not far away. A Mr. Dahleen there had a flock of oats that needed attention in the form of shocking. There was entry into the service of the old hammerhead at the rate of $1 per day. Bros. Norman, Williams and Bloch gave the oats a workout in the afternoon of Tuesday, earning a collective $1.50. On several days following some time was spent in the same pleasant fashion, despite lousy weather.

A decision was made to remain over the week-end. Daily campfires were in order and much enjoyment was received from this activity, especially when there was a roast. The days passed pleasantly. Eventful was a five-mile paddle by Gauer and Bloch with a storm threatening.

An outdoor cafe where the portable gasoline-powered camp stove provided manageable heat.

One morning Williams and Norman emerged from the puptent while the others were still in the arms of Morpheus. There was a dense fog. The romantic aspect appealed to Wms and Norm, and they decided to prowl about in the fog in the canoe. Feeling their way to shoreline they found the canoe conspicuous by its absence. As the wind was coming from the N.E. they went South, finding the river had risen several inches during the night. Paddles over their shoulders, they came on an old jimoke who volunteered the information that he had found the canoe and pulled it on shore. It had floated almost a mile downstream. The old bird wanted to know how to pronounce the name of the craft. It had been christened The Sylvester W. Skadietndapmn in honor of the Commissioner of Blue-Eye League baseball.

Suddenly Departure Day was at hand. Expected mail did not arrive (from Joe Pierce). Camp was cleaned up, the canoe again roped to the top of the car. The younger Gauer and Bro. Bloch sneaked into the women's outhouse with nails and a hatchet and crucified the latter's campfire-charred and no-good pants to the wall. Saying goodby to Papa Dahleen, we started off...

NORMAN T. GAUER

Stopping at the center of the Twin Falls bridge, Gauer applied a "Breep" - hideous Tarzan-like ululation - to the ambient air. He does not do that often as it causes his noggin to ring like a gong. And we bid so long to the Peshtigo Reservoir and Flowage for keeps. We decided to get as far as possible in the general direction of home the same day...

Lizzie chugged along in encouraging fashion, never faltering. A sustained drive carried us through Green Bay. Down the lake shore we babied the crate. Dizzy harmony greeted the air of various counties. Manitowoc and Sheboygan passed in review. It was getting dark. We limped thru Port Washington. It looked like Lizzie was gradually croaking! Eventually she sputtered and died. No amount of pushing would get her started.

In the blackness of midnight we pushed her onto the shoulder of the road no less than twenty miles from Milwaukee. A neighboring oat field (yee Gods, oats again!) was rifled for bedding. The shocks of oats were spread in the spacious ditch and the shelter-half covered them. Williams retired to the car and the others curled up in this excellent bed.

Awakening with cramped torsos the body waited as Gauer concocted pancakes and soup on the fender and running board.

It looked like the Fickle Finger of Fate was pointing at the idea of roughing it to the very end. The Gauer Bros. took off in search of technical advice and came back with a grizzled Swede who quickly diagnosed the disease - a DEAD BATTERY.

A second-hand battery was installed at considerable expense. Lizzy was cured and the party left.

It was pounding gaily through Fox Point, Whitefish Bay and almost through Shorewood before suffering the last mishap of the journey. One last final flat. Surrounded by curious urchins the innertube got a lozenge of rubber patch volcanized to it in a cloud of stink from the gizzer Gauer used, it was stuffed back into the tire which was forced back on the split rim with the tire iron, and in no time we had arrived at Joe Pierce's dive.

Ma Pierce dug up a message from the already departed Pierce and we ducked. The scroungiest bunch of hammerheads seen in a long time deposited the canoe in Col. Warren's backyard. The Gauer equipment was unceremoniously dumped on Brady Street. Bloch was hastily disposed of on Knapp Street and the incomparable Williams entered his dive to struggle with two week's of face foliage.

Williams looks back with intense satisfaction: It was good we brought the canoe. With the thick-handled paddles, broad blades. The yellow canoe bottom leaked very slightly. The sun reflects off the water into our faces. The water gurgles from our paddles. The Peshtigo stretches endlessly to the north. Two narrow slats make up the seats. Our shoes are off, and the water in the bottom is cool. Grasshoppers in a tobacco tin on the bottom of the craft scratch and thump. Man, that was livin'!

* * *

THE BLUE-EYE LEAGUE
The Incredible Baseball Games

On this day, October 28th, 1935, two hundred and twenty eight baseball games have been played in the BLUE-EYE LEAGUE. There are three teams which play regularly the year around. They are THE BLOCH FUNGULAS, THE GAUER MAGS, and the WILLIAMS STUGATCHUS. The league is presided over by Sylvester W. Skadietndapmn, who is, unfortunately, out of town.

A Welsh kinsman of Williams, one Bill Jones, came up with a game resembling this one, but Jones met with unfortunate circumstances, received several beatings at the hands of the Fickle Finger of Fate, and is now practically unknown.

Using that material, and after weeks of effort, Bro. Gauer and Geo. Graham brought the present method of calculation and scoring into being. In 1934 on April 10th, Bro. Gauer revised the schedule and introduced it for a trial season.

For the technical minded the MONSTER REVISED GAUER-GRAHAM BASEBALL CHARTER OF SIGNIFICANCE applied to the Deck of Playing Cards - which stands to the present day - is appended:

JOKER - Home Run (later eliminated). FIVE OF HEARTS - Home Run. BLACK ACE - Triple. RED KING - Sacrifice Fly. BLACK KING - Foul Out. QUEEN - Single (1 base advance). RED JACK - Single. BLACK JACK - Double. RED TEN - Error. BLACK Ten - Bunt Out. EIGHT CLUBS - Wild Pitch. RED SEVEN - Double Steal. BLACK SEVEN - Stolen Base. BLACK FIVE - Balk. BLACK FOUR - Caught off base. RED THREE - Walk. TWO SPADES - Double Play.

The schedule is so constructed that the general run of games closely approximates a real game. Cards are turned over three at a time as in solitaire, the top card representing the play. The Manager deals the cards for his team, turns the deck over to his opponent for his turn at bat. Changing a pitcher causes the deck to be shuffled and cut.

The results are scored on appropriately ruled paper as in the sample. At the conclusion of 15 games (The Quarter of the regular 60-game schedule) The Statistician computes the batting, pitching, sets forth the standings. From that the Managers can make decision about their line-ups and tactics. THE FOURTH MONSTER SEASON has started and since no changes can be made, according to THE STATUTES, after Aug. 19th, the permanent line-ups are here given:

BOOK 2

THE HISTORY

Approved Line-ups For The 4th Season

STUGATCHUS	FUNGULAS	MAGS
1b. Joe Aardvark	Sam Lapidus	Chas. Hovacoe
2b. I Sneekafeelia	The Maharaja	A. Stuquepuchu
3b. Liverlips	Lester Scranch	Gnu Face
ss. Buster Bladder	Jeffry Snarch	Osgood Stercore
1f. Joe Bustagut	Little Fungula	Hoyle W Struggle
cf. Waldo Gonad	Omar Kyoebleh	Merde Vous
rf. Sam the Goniff	Hungry Morriss	F W Yocshamosh
C. Dave the Dude	Regus Patoff	F. Gregory Coprophalia
c. Wun Dum Bum	Pop Eyeballs	Hotfoot O. Ouch
P. The Brain	Lous La Trine	Petey The Beep
P. Gaston Belch	Black Art	Lefty Feep
P. Hothorse Herbie	Luke the Puke	Fosco the Ruptured
P. Hairless Harry	Toofer Twice	Fracas W Melefite
rp. Herman Hormone	C. Horsefinger	Fastball Floogie
rp. Manuel Labor	Pedro Pheel	Hurrell W Tchetch
Ut. Oliver Optic	Sex Roamer	Jack FuGroin
Ut. X.T.See	Jaques Strapp	Stabber Fitznoodle

Manager of the Mags
Franchise
(from an old print)

THE BIG RAID
Part One

N.T.G.

It was the custom of certain uncouth-type no-goods in the Brady Street vicinity to use the Gauer's new ping pong table in the basement for immoral purposes, namely to shoot "craps" thereon and to engage in caterwauling with the window open. Which wasn't too bad, except that somebody must have been stabbed with a crusading mania because they complained!

And with that foul deed accomplished, **the cops came!**

THE BIG RAID
Part Two

The elder Gauer was "watching the store" and cutting a pan of caramel into squares. And wrapping each piece in a little square of wax paper. A most tedious task. Came a knock at the back door. A policeman.

"How dee doo" The Mag says affably.
"What's goin' on down there?"
"Where?" The Mag asks helpfully.
"Down there, inna **basement**!"
"Ah, I couldn't say, offhand ..."
"A **crap game**!" cries the flatfoot accusingly.
"Crap game?" exclaims The Mag, groping.

The evening was young, Danny Goose, Duh Beaver, was calling for snake eyes. Williams borrows heavily from Bloch to cover his bet. Col. Warren has a despairing look and Wallio grimaces stoically. The bones bounce over the green of the plywood as a local flatfoot waddles in and in an innocent tone wishes to know what the excitement is all about. Then he retires to confer with his Lieutenant.

Came The Honey Wagon and the criminals are loaded inside. The Mag closes up shop and decides to come along and sits up front with the driver, looking like a plain clothes dick. High class repartee with the cops.

At The Cell Hotel, Bloch, Williams, Wahlberg, Warren, and Duh Beaver are agiven cells #31, 32, 33, 34 and 35, all of tahem furnished with the comfort of home, H. Mag meanwhile trying to tell the jailers these guys are not so bad after all.

A drifter type inmate calling himself "Idaho" offers some advice nobody asked for. Wahlberg inquires loudly about bail. Bloch tells a Sam Lapidus story to lighten the atmosphere. Warren declares somebody "pulled the chain" on them, meaning he suspected foul play. Duh Beaver croons to himself.

It is chilly in the Calcutta-type hell hole and there are no seats on the toilets, and a feeling of going stir-crazy descends like a pall. Then in the middle of the night The Mag shows up with a bankroll, with which he springs Bloch and Williams at $20 a throw, that being all he could raise.

The ex-cons shake hands with Warren, Wahlberg and Duh Beaver, part with their last cigarettes and say they will pop around to the various domiciles to break the news. The Mag tries to take pictures of the victims in their cells but is foiled by the proprietors.

The above version is furnished by Williams
We now take up the narrative according to Bloch . . .

THE BIG RAID
Part Three

The law escorts us into the presence of the Smiling Lieutenant, his hands on the table, his feet in a gaboon, and his teeth in a glass of water. When we enter, his lips curl with scorn. The boys in blue drag us over to the desk.

"Search these guys," the Looie snarls. They drag a machine gun out of my pants leg. Warren disgorged his supply of opium and Whalberg lost his brass knuckles, revolver and tong hatchet. They found dirty pictures on Danny Goose. "Oh, goody!" cried a cop, "doidy peetchas!" The four bulls crowded around to see. Then the lights brightened and more cops came in for the third degree. Also some plain clothes men, an old-clothes man, and Nate Grinstein, Gent's Underwear. They put us in hard chairs. Spotlights seared our eyes.

They beat us, hosed us, punched us, ground lighted cigarettes in our eyes. Always questions. "We won't talk. You can't do this to us!" But they did. At last the cop who made the arrest came in. I rose to my feet and in a cracked voice I shrieked "I'll have you broken for this!" He laughed and hit me with a club. But we would not talk. At last they led us away.

To cells. Chained to the wall like beasts. Devil's Island. Breaking rocks in the hot sun. Striped suits, solitary. Ah, the agony of it all! It's lucky we didn't go there. You know the rest. Five minutes before the guillotine fell, the Scarlet Pimpernel came to our rescue. We got out on bail.

On Monday - *The Trial*

A crowded courtroom. As we entered, they cried "Hauptmann!" and "Rutkowski!" Somebody called for Augie Galan to come out and bat. We sat waiting. Several women stepped out to the ladies lounge. The Judge entered. He banged mightily. A chorus began the jungle song from Emperor Jones.

Cowering in our seats we saw him dispose of cases as easily as a bootlegger. We trembled. Did it mean Siberia? Then our names were bellowed. Up to the seat of justice we dragged. The Judge gazed at us with stricken, nauseated eyes. In a pained voice he asked us our names and the charge. We told him. He leered. The officer gave his story. They both leered.

"One dollar and costs." grated the contemptuous voice.

Out of court we lurched and into the sunlight. The prison pallor in our faces, the lines creasing our cheeks.

That night we left for the West, to start life over again under assumed names. . .

A History Of The Pong Table

No history of the Ping Pong Table would be complete without this picture of Brother Gnormie Gauer and Hoibie Williams in the Brady Street attic where the first table was a round one made out of an old walnut dining room fixture stored there. It made for exciting play of a sort as the players gained experience, but the accursed ball would roll on the boards to the edge of the attic floor and disappear atween the walls and also down knotholes. A real table was not in use until H. Mag. Gauer drove the Model T down to the Schroeder Lumber Company (getting it started by coasting down the Humboldt Avenue hill from J.C. Lehr's place on Weil Street where it was kept for a short time) - and purchased two 4 x 8 foot hunks of three-eights inch plywood. And a new net. There was a desperate wait, after it was set up and sanded, while the green stain dried so the white lines could be painted on. And after that more anxiety until it could be simonized. But eventually play started - in the basement laundry room. After that the plock ... plock ... plicky, plicky, plicky, was constantly heard and the thumb-flick service was practiced (until it was outlawed) and it made a great place for other occupants of the place to put washbaskets and laundry supplies. Meanwhile a fine overhead light was found, with a great, spreading bell reflector, which made a great "doing!" when struck by an errant spheroid. Much pong was had...

The Permanent Library

The library in the attic Labratory continues to expand with the acquisition of weird and exotic literature contributed by Bro. Bloch, fiction and technical works by H. Mag. Gauer and salvage from the estate of Williams' father. Gifts have outnumbered unreturned borrowings and The Authors (of this HISTORY) continue to comb book sales and rental library throwout events.

Sample titles: *Journey to the End of Night, Torture Garden, The Human Mind,* the works of H.L. Mencken, Somerset Maugham, James Branch Cabell et al, Also novels loathed by the public library such as those of Thorne Smith and Tiffany Thayer.

Fifty-five magnificent books in varying stages of decay, along with a formidable array of magazines - *Esquire, Reader's Digest.* Plus *Brutal, The Magazine for People,* bound volumes of Blue-Eye League scores, volumes of this HISTORY, the Precision Process Album of Stuff. And the Monster File of Unbound Manuscripts.

BRUTAL

JAN
FEB
MAR
1936

THE MAGAZINE FOR PEOPLE

PEOPLE HAVE MORE
FUN THAN ANYBODY

ARTICLES
BLACK ART
Buster Bladder
N. DROGYNE
Doc. LESSGLAND
THE MAG.

B. McFITTIN
OLD TRAPPER
OLIVER OPTIC
FLOYD SCRILCH
SUBCONSCIOUS
SIGMUND
Bert Stutred
GEN. VON der BUM

ART WORK
ANTON DIRP
Norman Gauer
COL. WARREN

EDITORIAL
CHAS HOVACOE
SAM LAPIDUS
DR. STUGATCHI

The Magazine For People

The first issue of BRUTAL, The Magazine For People, was completed in three months and came out in January, 1936. It was a huge success = with the editors. It carried 17 original photos, 35 original drawings and 13 original articles and stories. Also 53 advertisements. Makeup and binding courtesy Precision Process.

A sampling of the contents: **Care and Breeding of Minks. Are You Old At Ninety? Brutal's Spring Fashion Forecast. This Puzzling World. Hind Legs Of A Hamburger. News & Comment. The Sound & Phooey. Nine Pahts Devil. Three Poems. Practical Psychology. Blooie! = A Drama. Notes On Bidding & Play. Editorials. Letters From Readers.**

The Backstage Backache

Of February 12, 1936

Williams engaged in conversation with H. Mag. in the latter's back room of the candy store. He told him of a place where extra high class beer could be had by initiates. Two-bits the gallon, corner of Pulaski Street and Kane Place. They summoned Sister Alice and Gracie Toots and went looking for Bro. Bloch.

With the cast assembled, they opened the second act of the backache by bringing two gallons of the stuff to the little flat on Brady Street over the candy store and demolishing the first gallon. Then the assemblage retired to the Precision Process Laboratory and wellhead of the Federated Arts Council located on the floor above that, or namely the attic.

An entire can of Jolly Time Popcorn was popped over a Bunsen burner in the Laboratory and meanwhile and simultaneously the remaining gallon of beer went down and a lot of conversation with double-meaning gags was had, with much laffing.

ENTRANCE OF THE LITTLE FAUNS

Maybe they sniffed out the popcorn, but it was not long before Wallio and Dilly, Berto and Dolores and an unidentified person stumbled up the dark of the attic stair and across the stygian of the attic to the door of The Lab and made their presence known by despatching what was left of the beer.

There was a labored descent to the street level by way of thumping on behinders (in a ghastly imitation of Fred Astair with his legs around his neck), indulged by Warren and abetted by Wallio. Saner members were saddened by this. There was a determined exodus to Lee's Cafe, where. . .

SPOKEN:

Williams: Blahblahblah! Blah!
Warren: Have anudder BEEEEER ! ! !
Williams: Hello! (aside) Flotcccccch !
Gracie: Whyncha have black coffee ? ? ?
Williams: Hey HAMMERHEAD ! ! !
Waitress: [serves coffee]
Williams: Joe Aardvaark in the Ozards
Gracie: Drink your damned coffee ! ! !
Warren: Have anudder Beeeeeer ! ! !

Williams, heedless of counsel, fell in the snow and got a frozen ear.

The Matter Of The Wooden Bladder
and It's Aching Contents

MEMORIAL DAY was marked by the departure of Mammy Gauer to visit relatives in Pulaski (Wis.) The expression was to "Go by Chutka" (who spoke no English, only Polish) living on a farm about three miles from town. Mammy Gauer could also indulge in that fantastic exercise in linguistics and usually had a pretty good time.

So did those remaining behind. There was figolo soda, cherry cordial, apricot cordial, blackberry cordial, sloe gin, plus the promised delivery of a half-barrel of beer (with the gratis loan of a pump). And a pint of Old Farm rye whiskey. (Old Farm can do no harm).

There was Margie, Geo. Graham, an unidentified lesbian, Wallio, Dillie, Col. Warren, Delores Green, Young Gauer, Danny Duh Beaver, Madam Goose. Bro Bloch, H. Mag., and Williams since it was his birthday. It is understood that there would always be some coming and going, so this cannot be considered an iron-clad roster, nor can the historians be depended upon to given an accurate account of their own bewilderment.

There was a popping of corks and jocosity, funny questions. There was flowage. Banging on the piano, most of it untuneful. The same for the singing.

Several Volga boatmen carried the console radio from the candy store upstairs into the festive flat and there was dancing, in an ungraceful manner. Col. Warren and Green had disappeared. When they came back, Green had turned pink. A strange rash spread like a hideous fungus over her neck and adjacentae. Danny Duh Beaver had his shirt off and was displaying his muscular attributes, scowling at this bicep with a threatening demeanor.

The latter pulled himself together after a while, put beer and ice in a derby hat and wore that as he gibbered frantically. Other strange portents were observed. Graham, who had spent some time in the attic communing with cobwebs, reappeared to find his toots had gone home. Alice and Margie prepared and helped snaffle sandwiches.

The delivery truck was downstairs with the half-barrel. On hearing the news, Duh Beaver, who had momentarily relaxed in the pantry with an unidentified female, burst down the steps and thunder-bellied back up with what turned out to be, actually, a steel bladder, in his arms, his muscles bulging like crazy. The keg was not cooled. It stood on the congoleum of the kitchen gurling hoggishly with pent-up whoopee, hissing, like a bomb itching to go off...

"Watch me take her with one plunge!" Duh Beaver cried out, grabbing the beer pump with the mad intention of stabbing it directly into the bunghole. He put the barrel on its side and straddled it with knotted thighs and poised the pump shaft.

> You had to screw the cap of the
> pump onto the threads of the
> bunghole first. Then jab the
> pipe through. But he didn't
> know that - he had to do it the
> fun way.

A breathless hush fell over the embattled kitchen.

"Everybody ready?" Duh Beaver screamed. He lunged downward and everybody

93

cringed, but the instrument failed to penetrate. The keg hissed a menacing warning that was lost on the celebrants and Duh Beaver again cried "Everybody ready?"

He lunged once more and there was a horrid blast, followed by a gushing fountain of beer rocketing to the ceiling. Duh Beave's hands, like clusters of plantain, clapped over the geyser. That only nozzled the eruption to all corners. There was a cloudburst of suds.

Screams of the squirted echoed through the flat as the keg sobbed, blubbered and subsided. Duh Beaver, his sanity (sic) gone, lay on the congoleum and wept. Williams sat stunned in a puddle until he got himself together and screwed the cap down. H. Mag. helped adjust the pump and got some pressure up. Concerned citizens, worried what Mama Gauer would say if the beverage was left to sour and stink in the crannies, were running with towels and wringing them out in the bathtub.

A lot of the warm, spicy froth that was left was consumed with evident relish. The correspondent who was recording all this began to feel a warm affection for all of his good friends and a vast contentment with all that had transpired. It was comforting and enriching to to be a part of this wonderful group in this delightful social setting. He was getting stewed.

* * *

Madame Goose

94

Williams, Col. Warren and Gnormie put on a first-class act (for themselves) by coming down from the attic Lab in a bashi-bazouk of military uniforms, a gas mask, and two ancient Enfield rifles with rusty bayonettes. There was a latrine-digging detail, a short-arm inspection, a homosexual sergeant and the rest of the familiar routine. All laughed hysterically, probably because of the demented intensity that gripped the actors.

The Fucharello sisters, Congetta and Phileomena, and their brother, Cono, who used to play ball with the gang on Sobieski Street, came to join the party. They arrived in time to see Madam Goose demonstrating the bump and grind, and Duh Beaver, more than half-naked, lifting a girl to the ceiling with one hand under her bottom. They left again probably wondering if the whole gang would turn to pillars of salt.

The Mag. was grateful when the girl grabbed the chandelier, that it did not tear out of the ceiling. The military boys continued to nourish their starved sensibilities with variations of the close order drill and kept on being killingly funny, which made The Mag. forget that Mr. Jazdjewski might just take it into his head to rumble over and close the show down.

Mammy Gauer had left a gigantic angelfood cake, heavily frosted with caramel frosting, splendid under a bell jar, hidden under the bed in her bedroom. When this was discovered there was a surge to the kitchen with it and a copious brewing of coffee began. Then the cake was assassinated.

H. Mag., with Alice, went up into The Lab where the former smeared diluted LePages' glue on his jowls and stuck cushion-stuffing to it. Alice helped stick and deftly trimmed a nifty spade beard. The effect was so attractive that the armed forces, and non-combatants too, all wanted beards, and they came up and worked The Lab into a shambles, bringing half the angelfood cake and platters of baked beans with them. All of the glue and most of the cushion shortly adorned their muzzles.

Duh Beaver also technically augmented his armpits and had a lot coming out his ears, and wanted to go even further but was forcibly restrained. Attrition set in. Only a few were left, finally, and they carried on into the wee hours in Gnormie's den in the attic.

Madam Goose unwrapped a special present she had for young Gauer. It was a Turkish water pipe, and it was decided to have at it. All, that is, except the unidentified Strange Girl, who, wine-logged, lay on a pallet and refused to be disturbed by hell or high wassail.

The device was a jar to be filled with perfumed water. A ceramic cup plugged into the top which was loaded with tobacco. The contraption had four velvet-wrapped rubber hoses connected to it with mouthpieces on the ends.

Madam Goose supplied some Balkan Sobranie, an exotic pipe tobacco, and two gold-tipped Russian cigarettes about four inches long, which were stripped of their paper and also stuffed into the hookah. Williams, Gnormie, Bro. Blo. and The Mag decided to sit in cross-legged yoga positions and started to enjoy the new thrill.

When they blew, a cloud of smoke came out and gave them an oriental-style feeling of asphyxiation. When they sucked, the smoke bubbled through the water, which did it no good at all, and traveled through evil-smelling neoprene rubber to reach their palates like air being sucked from the lungs of a decomposing dead horse. Suck or blow, it was awful. Duh Beaver picked himself up from wherever he was laying and inhaled deeply from the hose dropped from The Mag's limp fingers.

The Mag., not knowing if he was swimming underwater or picking out wallpaper, wrapped his head in a towel, claiming to be the Grand Vizier of Brady Street, stroked what remained of his beard, clapped his hands, and commanded nauch girls to dance.

It was a cue for Madam Goose and she danced. She danced wickedly, making the orient seem quite splendid. The smokers puffed some more and clapped in a bolero rhythm.

It was all the white port. Or maybe the foul warm beer. Or both and the oriental water-sickener. Something volcanic arose. An erupting army of two, Williams and Duh Beaver, burst from the seraglio, eyes bugged and lips empurpled. They thundered to the front attic window. They puked!

It was no ordinary exgurgitation, it was a soulful, primeval upchucking, an orgiastic convulsion. The stomach of observers like that of H. Mag churned convulsively. Crashing combers of nausea washed the beaches of his inland lake. Madam Goose vented a sob and a warning:

"They are going to fall out the window!" she keened. Rescuers ran across the splintery attic boards in order to grab the pukers by their belts and hold them to the sill. It was three stories straight down.

They should all have gone overboard, because the next day the whole world could see what had happened to the new paint job that had just been put on the building.

A brutal, searing lava-flow of shame had cascaded down the front all the way to the little cupola over the street entrance, where it divided into two slobberous tributaries, almost to the sidewalk!

The sun baked it into a monstrous speckled maroon scab!

* * *

A PERSONAL VIGNETTE

**Williams on the Railroad
And
Williams in the National Guard**

Williams' first day of work on the railroad came on July 3, 1936 at 5 a.m. It concluded at 11 p.m. He got the job, on the week-end Flambeau, through an old high school pal name of Wenninger. The C&NWRR, it seems was hard up for pearl divers, and Williams did nothing but wash dishes, fill tea pots, complete orders, toast crackers, toss pie, and ultimately darn near fall down. No forced march was ever that hot or that tough.

The off and on work continued from July to December. It was to the tune of clicking trucks, swaying cars, nasty burns, blisters, flurries and quiet sessions of dead heading. But even as a third cook, you met a lot of interesting railroading people.

When you went around a curve at 90-miles per, everything on the work tables went flying and if you didn't keep the overhead cupboards closed, all the crockery came zinging out of there, too. It was murder. The cookstove was fired with coke. Williams had to tend that. It would all hop out of the grate on top of him if he didn't work on a straight stretch of track or in the station.

The dishwasher in the sink was heated by turning a valve to let live steam from the locomotive squirt in to heat it up, which accounted for several bandages on William's grabbers. Old Man Wenninger could be one of the meanest bastards in the Brotherhood of Railway Trainmen while on duty, though a real sweet guy otherwise.

Williams also had a smashed fingernail and a cut from falling in the flour can, but the real hurt did now show. Like the rule they were not supposed to go through the passenger cars in their greasy aprons to get to the toilet compartments.

They were supposed to hold their water until the end of the run, which was insane. The second cook told Williams to urinate in an empty can of peaches and throw that out the vestibule. He tried that, but sloshed it out the wrong side of the car like a lousy landlubber, with disastrous results to his costume and personal daintiness.

"It seemed to rain piss for about five minutes!" Williams complained lugubriously.

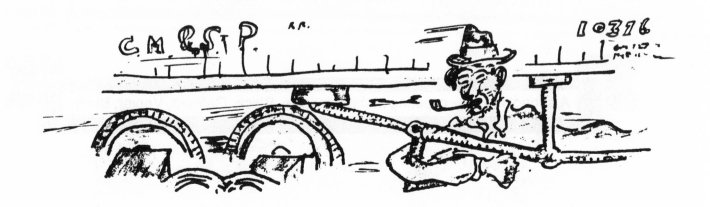

"It was a Saturday night,
We thought that we was hard
We went down to the armory
And joined the National Guard
-old army ballad

In the ranks of the Guard there are many species and varieties of humanity. In June of 1933, Williams decided to become one of the specimens. After passing a course in swearing and encampment, Williams was automatically considered a militiaman. It was then the privilege of Private Williams to pass the bucks, use foul language, perform menial duties, kick about the grub, view with disdain all army cooks, shavetails and other forms of lowlife in the military service.

The first field encampment was a decided thrill. A massed brigade parade was a spectacle Wms. never will forget. It is a busy two weeks - at a dollar a day - many phases of training are covered. Shooting, drilling, and field operations are the major divisions. Headquarters units (Reg H.Q. 127 inf.) spend much of their time in the field establishing communications with both entrenched and mobilized troops.

May 6, 1933 found Pvt. Williams and cohorts on strike duty at Shawano, Wis. Seems that the horse marines were getting beat by the farmers, so they called in the doughboys. Five days were spent with little or no sleep on sentry duty during pitch black nights, on flying patrols, tangling with barbed wire, searchlights and machine guns.

On June 2, 1933, Williams was discharged so he could join the Civilian Conservation Corps. When he reenlisted in the Guard in 1934 he had to wait until the 1935 encampment, at which he suffered a direct hit by lightening and was laid low. The quartermaster corps replaced his ripped uniform and he recovered without ill effect.

Williams waited until 1936 when the ordinary encampment was replaced by a gigantic mobilization of the second army at Camp Custer, Mich.. There were troop convoys across Lake Michigan, train rides, marches, night movements. Tanks aeroplanes, battles and gas. Anti-aircraft demonstrations. Sleeping on the ground, in rain, bad grub, grub shortages, blisters slogging in sand, observation balloons. Casualty reports, questionsing of prisoners. Just like in a *real* war!

A personal vignette
The adventures of Sam Lapidus

Bro. Bloch was looking through the newspaper trying to find his lunch when he sees a startling announcement:

 RIVERSIDE THEATER
Roy Atwell in person
Amateur night Monday

The next thing is, Bro. Bloch is in a room. Around the piano stands Eddie Weisfeldt, the orchestra leader, the MC, and the piano player. They have one cigar between them. Which they are passing around self conciously. First Weisfeldt takes a puff and leers. The orchestra leader takes a puff and coughs. The MC takes a puff and runs for the washroom. The piano player takes a puff and throws the cigar butt in the gabboon. From where Bro. Blo. fishes it out.

In between puffs they are rehearsing the amateurs. Bro. Blo. begins to perspire. Some of these acts are being treated very brutal. At last Weisfeldt bawls Bro. Blo's name and Blo. staggers over and does his Roy Atwell imitation. He is much surprised at the subsequent applause. After doing a Lou Holtz he is surprised again, and Papa Weisfeldt puts him on the radio broadcast half of the show.

Then Bro. Blo is taken to dressing room #1 and introduced to Roy Atwell himself - a tall, grey-haired citizen with a semi-intelligent pan, and a cordial manner. They gibber at random. Then it seems that he has a performance coming up. So Bro. Blo. pops, promising to see Atwell again on Monday.

VERY BRUTAL ... PART II

The acts come on — trombone smears, accordion throttlers, banjo garroters. Also several vocalists who abuse the lyrics of popular songs. They collect a large hand. Bro. Blo. does the Atwell piece. It seems to go, and the MC calls for an encore. Bro. Blo goes into his Louis Holtz. At the finish it is so quiet you could have heard a cough drop. Blo. lurches back to his seat. But then the brutality breaks. On comes an old duck - a shunnamite - who plays the harmonica and piano at the same time. He tries to get a piccolo in his nose, but fails. Then a Laurel and Hardy act which is funny at first, but gets so feeble it is yanked. Followed by some very brutal tap-dancing.

Comes the awards and Bro. Blo. gets a not. But all is not phooey, as Atwell has caught Blo's act from the wings and is very cordial and wants Bro. Blo to leave his script. Which he does. Then a little guy in a brown suit with checks gets Bro. Blo and six other acts to go out to the Club Kilkare with him in three taxis.

And here is brutal night life in the big city. All sit around a table - two accordionists, two soloists, Laurel & Hardy, a tribadist, and Bloch. About 200 people, or about 20 souls are out in front. Bro. Blo. goes on last and collects the prize, a finn. He gets home in a taxi after turning down a Cudahy a night for a week's work.

The next day Atwell likes Bro. Bloch's work. He offers to broadcast one of Bro. Bloch's scripts over WISN and give credit. Also he will talk to the studio about same. So he buys the script and does the stuff, offering a good plug, including name and address. And at Gaynors there is another mob of amateurs - Brutal. And an MC - Phooey! Such a bonch of doidy gegs, wit a farmer tsoot on yat, wid a straw het! Phooey. Bro. Bloch is so nauseated that he barely wins first prize, obliging with "The Maharajah" as an encore.

And the next morning, Atwell having plugged, WISN summons Bro. Bloch. And he is scheduled for an appearance next week. And gets to the Highland Cafe and another hangover show. A Weber & Fields act and after its smell drifts away, a singer with a voice like King Kong. And the guy who does slow motion sketches. Then Bro. Bloch with Atwell. Encore, Lapidus and the Havey Braadd, encore The Maharajah, and receives the prize.

At WISN Bro. Bloch is accompanied by Hoibie, Alice and Gauer. Two Sketches, the second being cut for time. And out into the night. The next morning our hero woke up with a brown taste in his mouth, having swallowed a horse blanket.

A Personal Vignette
Gauer Among The Wood Butchers

One day the Overlord of Brady Street hired Gauer into a decaying building at the foot of Marshall Street at $2 a day, Gauer to supply the overalls and a hammer. This was done at the will of Mammy Gauer, matriarch of the Gauer household in the summer of 1936.

With the sun yet young, H. Mag found a wizened and bent Polish carpenter, non-union in character, crouched in a littered yard, who set him to tasks the nature of which were:

To rip away clapboards from the outside and then rip out the underboards. To cut 2x4s, bust out plaster, saw out sections of flooring. To remove an entire crop of shingles from the roof and the boards under them. Then to smash down the chimney. To nail on a new roof and nail on a new siding. And to do a good bit of etcetera, including to liberate all the cockroaches established under the sink by taking out the sink.

Certain boards from on high accidentally landed on or near the old carpenter. There was an impromptu bombardment of the yard with chimney bricks and other acts causing displeasure. But The Mag learned during that brief training period to tear down and rebuild a house. It would guide him on his journey thru life.

He also had a week of shoveling sand and gravel into a hungry concrete mixer, and was beginning to suffer delusions of adequacy when the old carpenter, one Saturday night, got drunk and was thrown into the county tank, where he hung himself by his suspenders until dead and that was the end of that.

Gauer And The Swinging Pigments

Let it be known that thru the same channel of employment, H. Mag became an aerial artist of the first pigment when The Overlord Of Brady Street (Papa Jazdjewski), again gave him employment opportunity, this time   with his Painter From The Faraway Hills who owned the truck filled with paint-stiffened dropcloths and cans of slobber in assorted colors. The truck itself looked like it had been heavily desecrated by pigeons that could excrete in muddy versions of the colors of the rainbow and was ready for mounting as a monument in a public park

At the same wage of $2 per diem, for five days, he climbed towering ladders to wield brushes of a large bore with thick painter's cream - if nobody specified otherwise it was always the same depressing color of porkchop gravy - applying it to the withered and blistered exteriors of the residential structures in the Brady Street neighborhood.

It didn't take any particular skill. Anybody could dip a brush in a can and slap it against the inside to shake off the excess that would otherwise run down your arm to the elbow, reach out thru the rungs in the ladder and muscle the mucilaginous kaflooie back and forth in the baking sunlight onto the reluctant clapboards.

An Employment Turntable Of Old

It wasn't like that in the pre-Depression days when the late John N. Gauer (father to the Gauer Bros.) earned a living as a machinist and roundhouse foreman in the Chase Ave. yards of the Chicago and Northwestern Railroad. It was a skilled trade and the work was steady and the pay was no doubt adequate. When a switch engine fell into the pit, the guys could haul the enormous bugger out again and if it was busted they could fix it.

None of that apprenticeship or job experience was now available to the Gauer Bros. and nothing much, certainly not an estate or family wealth had been passed on to them and there were no influential relatives in the background, either. The Future, if it was to be hewn from the carcass of The Present, would have to be accomplished by dumb luck, happenstance, and of course, by exercising advanced optimism ...

At the wheel of a Checker Cab

[Low zone rates]

A Checker taxicab of the 1930s, with the driver, passenger and cab
all showing signs of the decade's wear and tear

Taxi-driving, the lowest form of living-making was no novelty to H. Mag Gauer. In fact
the fall of 1936 marked his third stint at that odious occupation. This time he made more
faithful notes and this History is the only place they can be set down as a guide to those who
follow. . .

Sept 15 — I am second out at the Belmont Hotel and the man on the pin looks aged and
rooted. The phone on the wall isn't ringing. The same old juice, nothin's movin' ... People go
past, women pour out of buildings headed for lunch. Old guys lurch along, guys in suitcoats
walk in gangs toward the auditorium with convention badges on their lapels. A drunk comes
out of the hotel eating peanuts. He stops to give some to the pigeons. The birds look kind of
drunk also.

Sept. 16 — The idea is to pick up drunks. I get one just before the rain, loud-talking and
stumbling, with a fistful of money. He wants to tour the taverns. The profit on that is 85 cents.

Thursday - A guy throws an epileptic fit at 2nd and Wis., attracting hundreds. A fat greengrocer and his fat ladyfriend ride into the far suburbs and I rot out there for 2 1/2 hours. What ennui!

Sunday — One of the drivers tells of getting a $5 bill for a two-bit fare. My fare from the Milwaukee Road depot to the Schroeder Hotel was short but dangerous as I left the flag up, thus enabling myself to pocket the entire fare. The fare told me about his waning vital powers in a blurred monologue.

The law of averages turned against me with my first load of nuns. They went from St. Mary's Hospital on the east side to the farthest corner of the 20 cents zone at 27th and National on the south side. Then they got out and walked the additional two blocks to Sacred Heart, saving themselves a cool 15 cents "extra" for the 2nd zone. Less tip. Aaargh!

When you did cross a zone the taxi company deemed it mandatory that the driver turn a knob on the meter to register that. The drivers considered that optional, for how otherwise could one make a living? It depended on one's estimate of total mileage against total fares registered on the meter, how much cheating one could get away with.

Tuesday - A load going from the Schroeder to the Tourist Inn, out in Cudahy doesn't know it had shut down as a disorderly house. (and I don't tell him). Later I enquire of other drivers about whorehouses in Cudahy. The Flag Station, the Liberty Bar and the 909 are supposed to be where you take that trade.

Having a slab of pie at an eatery at K.K. and Mitchell, the toots sliding the pie got to talking. She had a new way to gyp the pinball machines. Her method is to dig out the packing strip around the glass top and insert a stiff wire spring. Before I could tell her my method with the scotch tape over the nickel slot my phone pops on the pole outside and I have to blow.

Friday — A Yellow driver jumps in the wrong cab, meets the guy in his cab later in the day. He has one more load on the meter than the other guy so he gets two bits and they trade cabs.

A toots on Marlborough Drive has all her stuff lying out on the front steps. She says: "When you leave 'em on the spur of the moment, you got to expect this!" I take her to the Medford Hotel.

Monday — The crowd is yelling inside Borchert Field. then they pour out as the Brewers defeat the International League Champs from Buffalo. One happy fare affords me a shot of rare brandy. The Buffalo team pulls up in front of the Schroeder Hotel, crowding me from a spot in front.

I wait on Fifth Street across from the hotel to pull into the 3-cab line-up across Wis. Ave when a yellow screws across real fast and ootzes in ahead of me. I get sore and holler:

"Professor Einstein says there is nothing in the Darwinian Theory that justifies destructive competition in order to live up the the Survival of the Fittest doctrine!"

The slant-head in the yellow thinks about that for a minute and he replies: "You are right, Kropotkin, in his Mutual Aid A Factor in Evolution agrees that those who help each other are the ultimate survivors!"

In a pig's keister!

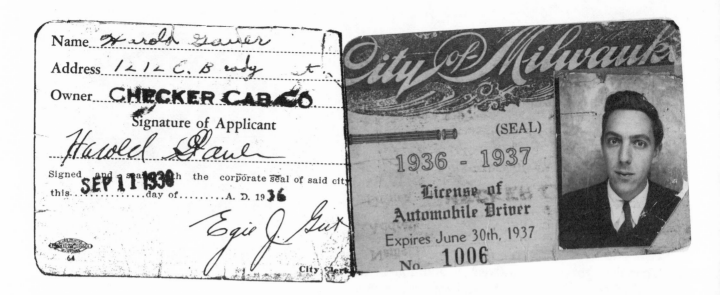

Wednesday — an out-of-town drunk is taken over the rocky road by the bartender and four come-on girls on N. Third Street ...

Drunks hold a fist-fight early in the cold morning. But the people watching are more interesting - an old guy with horrid gold fangs - a wizened negro woman with a police dog - a fat man who can't walk without puffing - a guy with a cigar sticking straight out of his muzzle like he had been hit square in the mouth with a potato ... a guy with a derby hat that doesn't fit.

A drunk stands next to the cab fumbling in his watch pocket with two fingers, bending stiffly at the knees, his face a bewildered muddle. When he gets in he can talk about only one thing - ol' Ernie Lambrecht, the greatest ketcher ever lived (himself) as he reviews the wavering images in his cracked brain.

One drunken dame has a fixed idea she can't let go of - she is going to "fix the clock" of a bakery salesman who had squealed to the County Aid about her having a job.

Eleven hours of cab driving
is enough to kill any man.

* * *

A personal vignette
Ghouls & Gunk

Bro. Bloch, attracted since childhood to WEIRD TALES MAGAZINE, tried writing for publication shortly after high school. Aided and abetted by H. P. LOVECRAFT, a greatly esteemed correspondent, he submitted a number of stories and in July, 1934, had his first acceptance. Since, Bro. Blo. has sold a number of yarns to Weird Tales as set forth below:

Horrors!

THE FEAST IN THE ABBEY
THE SECRET OF THE TOMB
THE SUICIDE IN THE STUDY
THE SHAMBLER FROM THE STARS
THE DRUIDIC DOOM
THE FACELESS GOD
THE GRINNING GHOUL
THE OPENER OF THE WAY
THE DARK DEMON
MOTHER OF SERPENTS
BROOD OF BUBASTIS
THE MANNIKIN
THE CREEPER IN THE CRYPT
FANGS OF VENGEANCE
THE SECRET OF SEBEK
FANE OF THE BLACK PHAROAH

* * *

FAN MAGAZINES (*Marvel, Fantasy, Unusual, Phantograph,* etc.) have or will publish the following tales and articles:

Lillies — The Laughter of a Ghoul - The Black Lotus — The Escape - Madness of Lucian Gray — How to Write for W T — A Master of Weird Fiction — The Ultimate Ultimate - A Visit with H P Stoopcraft - How I Got My Inspiration — Macabre Music — The Feast — I, The Insane

* * *

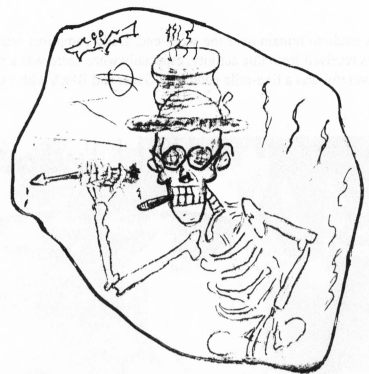

In addition to all that ...

Bro. Bloch has contributed to perhaps twelve Funtasy humor columns for Fantasy Magazines. He also has in his possession some fifteen factory throwouts or rejected stories, including an unpublished novel, allegedly humorous. Bro. Blo. has also perpetrated some radio comedy work, which was used, but for which he was greatly underpaid by Roy Atwell and Stoopnagle & Budd. He plans submission to other markets, including Thrilling Mystery.

* * *

A FLASHBACK

The Battling Stugatchus

The Blue Eye League inaugurates its Fifth Season. In this scribe's opinion, not all of the new line-up changes were a good idea. Last year saw three evenly-matched teams whooping neck and neck to the finish line with the Champion Fungulas nosing out the Stugatchus by a slim 2-game margin. And with the Mags following by another two games.

The lowly Mags may be excused for desperately trying to bolster their line-up, but the acquisition of Cecil Slotch was no stroke of genius. Slotch is slow on ground balls, swings like he was hung, and is as shifty as a pregnant hippopotamus. Marshall Mandrilljazz is all his name implies and won't help the Mags either. Manager Mag must be given credit for his unswerving loyalty to the failing ecclesiastics. I predict the Mags won't win a pennant until J.J. and his relatives are kicked upstairs into desk jobs. And the coaching staff of the Mags couldn't make a pitcher out of The Overlord, but they tremble now when he comes into the park with the Stugatchus.

Williams, Stugatchu Mgr.
on the road

On reviewing the Fungulas we see that the return of two foul balls to the roster means that The Big Boob and F. Gregory Coprophalia are being given another chance. And another no-good, Raskalvikov, is appearing as a pitcher in a starting role. Jeffry Snartch is another past master at throwing ball games recalled to the Fungulas 1936 team. It seems very plain to this writer that something is wrong. The Fungula management owns the largest farm of promising young ball players in the league and these men are being given the finger. Maybe the Fungulas are tired of winning pennants.

Lester Scranch

Soon, we will have the pleasure of seeing the Stugatchus in action. Manager Wms cleverly took advantage of The General's hitting power, converting him into a 2nd-baseman. Watch him. The Armless Wonder is no longer a pitcher, but is trying to plug the weakness at short. The Dude and The Brain were released. In their stead is an old Fungula pitcher, Lester Scranch, who twice already has licked his old teammates. With the powerful Joe Duck, Goniff, Fumblekeister and Sneakafeelia, it looks like another great season for The Battling Stugatchus - barring injuries!

109

Some very lousy fangs

Ravaged by a heavy diet of bon bons, chocolate fudge, Mexican penoche, fairy food, coated nuts, caramels, brittles and drops, Gauer's oral cavern sported teeth resembling stalagmites, which had to be withdrawn from his goozle.

Bro. Bloch and Mim Powell enter into a *pose plastique* to dramatize. The Mag's dental travail and at the same time provide a picture series symbolizing life in general and growing up on Brady Street in particular. Unfortunately the editors of the nation's picture magazines didn't understand Brady Street symbolism and ran a lot of shots of Gina Lolobrigida instead.

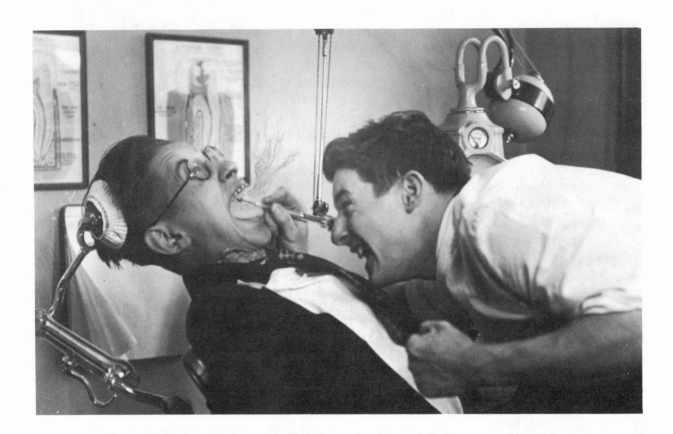

1936 - A Pantomime

This pantomime is different. It has spoken dialogue! 365 days were required for its 1936 performance. The cooperation of Sylvester W. Skadietndapmn is acknowledged and thanks extended to Mammy·Gauer and also to the Overlord of Brady Street for set decorations and background music.

SCENE ONE

A basement on Brady Street featuring a pingpong table. Jan 4th 1936, 10 P.M. Of a Saturday night. We discover Williams and a group of satchellites rattling the bones. The dice pass to Danny Duh Beaver and (FLOURISH) ...

A policeman enters. Pandemonium. General tumult. The lights fade. Williams, Bloch, Warren and Goose advance to center stage and sing. (Song: Four Boys With a Guitar).

SCENE TWO

A prison cell, left. In four separate ninny bins stand the song birds of Scene One. They flush their booming birds. Enter Bro. Gauer with $40. The prisoners are released. Exeunt omnes leaping and capering to the tune of (Song: Durance Vile Blues) as (Curtain falls)

SCENE THREE

Felons face Judge Page. Chorus of wailing Warren family, betrayed Blochs, unaware Williams' and depressed Gooses. (Dance: The Frenzied Familas)

SCENE FOUR

Kitchen, dining room and parlor of the Gauer flat on Brady Street. Enter: Gauer, Bloch, Williams, Bedard. Each places a bottle on the kitchen table. Break into song: (Song: All I Have Are Sunny Weather Friends).

Enter: Tootsae. Ballet. Bro. Gauer plays a lively tune on the piano (Nola - it is the only tune he knows). The entire body suddenly goes into double time and exits toward the washroom (Stage Left).

SCENE FIVE

Same kitchen set, seen through a fog of beer smoke,. Col. Warren in a living fountain sequence, followed immediately by Bro Gauer with a mop. Enter: Danny Goose Duh Beaver with a derby hat.

Goose: (Song) We Thought That We Was Hard from the Opera Horse Collar.

SCENE SIX

Precision Process Laboratory, a murky den, festooned with a host of stuff, this in turn being covered with more stuff. The authors of THE HISTORY sit around a table. Gloom. Purple lights, A clock shows 11 P M but it is really midnite, radio time.

They peer over their shoulders nervously. Nothing. It is uncanny. Weird. Williams falls down, saying:

Spoken: "It is the witching-frigging-hour ! ! !
Echo: "Aaaaaaargh!"

Bloch: Nird, what was that? A wreath of ectoplasm takes nebulous shape in midair, forming the fickle finger of Fate. Ghostly noises are heard in the gloom such as Gauer rustling his corduroy pants. Thorugh the adumbrated nigrification the supernatural appendage strikes, goosing all.

Pounding: Boom — Boom — Boom Boom. Boom — Boomboom!

Voice: You should put on 20 pounds, be fireman! (Coughing).
Other voices: Not! Fake!

Pounding: (Mammy Gauer pounds on ceiling with broom-handle from kitchen below.)

The ghosts yammer and scream, grimace unspeakably. They cough up a horrible syrup from their lungs and it hangs in the air, foetidly to enfold scene six, which fades to a deep purple and goes out.

In the darkness: (Gauer) All right then! I'll go back to the goddam taxi company! (Falls down).

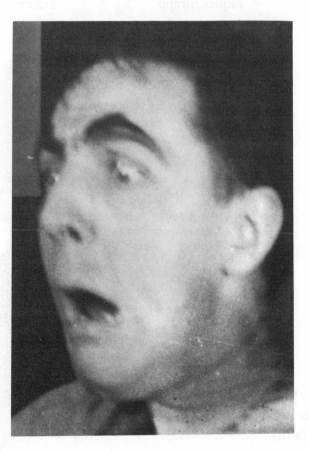

SCENE SEVEN

Dining Car Kitchen, C&NW Railroad. In haggard array stand The Chef, Second Cook, Third Cook, and WILLIAMS The air is thick with profanity and steam. Williams is also thick. (Sound effect: clicking of trucks on trails, banging of utensils and trays warmed over in an orchestral sauce). The stage rocks and sways constantly to this racket.

WILLIAMS (To Chief Cook) Don't beat me, boss, you lardhead, please, Sir!

Chef to Williams: Peel those spuds. Wipe those pans. Stir that gravy. Lift those bars. Tote those bales.

Entire Cast: Suddenly turns to face the audience and with aprons tossed over their heads, sing.

Song: Avez-vouz du chocolat.

114

SCENE EIGHT

Bedroom of Bloch. Lesbian Arms Apartments on Knapp Street. Bro. Blo. is writing a story, sitting at a cardtable wobbling with a Woodstock typewriter, many papers and a pile of assorted stuff. As the curtain rises, Block twists around in his chair and sings:

Song: You're F.W.Wright!

Bloch: 'Writes as orchestra tries to pick up his tempo. Rising, Bloch advances to miror, grimaces frightfully into it. Trembling, in every limb he starts typewriting again, leers insanely.

Exits (Left) Returns in vampire costume. Dribbles for atmosphere. Exits once more, returns in garb of Frankenstein Monster, Writes some more, climbs out the window into a tree and trembles in every limb. Gets back inside.

The threshold opens and there stands a ghost - The Green Goof! A horrible mockery, a ghastly caricature of the human form.

Bloch: advances to mirror and cuts throat. Smiling happliy, returns to card table and begins typing where he left off.

* * *

"PRECISION PROCESS"
PHOTOGRAPHERS
1212 EAST BRADY STREET
MILWAUKEE, WIS.

THE HISTORY

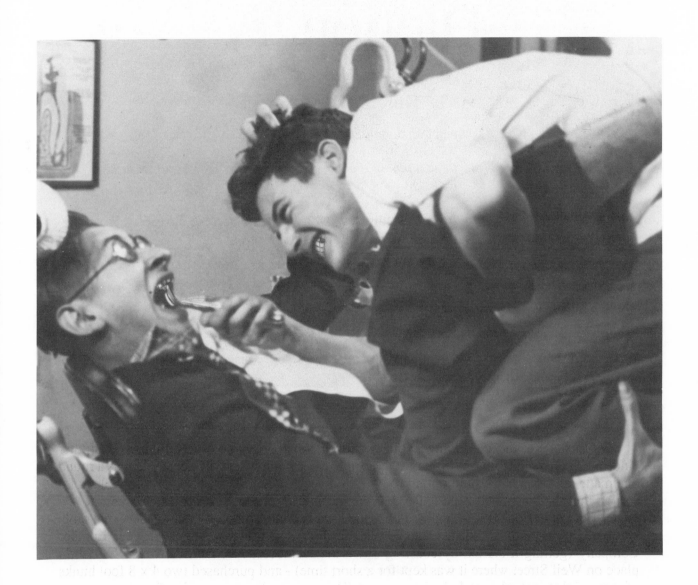

BOOK 3

The new Dictionary

1937 Third Revised Edition

AGED PROSTATIC	Ancient dodderer. Any crusty, rheumy, pooped adult.
ANCHOR PANTS	Person whose center of intelligence is located in the hinder parts.
AND A STORM CAME UP	Impending disaster. Indicative of a burst in the offing. Looming doom.
ANENCEPHALY	Total absence of the brain.
ANTS IN THE PANTS	Uneasienss. Fidget. Unrest. A bug has crawled into the person's fundament.
APPETITE PERVERT	A grub androgyne. Consumer of uncommon food. Ostentation, gourmandizing.
ARCHIVES	The voluminous collection of stuff. Hence: "Stuff this in yr archives". An uncouth directive.
ARE YOU SAVED?	A greeting.
AVID	Greediness characterized by drooling, slobbering, dribbling. "hungry".
BAG	A particularly odious and repellent species of female. A nasty piece burlap.
BABES	Any females
BIBLIOMANIA	A craze for possessing rare and curious books, such as those in the history library.
BLACK MASS	A big pile of stuff.

BLOAT	A liquid or semi-liquid uzz which, when rapidly guzzled, causes tumescence of the gut.
BOGGLED	Paazed. Or just plain dronk.
BORN UNDER THE WRONG SIGN	Born under the sign of Uranas..... or Uranus.
BRUTAL	The Magazine For People.
BREEP!	A weird cry, eructated on special occasions. Irritating to canines.
BUGGERY	Vile wretchedness. Unnatural diddling. Socialogically: rocking the boat.
BULEMIA	Morbid hunger. Craving for choc. malts.
BUST A GUT	Demonstration of mirth or indignation, accompanied by convulstions and pueling.
CARNAL CLUTCH	Avid grasp, letcherous seize, mostly faked, with appropriate outcires.
CLOACA THEORY	Infantile belief that the brains are in a remote section of the anatomy. Immature speculation on sexual matters.
CLOWNISM	Hysteric display of contortions and poses.
COPROPHAGY	Eating of forbidden frucht. Fondness for revolting foods.
CONSCUPIENT	Lecherous, full of avid.
CONSTUPRATION	Obscenity, lewdness.
CONSTRUCT	to make good out of from stuff that aint.
COPROLALIA	Insane use of obscene prhrases in the course of an ordinary conversation.
COPROLITE	Petrified details of carnivorous reptiles often found in cheap pipe tobacco.
CRAZZY-NOTZ	Catatonic rage. Violent & unhibited impulse to destroy following demonstrations of dubious humor. Drooling a symptom.

CRAWLING OUT OF A BIG PIPE	Happy ending to an unfortunate accident.
DIDDLE	Ineffectual futzing. Piddling. Indolent scrounging. Endless capering.
DOIDY PEETCHAS	Feelthy futtygrafts. History photography of distorted faces.
DON'T GIMME NONE O' THAT	Rejection of a suggestion the execution of which is impossible.
DRAGGED	Process whereby tootses are brought to functions. Also a paazment.
DRUNK AS A POPE	Of course The Pope isn't drunk, but boy are those who are as drunk as !
ECHOLALIA	Mechanical repetition of catch words and compulsive use of cliches.
ECHOPRAXIA	Mechanical repetition of the movements of another. Mass impulse to frenzy.
EOMANGIA MINGIA	Rare disease. Itching & scratching visitation.
ERETHRISM	Morbid degree of excitement in the ego. Muscles in the head.
EUPHORIA	A feeling of well being and satisfation in certain phases of endeavor.
EVIRATE	Render sterile. Extract virility from a social gathering. Also, disipation of liquid potency with tsody water.
FACTORY THROWOUTS	Dubious characters. Or, slightly damaged but high-class books. Slightly smoked but havy cigars.
FAKE	Absence of class in an individual. Immature. Ineffective consumation of an ambitious project.
FIGOLO SODA	Tsody Wodder.
FLIGHTY	Mentally unstable. Chronic veering into semi-hysterical conversation. A revolving brain.
FLOTCH-TCH-TCH	Hiddious resurrection of hastily digested uzz. Product of certain human fountains.

FOICHTBOINDERS	Things (and stuff) whose description is not covered by any other term.
FOOZE	Frothy substance dried-out. Frequently noticed in its dried state on books and photos. (You can't use mine, it has fooze on it)
FRONGE	Nasty stuff spit out while smoking pipes or cigars. Frequently swallowed, with consequent bogglement.
FULL IN THE FACE	Having a fat behind. Also having over-stuffed jowls or foolishly flushed Phiz.
FUSTIGATE	Pummel doghouse. (See: tap on horn)
FUSTILARIAN	Stinkard. One who stinks. Badly odored attitude.
FUN BOX	Radio or phonograph that gives happy stuff.
F. W. WRIGHT.	A much-quoted authority in emphatic statements. E.g. - "You're F.W. Wright!"
GASM	Convulsive rictus. Shuddering in the head. Intense excitement.
GIBBER	To deliver a rambling monologue on an irrelevant subject. To babble or blubber.
GREEN HEMMORHAGE	An inexplicable, unnatural occurrence or sight, offensive attitude or action, will cause revulsion of feeling resulting in a green hemorrhage.
GRAB LOOSE	Unclutch. Let go. Release.
GUNK	Great variety of minutia, mostly inoffensive, but given unfavorable aspect because of its failure to fall into a readily classifiable form.
GOOF	To eat rapidly.
HAMMERHEAD	Genial moron. Term embraces most snatches ranging from minor scrounge to troglodytic tworches, all resistant to suggestion. Similarly: hardhead.
HAVING A DUCK	Fantastic excuse for tardiness.
HIGH CLASS	Of the first water. A superior grade of humor. An obscurely amusing situation relished by the initiate. Subtle stuff.

HIGH KNOCKER	Crude boaster. Idle egotists. Arrogant chief.
HISTORY	The bound archive. The monster record of eventful stuff.
HONEY WAGON	Any conveyance, but usually one in a decrepit state, such as The Car. Or, any emergency or police vehicle.
HOOP	A cough or sneeze out of proportion to irritation causing its utterance. Produced with such bravado as to obviate an apology.
HOPE THEY ALL GET IT	A pious wish that clapping affect the applauders.
HORSECOLLAR	Minced oath. Polite expression of adverse criticism.
HOT FLASH	Pains of a good idea in labor.
HUNGRY	Avid desire for female attention.
INCUBUS	Symbolic bringer of havy trouble
I DUNNO WHAT'S THAT	Inability to comprehend. Defective retention of instructions or ideas.
I HAVE BEEG JOKE	Appreciation of comic situation.
IN A SLING	The mind in rupture. Defeatist mechanism indicating melancholia. Suspended.
JILOOKEY	A passing stranger
JIMOKE	An ordinary person.
KYOEBLEH	Unfamiliar tworze. Distasteful material usually in writing, causing retching and digital demonstration.
LARDHEAD	A person with wrinkles in his crisco. One who's meninges have been fried in deep fat. A poop.
LAY ANALYSIS	Therapy by non-medical practitioners.
LEGISLATIVE BODY	The Sexual Congress.
LITTLE FAKES	Minor attaches, stooges, parasites, satellites, under-age pseudo-people.
LUBRICIOUS	Libidinous, lewd and greasy

LUMBUCKAROO	Disease striking with mercurial swiftness. Symbolic indisposition.
MILWAUKEE SUBWAY	The fallopian tubes
MORBOSE	Condition proceeding from siege of either Eomangia Mingia or Lumbuckaroo. Inattentive state proceeding from havy thinking.
NIRD	A person or thing.
NOSTOMANIA	Excessive nostalgia. Morbid looking-back.
NYMPHOLEPSY	Condition seldom found in local females.
O FECAL FATE	Dolorous lament. Outcry against perverse fortune.
ON THE FLY	In a great haste. Or: located on the front of the trousers.
ONEIRODYNIA	Painful dreams with nightmare & somnambulism. Gaston Belch's remedy: "Partake of not le chile and le hamburgaire to the same time both".
ON THE FLOOR	Unfortunate predicament resulting from a reaming or brutalizing of Fate.
PHALLOCRYPT	A pair of trousers.
PRECISION PROCESS	Method of taking pictures with out-dated film of contorted subjects in a bad light, and printing them on the wrong kind of paper.
PUELING	Involuntary cachinnation, with occasional maniacal hooping.
SATCHELLITES	Minor toolbearers, in The History.
SATYRIASIS	Overabundance of letch.
SCHTAAZ	Voluble person lacking conversational class. A conversation of no consequence. (2) The planets and suns visible to the naked eye.
SCATOLOGY	Pertaining to filth. Used in all normal conversation.
SCHIZOIDS	Unsatisfactory personalities with maladjustment to ideas who constantly resort to frenzied yammering.

SCOPTOPHILIA	Act of looking at objects d' art. Voyeurism. Public eying of wenches.
SCOTSBOROUGH CASE	Any gathering or party at which males predominate.
SHAKE THE GRATES	Get busy. Get high-class. Put muscles in.
SKUNDJE	Embolophrasic word typical of many senseless words and phrases in current use.
SNATCH	An individual of fleeting worth.
STEATOPYGA	Projecting protentiously behind. A lard-hinder.
STEENK!	A shrill, piercing cry directed at conventional monotony. Criticism uttered in a tone of aggrieved surprise.
STOOGE	A dope used as a pawn. A stoopid.
SCROON	A hag, crone, wizened wench. Nogo toots.
STORKED	Unwanted responsibility of a parturient nature. Brutalized. Reamed.
TANGLE	Engage in combat or come to grips with females.
TOOTED	Extreme exhaustion. Pooped. Paazed.
TRANSVESTITES	Those strangely garbed and of indeterminate sex.
TUMESCENCE	Early rising. Out of bed early.
UNCONSCIOUS	Falling into good luck by sheer accident.
VERBIGERATION	Continuous repetition of phraseology with little comprehension of its significance.
VERY BRUTAL	At attempt at wit so hiddeous as to affront the sensibilities. Trite gags, senile humor and amateur stage performers are all very brutal.
VERY TENDER	A dearth of return. Nothing moving. Things at a standstill.
WHY WEAR A TRUSS?	Why be obscure? Why cloak your meaning? A plea for bald statement. An appeal for pithy facts.

WOOD BUTCHER	A Carpenter.
WOODEN BLADDER	A barrel of beer.
WORD PERVERTS	Persons who use incongruous verbiage, esp.: those who inject extraneous word for emphasis, splitting another word for this purpose. Example: "The Conser—stinkin' - vation Corps."
YOU'LL BE SO KINDLY	A polite interjection into an uncomplimentary invitation.

SOME PROPER NAMES.
And some not so proper:

Chas Hovacoe
Dr. Stugatchi
Sam Lapidus
Lefty Feep
Unnatural Tom
Floyd Scrilch
Doc. Lessgland
Hugo Monsterberg
Antsmosh Strandnagle
Sex Roamer
Buster Bladder
The Little Fungula
H P Stoopcraft
Poopse W. Tewya
Antop Dirp
Fake W. Nogo
Gaston Belch
Hoyle W. Struggle
Dominic Snatchatcha
Jno. Semipopo
Fileding W. Yocshamosh
F. Gregory Coprophalia

The Maharaja
Mr. Stoof
Subconscious Sigmund
Chalres Brutch
Mary Kajaadj
Cloven W. Hoof
Anton Stuquepukchu
Fracas W Melefight
Marshall Mandrilljazz
Black Art
Osward Drizzledrawers
Ecclesiastic W. Omigod
Lumpatsias Fadjumbrundis
General Von der Bumm
Fadder Kaufmann
Plentygone W. Notmuchleft
Caspar the Naked
Tubal Scrotus
Stabber Fitznoodle
Gilbert Spooldripper

Medical Supplement

ABALENIATION - Physical or mental decay

ABOLUIA (ABULIA) - Loss or defect of will power

ACATAMATHESIA - Morbid blunting of perceptions. (2) Inability to comprehend speech.

ACEDIA - Apathy

ACONURESIS - Involuntary voiding.

ACORIA - insatiable hunger

ADIPSOUS - tending to quench thirst

AEROPHAGY - swallowing of air.

AGENESIA - sterility

AGENOSOMIA - Poor development of the reproductive organs

AGRAMMATISM - inability to form grammatic sentences.

AGOROMANIA - Morbid desire for solitude.

AICHMOPHOBIA - fear of sharply pointed instruments

ALEXIA - word blindness - inability to read.

AMBLOSIS - miscarriage; abortion

AMENOMANIA - Mania with joyous delirium.

AMUSIA - inability to distinguish musical sounds.

AMYOUS - wanting in muscle.

ANADIPSLA - Intense thirst.

ANAMNESTIC - Remembering.

ANDROGYNA - Hermaphrodite-female type

ANDROGYNUS - Hermaphrodite Male type

ANDROMANIA - Nymphomania

ANDROPHOBIA - Morbid fear of men.

ANHEDONIA - Complete loss of sensation of pleasure.

ANOREXIA - Loss of appetite for food

ANTEPHIALTIC - Preventing nightmare

ANTHROPOPHOBIA - Fear of society.

ANTIPERISTALSIS - abnormal movement of bowels toward stomach.

127

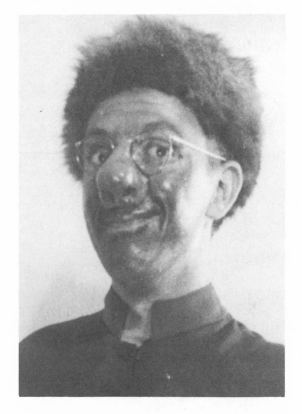

APHRONIA - Morbid lack of practical judgment.

APOSITIA - Loathing for food

ATAXAPHASIA - Inability to arrange words in sentences.

ATAXAPHOBIA - Excessive dread of disorder

ATAXIA - Marked incoordination, physical or mental

AUTISM - Morbid or phantasmic daydreaming

BARYSHMIA - Gloomy state of mind

BESTIALITY - sexual object is lower animal

BICAPITATE - has 2 heads

BULIMIA - Inordinate appetite.

CATATONIA - Compulsion to assume peculiar postures

CONFESSION COMPULSION - Abnormal need to confess (2) Compulsion to commit symbolic acts.

COPROPHILIA - morbid liking for filth.

COUVADE - man who takes to his bed and simulates pains of his wife in labor

BOMBUS - Intestinal rumbling

BORBORYGMUS - Rumbling of intestinal flatus

BROMIDROSIPHOBIA - Morbid fear of bodily odors

CACHINNATION - Immoderate laughter

CACOSMIA - Offensive odor

CACOTHYMIA - Disordered state of mind.

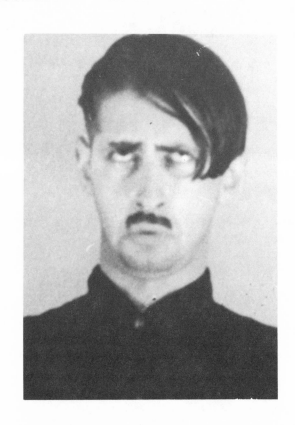

CADUCITY - Senility; feebleness.

CATAPHASIA - Senseless repetition of same words.

CEPHALODYNIA - Pain in the head.

CHEIROSPASM - Writers cramp Scrivener's palsy.

CLUNIUM - Buttock

CRYPTORCHID - Individual with undescended testes

DAMIANA - Certain powerful aphrodisiac leaves

DESUDATION - profuse or morbid sweating

DIABOLEPTIC - Insane person professing to hold supernatural communication.

DIDYMODYNIA - Pain in the testicles

DINOMANIA - Dancing mania.

DIVAGATION - Delirium; disconnected speech.

DOMATOPHOBIA - Insane dread of being in a house.

DYSBULIA - Impairment of will power

DYSGEUSIA - Perversion of the sense of taste

DYSLEXIA - Ability to read, but not understand

DYSLOGIA - Inability to reason

DYSOREXIA - Depraved or unnatural appetite

ECPHRONIA - Melancholia bordering on insanity

EGESTA - Discharges of bowel

EMBOLOPHRASIA - use of senseless words or sentences

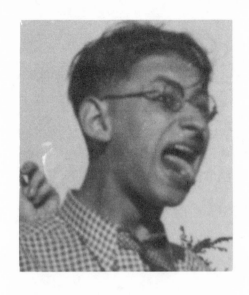

EMICTION - Micturation

ENTHEOMANIA - Religious mania

EPHEBIC - Pubertal period

ESCHROLALIA - Coprolalia

ESTRUATION - Sexual desire. Orgasm.

EUCRASIA - Sound health

GEROMORPHISM - Appearance of age in a young person.

GRAPHOSPASM - Writer's cramp

GYNANDRIA - Hermaphroditism

HEBEPHRENIA - Peculiar insanity incident to the age of puberty

HETEROPHASIS - Misapplication of terms in mental diseases

HIDROPEDESIS - Excessive sweating

HYPERCRYALGESIA - morbid sensitiveness to cold

HYPERMNESIS - Abnormal memory

HYPERMYOTROPHY - Excessive development of muscle

HYPEROREXIA - Bulemia Hyperphagia

HYPNOLEPSY - Morbid sleepiness

HYPOSTASIS - Excretion (2) sediment (3) deposit

HYSTRICIASIS - Disease of the hairs in which they stand erect.

ICHTHYOID - Resembling a fish

INSPERGATION - act of powdering

JACTITATION - Restlessness; moving to and fro

LECTULUS - bed or couch

LIMOSIS - morbid or depraved appetite

LOGORRHEA - Abnormal rapidity of speech

MACROESTHESIA - abnormal capacity for sensation.

MACROPODIA - abnormal size feet

MEGALOGASTRIA - Abnormal size of stomach

MELOMANIA - Insane love of music

MOGIGRAPHIA - Writers cramp

MUIRAPUAMA - Brazilian wood said to be powerful aphrodisiac

NECROMETER - Instrument for measuring dead organs

NUBILITY - State of sexual development when marriage may be consummated

OINOMANIA - mania of intoxicating liquors

ONYCHOPHAGY - biting of the nails

OZOSTOMIA - foul odor from the mouth

PABULUM - Food: anything nutritive

PACHYCEPHALOUS - having a thick skull.

PALPEBRATION - act of winking. Nictation.

PANDICULATION - act of stretching. Yawning.

PANTAPHOBIA - absence of fear.

PAPPUS - first downy beard

PAPPOSE - covered with down

PARALOGIA - faulty reasoning

PAREUNIA - coitus

PAVE - Fright

131

PAVOR NOCTURNNIS - Nightmare

PECCANT - Unhealthy, morbid

PECILONYMY - Use in writing of different names for the same thing.

PERIBLEPSIS - the wild look of delirium

PERIZOMA - a girdle, as a truss

PHRENESIS - delirium; frenzy

PHRENOPLEGIA - Sudden loss of mental power

PLEONEXIA - Morbid selfishness or greediness

POLLAKIURIA - Abnormal frequency of micturation

POLYPHRASIA - Excessive garrulity.

POLYPHAGIA - (Bulimia)

PROCTALGIA - Pain in the anus (Procto-dynia)

PROLABIUM - Red exposed part of the lip

PSEUDOMNESIA - Things that never occurred seem to be remembered

PUBERTAS PRAECOX - Puberty at an early age

PYGAL - Pertaining to the buttocks

RAPTUS - Any sudden attack or seizure

RUCTUS - Belching of wind from the stomach

SALTATION - Dancing, leaping, skipping

SCORACRATIA - involuntary evacuation

SITOMANIA - periodic bulemia

SOPOR - Sleep

STERCORACEOUS - Having the nature of dung. (Stercus.)

STERNUTATION - Act of sneezing

STRIDOR DENTIUM - gnashing the teeth

SUBLIGAMEN - Truss

TABACOSIS - Poisoning by tobacco

TABAGISM - The tobacco habit

TARANTISM - The dancing mania

TENTIGO - Lust

THERIOMIMICRY - Imitation of the acts of animals

URACRATIA - Enuresis

URANIST - A sexual pervert

VAPORS - Lowness of spirits: Hysteria

VESANIA - Unsoundness of mind.

VIRILESCENCE - Assumption of male characteristics by an aged woman

YOHIMBINE - An alkaloid used as an aphrodisiac. Also as an local anesthetic (Dose: Youhimbine Chlorid, 1/10th gr. Sol. in W.)

ZOOID - Resembling an animal

132

THE PRECISION PROCESS TAKES ITS
ANNUAL INVENTORY
Jan 4 1937

EXCERPTS FROM THE SATYRIASIS OF PETRONIUM

1937 Version Of The New Year Classic

TYPICALLY, there were no preparations to accouch the 1937 New Year. There was only Bottoms W. Up and faulty information that the Gauer flat would be occupied by celebrating adults. But when a unit sallied forth from The Lab above, the place was well right now empty after all.

Bro. Gauer, Corp. Williams, Bro. Bloch and Sister Alice took over. Facing them in the kitchen were Madame Goose and Gnormie and they said tidings. Expected, with more drinking fluid were Duh Beaver, Health, and Menos.

Bro Bloch played a version of *Manhattan Serenade* on the piano whilst Bro. Gauer performed it on the cocktail shaker and two rounds of manhattans were had. Then a shaker of Tom Collins. The entrance of Health was announced by loud blasts on a pint of Applejack and some Rock & Rye. And figolo soda, with shrill tootings likewise on some beer. An air of whooie became apparent.

Enter Menos, Duh Beaver, and what might be called a third party. At Midnight the OLD YEAR was heaved out, together with whatever Williams had been drinking. Bro Gauer brewed coffee downstairs in the candy kitchen. Heath, now on a first name basis with Tom Collins, fell down.

At Gardner's Tavern on Franklin Place the world had gone mad. So had it in Lee's Cafe on Ogden Ave., where the lights went out. That was ascribed to *The Little Man With The Hammer*, but it was an actual and real power blackout, all over, including the street lights. The group departed the adumbrated Lee's Cafe and went into a stygian Green Parrot, from which panic-stricken customers had fled, leaving behind four onion sandwiches, upon which the group nourished themselves.

On returning to New Years Eve Headquarters on Brady Street, Madame Goose was found cleaning up the place. Heath, Menos and Duh Beaver had departed, destination unknown and whomever else had been on the premises had also flown. It was time to go home by the stumble and grope method, perchance to dream and postively to see what the future had in store in case the lights came on again, or that if they didn't, there would be another day's dawning or any trace of the year 1938 . . .

A RESCUSCITATION EFFORT FAILS

Two years ago, in 1935 the Federated Arts Council was at its height, flourishing three floors above the Milwaukee River only to collapse in 1936 of overweight and ennui. Legend and fable remained and in early Feb of this year, 1937, Bro. Milt Gelman started to talk it up again.

He approached H. Mag. and Bedard in a low dive called Unnatural Tom's one night after they had been cavorting at the Riverview Roller Rink. Then he cornered Bro. Bloch and Bro. Gauer who were among beers, listing on pieces of blotting paper the probable line-up for the Blue-Eye League baseball season..

Hence there was a gathering at the Carleton Hotel where Bro. Sprague Vonier dwelt. However, Bro. Gelman was not present, since he suddenly came up with a very heavy commitment involving a ginch. But seated on the chairs of a many were Paula Kovack, Col. Warren, somewhat late but plenty heavy with the feet, Cousin Sherm, dead pan, and a lout from high school now unknown and never seen again, Mert Koplin and as well, Bro. Bloch, Bro. Herbie Williams, Sister Alice and Bro. Gauer, the latter bringing along some psychological stuff and a bunch of philosophical credos including the outlook on life of such jimokes as George Jean Nathan, H.L. Mencken, Sir James Jeans, Albert Einstein, and a host of other guilookeys.

There were 8 or 9 of them and each delegate present was given one of the credos to read aloud to the entire group. Well, and ... everyone read the material dutifully. But discussion was forthcoming to the extent of not.

Bros. Bloch and Gauer carried on a sporadic cross-chatter liberally sprinkled with leading questions and direct inquiries of the participants, but only a few irrelevant and pointless beatings of the obvious were had.

There was nothing to be done.

The FAC slumped to the carpet and lay there with its gills working like a beached carp. Sprague came with some old newspaper and it was taken down into the alley.

The second coming of the FAC was not to be.

Sprague Vonier

135

Easy Winner;
Gauer in Fast Knockout

Gauer Wins Stiff Fight

Norman Gauer found Art Greer, Chicago Negro, a tough and willing foe, but punched out a victory in six rounds. He had Greer bleeding at the mouth and very tired from left hooks to head and body. Bobby Fadner, Fond du Lac. handled an awkward job well in decisively beating Charley Mack. He knew the answer to Mack's crouching style—a left uppercut—and had Mack in a bad way before the four rounds ended.

Gauer Rematched to Wipe Out Kayo

136

Tonight's Card

Max Chowaniec, Cudahy, vs. Chet Leverre, Chicago, eight rounds, 175 pounds.

Al Schwartz, Milwaukee, vs. Joey Mandell, Rockford, six rounds, 161 pounds.

Augie Kluborg, Milwaukee, vs. Johnny Tecovitch, Chicago, four rounds, 143 pounds.

Harold Gerarden, Green Bay, vs. Henry Hamburg, Chicago, four rounds, 154 pounds.

Norman Gauer, Milwaukee, vs. Honey Mellody, Chicago, four rounds, 135 pounds.

Ray Blum, Janesville, vs. Pat O'Brien, Chicago, four rounds, 126 pounds.

The Results

Al Nettlow, 133½, Chicago, defeated Roger Bernard, 132¾, Flint (8).

Al Schwartz, 159½, beat Elby Johnson, 159½, Moline, Ill. (6).

Joe Richards, 142, Chicago, outpointed Augie Kluborg, 136½ (4).

Ed Maleski, 147¾, Chicago, beat Henry Hamburg, 152, Chicago (4).

Norman Gauer, 134¼, knocked out Honey Mellody, 131½, Chicago (1).

Pat O'Brien, 123½, defeated Willie Dudlik, 127, Chicago (4).

down with a left hook. He put Hamburg down again in the fourth and had him practically out. Norman Gauer's left hook winged Honey Mellody's chin in mid-air and brought him down so hard that his head thumped the floor and he was taken across the road to emergency hospital for attention to a brain concussion. The knockout took just 45 seconds.

Tiger Markos of La Crosse, who turned in a surprise recently by holding Norman Gauer to a draw in four rounds, was pretty thoroughly punched around in six but was still trying at the finish and bothering Gauer, too. Gauer forgot all about jabs and straight rights, relying almost entirely on his left hook.

Wilbur Dunn of Fond du Lac found chunky Mike Percira of Houston. Tex., too rough and busy in another six-rounder and lost the decision.

FOUR ROUNDS

Art Halamka vs. Eddie Moleski, Chicago, 152.

Augie Kluborg vs. Hal Mollison, Quincy, Ill., 143.

Norman Gauer vs. Jack McCarden, Chicago, 135.

Pat O'Brien, Chicago, vs. Ray Blum, Janesville, 126.

**Golden Gloves Champion Norman Gauer
with his mentor, Richie Mitchell**

The Results

George Black, 160, defeated Bob Turner, 155, Virginia, 10.

Baby Joe Gans, 160½, drew with George Burnett, 154¾, Detroit, 6.

Baby Face Breese, 133½, Manhattan, Kas., defeated Harry Booker, 135, Chicago, 6.

Norman Gauer, 131½, beat Tiger Markos, 131, LaCrosse, 6.

Mike Pereira, 150¾, Houston, Tex., beat Wilbur Dunn, 154 Fond du Lac, 6.

Wilbur Van, 126½, Green Bay, defeated Jimmy Mason, 129, Milwaukee, 4.

Receipts, $2,495. Promoter, Auditorium A. A. Matchmaker, Tom Andrews.

FIGHT RESULTS.

Larry Greb, 135½, Milwaukee, won by technical knockout over Al Nettlow, 133½, Chicago, in the fourth round.

Al Schwartz, 159½, Milwaukee, defeated Sweeney Byer, 161, Oklahoma City, six round decision.

Eddie Moleski, 151½, Chicago, knocked out Art Halamka, 151½, Milwaukee, second round.

Augie Kluborg, 139½, Milwaukee, defeated Hal Mollison, 144¼, Chicago, four round decision.

Norman Gauer, 130¾, Milwaukee, defeated Jack McCarden, 134½, Chicago, four round decision.

Pat O'Brien, 125½, Milwaukee, and Ray Bluhm, 127, Janesville, four round draw.

SNAPPY SHORTS and CASUAL SPORTS COMMENT
(From the Sentinel)

Norman Gauer, Richie Mitchell's novice, has one of the best left hands around here in some time . . . The lad knows how to relax while boxing and should go places . . .

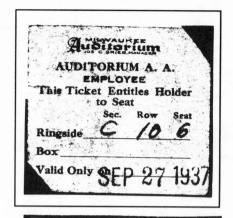

Tonight's Card

Max Chowaniec, Cudahy, vs. Chet Leverre, Chicago, 175 pounds (8).
Tony Bruno, Milwaukee, vs. Billy Miller, Milwaukee, 158 pounds (8).
Al Schwartz, Milwaukee, vs. Jackie Reed, Berwin, Ill., 162 pounds (4).
Art Halamka, Milwaukee, vs. Louis Doelke, Milwaukee, 152 pounds (4).
Augie Kluberg, Milwaukee, vs. Billy Gladstone, Chicago, 143 pounds (4).
Norman Gauer, Milwaukee, vs. Hal Mollison, Quincy, Ill., 135 pounds (4).

The Results

Max Chowaniec, 170¼, defeated Chet Leverre, 171½, Chicago (8).
Tony Bruno, 156, defeated Billy Miller, 150 (8).
Al Schwartz, 158, defeated Jack Reed, 157, Berwyn, Ill. (4).
Louis Doelke, 116, Chicago, defeated Norbert Gerarden, 145, Green Bay (4).
Augie Kluborg, 131½, drew with Billy Gladstone, 140¼, Chicago (4).
Norman Gauer, 131¼, defeated Charley Mack, 131 (4).
Attendance, 2,058. Receipts, $1,371.55.

Tonight's Card

TEN ROUNDS
Larry Greb vs. Dominic Mancini, Pittsburgh. 135 pounds.
Roger Bernard. Flint, vs. Sam Angott, Louisville, 132.

SIX ROUNDS
Al Schwartz vs. Elby Johnson, Chicago, 160.
Johnny Barbara, South Bend, vs. Don Custer, Peoria, 148.

FOUR ROUNDS
Norman Gauer vs. Duke Davis, 135.

The Results

Al Schwartz, 157, beat Jerry Hayes, 158, Chicago (6).
Augie Kluborg, 137¼, defeated Joe Richards, 140, Chicago (6).
Norman Gauer, 131½, outpointed Art Greer, 135¾, Chicago (6).
Bob Fadner, 129, Fond du Lac, beat Charley Mack, 132 (4).
Henry Hamburg, 153½, Chicago, beat Harold Gerarden, 151½, Green Bay (4).
Willie Kirkpatrick, 136, Chicago, defeated Ben D'Amico, 132½ (4).

RICHIE MITCHELL walked kind of funny and when you shook his hand you realized it was all busted up. He was a fighter in the old days, his best known opponent was Benny Leonard, from Chicago, whom he could never beat. He runs the gymnasium at 3rd and wells, upstairs, where Bro. Norman started to work out.

Richie told Norman to try for the Golden Gloves at the old South Side National Guard Armory and Norman did that. He got into the 135-pound (lightweight) class, won all 5 of his fights and won the Golden Gloves Award. He had to go to a jewelry store downtown to get it. He gave it to Trinket.

That's where Norman met Duh Beaver - at the South Side Armory. When Norman turned Pro he had some 10 bouts in all and got knocked out in one - he won all the rest handily. About the kayo, he said: "I was looking for a place to drop him when he hit me by mistake!"

There were bouts every two or three months, at the Armory, the Eagles Club, at the Riverview Roller Rink. Guys willing to travel - Chicago, St. Louis, got more fights. Norman got $25 to $30 per bout, net.

Some guys, said Norman, were 'Club Fighters', like Tony Bruno, big, strong, but not a hell fo a lot of talent. But everybody did a lot of training. Bruno, he related, used to go out on the Government Pier, hop off, and swim across to the Northwestern Railroad Depot (which was pretty close to the water at the time).

Norman says of Mitchell's tutelage, "It was probably something of a handicap, he had an old-fashioned upright stance that wasn't all that great, but he insisted on it, and a lot of guys got conked that way".

"Getting pounded doesn't hurt". he said, which let a lot of guys take beatings without knowing they could get punchy.

Norman was a clever boxer, never got pounded. He didn't quit because of a busted nose or missing teeth or a cauliflower ear. Although the training and road work were good body-building etc., he just lost the feeling for the game. The atmosphere, of course, was awful. And unless you had a head of cement, a good, hard punch will drop you. Norman just didn't have one of those heads.

He remembers a bout at the Riverview Roller Rink, which he won, and afterwards decided to do some skating in the outside rink overlooking the river. He had a bleeding eye from a headbutt, with collodion smeared over it, and while he was standing in the entrance to the bar, the fight doctor, also on roller skates, pulls up. He takes the rubbery collodion off Norman's eyebrow, puts on a clamp, takes two stitches of catgut with a gizzer he carried, and told Norman to carry on. They resumed skating to the wave-lapping rhythms of Blue Emil at the console of the mightly Wurlitzer.

**Emil Cords (Blue Emil) at the console of the
Riverview Roller Rink's mighty Wurlitzer**

INTRODUCING ⦂⦂⦂⦂⦂

CALIFORNIA
AND
HENRY KUTTNER

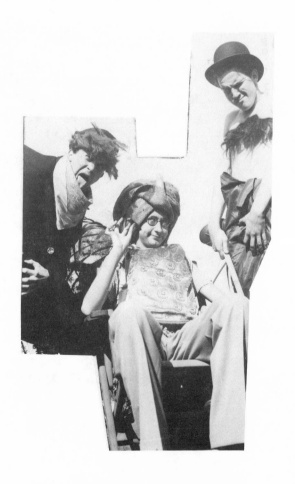

For several years Bro. Bloch had been in correspondence with other writers - August Derleth, Clark Aston Smith, E. Hoffman Price, and among them, *Henry Kuttner*, a contributor to Thrilling Mystery, Thrilling Wonder, and the doidier pulp magazines. That inhabitant of Beverly Hills was fascinated by such items as *The History, Brutal Magazine, and The Dictionary*.

With the result that in April, 1937, Kuttner was so illadvised as to jokingly invite Bro. Blo. to spend a month with him at his home in the west.

Bro. Blo. clutched the invitation to his bosom, wrote to F.W. Wright, who sent a hundred dollars, then made for the west coast and stayed from May 11 to June 24 - some six terrific weeks under Pacific skies, pink beards, redheads, scotch, roller coasters, and weird uzzings.

This tale is told in an exchange of letters between H. Mag. Gauer and Bro. Bloch:

Dear Mag: May 18 1937

Tuesday morning the Ford V-8 pulls up and it has four share-the-expenses-to-California jimokes in it — Joe, Chuck, Mac and Russ., all funny guys talking like W.C. Fields.

Down to Rockford and across the Mississippi. Into the hills of Iowa, the monotonous plains of Nebraska and we reach Omaha at dusk. So Joe says "let's drive on" and by morning we had reached Cheyenne, Wyoming.

"On to Laramie!" was the boggled suggestion, taking us through a land of coiled rattlers, prairie dogs and hawks, sheep ranches, long-horn steers, chuck-wagons. The Mountains! Laramie. Lunch. "Let's Drive On" O.K., cross the Great Divide and to the Great Salt Lake in darkness, Supper. "Let's move on to Provo!" Through rocky mountain passes, canyons, precipices, and at 1 A.M., Provo, Utah. Fifty miles without seeing a soul, 1500 miles from home, 42-hours of continuous driving. Hotel. Sleep.

10 A.M. - Off in a cloud for Las Vegas all day thru Utah. Helldorado Day in Las Vegas, the streets thronged with red-shirted, black-bearded men, cowgirls, tarts. Guns roar, Indians whoop, women scream, everybody is horribly, lurching dronk. The main street is eight blocks long, lined on both sides with neon-lighted saloons and gambling houses, eighty of them.

We stop, go in. Faro. Poker, 21, roulette, dice. It is silver dollar country. The old deacon, dealing stud. The painted wimmin, the suckers. Fifty dollars in a stack pushed forth on one bet. Piles of dollars changing hands each minute.

The air is filled with smoke, the odor of perspiration, whiskey, whore perfume. Obscenity, clicking wheels, the litany of the dealers, mechanical piano music, the tinkle of slot machines.

Then it was across the Mohave Desert at midnight. Hot. We stop the car. From afar the ululation of coyotes, no other sound. The lights of an approaching car can be seen thirty miles away over the cactus flats. Morning. California, here we come ! ! ! Down the mountains, racing the sun along Wilshire Blvd, 2400 miles and 71 hours.

You'd like Henry Kuttner. You'd like his house, his electric phonograph. His Ma is like Stella, need I say more? No lousy formality and things are swell at 145 Canon Drive. A bed of my own, Henry doesn't snore, the windows are open at night. There is no damned alarm clock. I get up when I please. The cooking is like home and the California sunshine is the nertz. I have my own key.

Henry works in a literary agent's office, so he goes to work. I wrote up The Body and the Brain, our first collaboration, Hank to revise. Also sent off a humor item to Ballyhoo Magazine. Worked all day.

We visited the home of Fritz Leiber, son of Shakespearean actor now in films. He is a swell guy, about 28, big. His English wife, Jonquil, isFriday, May 21 1937Friday, May 21 1937Friday, May 21 1937Friday, May 21 1937Friday, May 21 1937Friday, May 21 1937Friday, May 21 1937Friday, May 21 1937 tiny. Beautiful home. Lovely books. They know Lovecraft, they like us. Scotch.

Write if you get work & hang by yr thumbs!

— Bob

Dear Bob: Friday, May 21 1937

What's happening here (back home) is I am renovating The Lab with hammer and tongs. Also, Vernie's Home Made Candy Store is FOLDING. Norman and I have been taking down shelving, lugging cases of stuff into the attic. We can hear clashing of kitchenware and the raucous cackle of Aunt Annie below ...

Williams was in, off the railroad ... encumbered with a rather offensive tsoot of brown rapidly subdivided with stripes of green twirz. Within that garment Doidy Hoibie maintains a bankbook inscribed with a $15 net. Our old friend is not what you might call happy. He likes to give out with the Damon Runyon talk, and can work up some enthusiasm for whatever glamor there is for him in railroading, but I think the life is essentially hard. And probably lonely. I wish he might say that he misses our company and rolling cigarettes with the Target roller and camping - but he doesn't. He's got his eye on the future, not the past - which is a healthy attitude - but its a wary eye.

— H. Mag.

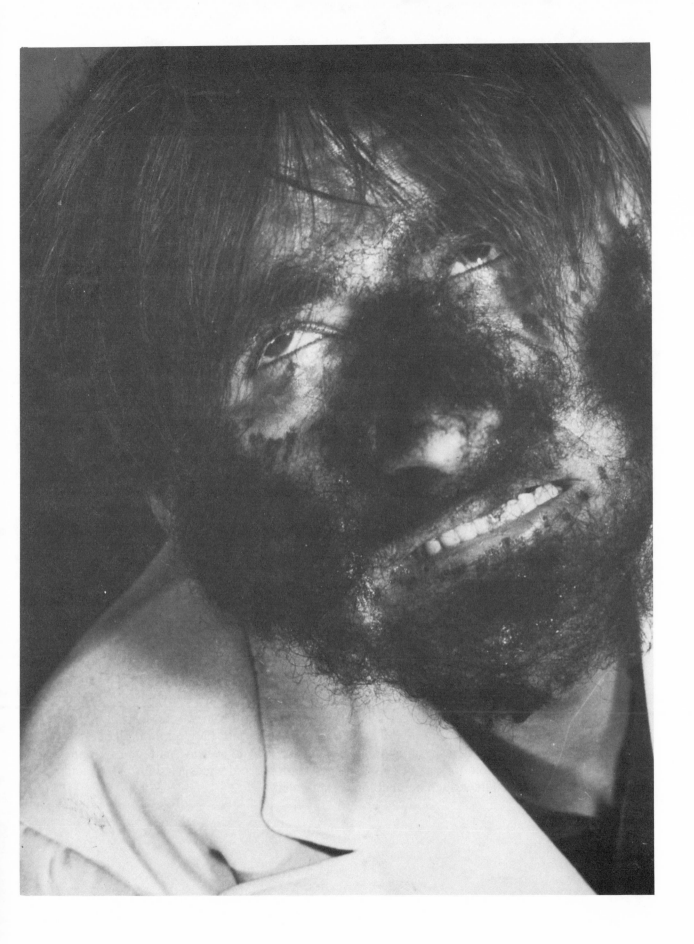

Dear H. Mag: May 23 1937

Western front news: We were invited to the home of Laurence D'Orsay in Topanga Canyon. He has a 12-acre rancho, is related to Mrs. Kuttner and is Henry's boss (which is, as in Milwaukee, the only way to get a job).

D'Orsay drives a Mercedes sports roadster, imports gold-tipped cigarettes from Cairo, his wife is an artist, his hobbies are European phono records and imported liquors. Roaring fire in the stone fireplace, an evening of real conversation. Tiers of books in a massive room.

Ebony figurines on a sideboard. Monkeys, parakeets, cockatoos. Russian, Egyptian, Turkish cigarettes.

I worry about Williams, too.

Everybody here is yammering to see the photo montage, so gat beezy. Gawd help the defunct Candy Store. Gawd help Aunt Annie. Gawd help young Gnormie. Gawd help you.

Henry hates almost anybody on sight, is more isolationist than we ever dreamed of being. He does, however, worship the Brutal photography of Sister Alice and yearns to meet her.

                                                                       — Bob

Kindly Snurbfleagle: May 27, 1937

The requested photo montage is on the ferrotype and I expect it to spring off before I finish this letter. Pappy Bedard gave me a recipe for black fig wine. It will be ready for consumption 14 days after birth. The photos submitted to Coronet Magazine came back, alas.

Rumor flies that Mammy and Sister Annie are week-ending it in Pulaski (Wis) over Memorial Day, but with hardly anybody present, Brother Gnormie and some of his friends will no doubt celebrate with some enfeebling liquid and forced marching in the attic.

The Falstaff Press made me another startling offer today. All four works, including that of Professor Paolo Mantegazza for only $2.50 net. I am waiting until they send me a check!

I must say that I am a restraining influence on those who would mail you obscene literature, prospectuses from makers of suppositories, orthopedic devices, sanitary goods and mashed potatoes and letters written on uncommon stationery.

                                                                       — So!

Dear H. Mag:

Bro. F.W. Wright bought *Return to the Sabbath* for Weird Tales for $55. Also Henry and I have finished another collaboration. I bought a beautiful edition of Cabell's *Cream of the Jest* we saw with the classy interlocking illustrations, marked $5, for $1.50. I also bought *The Circus of Dr. Lao*

To San Diego for supper - and for once I bite into a $2 dinner. Eemagin ! Then over the Rio Grande to Tia Juana, very sad, a tourist trap. We had an absinthe in one of the saloons, the notorious drug drink verboten in the States. The green goo tastes like crushed coughdrops. Wormwood. But mild. Another, then a glass of fiery tequilla, the Mexican ninny-water. And suddenly the little man with the hammer playing Nola on the skull. Not dronk stuff, but stooooopor.

They like the Fiddlestuffer routine out here, especially the "turn in your truss, Fiddlestuffer, you're fired!" The new routine features, "Turn in your grave, Fiddlestruffer, here comes a necrophile!"

An aged prostatic in the box overhead at the Burlesque slobbered on my hat.

— Yrs in brotherhood.

Dear Expatriate: June 5, 1937

I have turned a distinct brown from blowing smoke rings for pictorial purposes. And I have been doing some reading. Sample:

"... and this is the hardest of all to tell, Ellen, I love Mary!" "What, Jacob, you love my sister?" "Yes, Ellen I fought against it: we both fought against it, but well..." "Don't touch me, ptheh!"

I think "Aint a fit night out for man or beast" came from East Lynne, by dog team. I've heard W.C. Fields use the line. About buying books, I am somewhat bereft myself, having invested in a tsoot and will have to leave an odd 26-lumbuckaroos for it, extra pair pants, $4 more. The Montage has caused tizzies in these parts also, including at the Sanders Bros. Drug and malt dispensary.

Earl Pierce Jr., writes, returning the borry of The Historical Dictionary. He recommends Tiffany Thayer's *Doctor Arnoldi*. But about this beetle ... I found him on Pulaski Street and took him to The Lab to photograph him on a blade on grass. I spent the best part of an afternoon diddling with lights and camera. But the little bugger could not control the trembling of his antennae. So I put some Fuchsin Red on him in a solution of ethyl alcohol just to calm him down, and the little sonofabitch croaked!

But I see the conductor is raising his baton now, and
-Flotch-ch-ch !!!

Response from California: Dear H. Mag., Gnormie, Beaver, Mme Goose, Powell, Col. Warren and three others — Your wonderful postcards arrived just in time as we were running out of paper. Your cards saved us. Yes, I am writing much more that I would back home and I guess most of it will sell.

Out here you run into Iowa farmers, fake spiritualists, snotty clerks, perverts, bums, moochers, blackmailers and National Guardsmen. Hollywood Blvd is filled with queers painted and powdered, but they don't molest the gawking tourists. I shall probably return around June 1st. This is really the life! Whooie!

Dear Bob: Early July 1937

You know the old saying: absinthe makes the heart go faster, and I absinthed myself from the premises over the Memorial Day weekend when Doidy Hoibie got me a 17-hour-a-day job on the C&NW Flambeau run. Third Cook on the dining car, already, and it was lurch all the way!

Now I know why Wms doesn't know what's that. He's a fatherless child, as you know, lives with his Ma and sister, with no visible means of support, so its got to be very tender for the guy. He's got to take whatever employment he can get, stick with it no matter what, and duck the fickle finger of fate when it points at him . . .

Come to think of it, Alice is fatherless (and a working girl, sole support of her aged mother), Bro. Vail is fatherless (living with grandma Hassmann, Uncle Frank Flumey and aunt Rose), and, of course the Gauer Bros. are fatherless (living with Ma in the candy store).

Danny Duh Beaver is motherless (his father, Sam, works at the London Hat Shop), and Bro. Vonier is motherless (living with his father, Chet, at the Carleton Hotel).

Lucky's father runs a Blind Pig on Juneau with a supply of "B" girls and he hates the sound of Lucky's saxophone, which Lucky needs to practice to become a musician. (I got all this from Vonier the other day). He has to clean up around the tavern and to practice his sax (or maybe it is the clarinet) he has to open a trapdoor in the tavern and go into the unfinished cellar, prop his music on some beer cases, sit on a stool and do his tootling by the light of a plumber's candle while the old man hollers shut up down there!

Who else? Berto Warren has a full deck, with both parents and two sisters (Winnie and Frances), Milt Gelman has both parents and his sister, Edith, and Mert Koplin lives on Prospect Avenue in a nice apartment with his parents and his paw is in finance and they are in good shape. And of course, we have Bro. Blo. in possession of Stella and Ray with sister Winnie.

The remarkable thing is nobody in this cast, or any ancillary spear-bearers either, have met with fatal accident, died of natural causes or been murdered in their beds. Nor have they been convicted for any felonies, been swindled of any holdings or met with any great good fortune during the period.

In excram tootam

— Harold

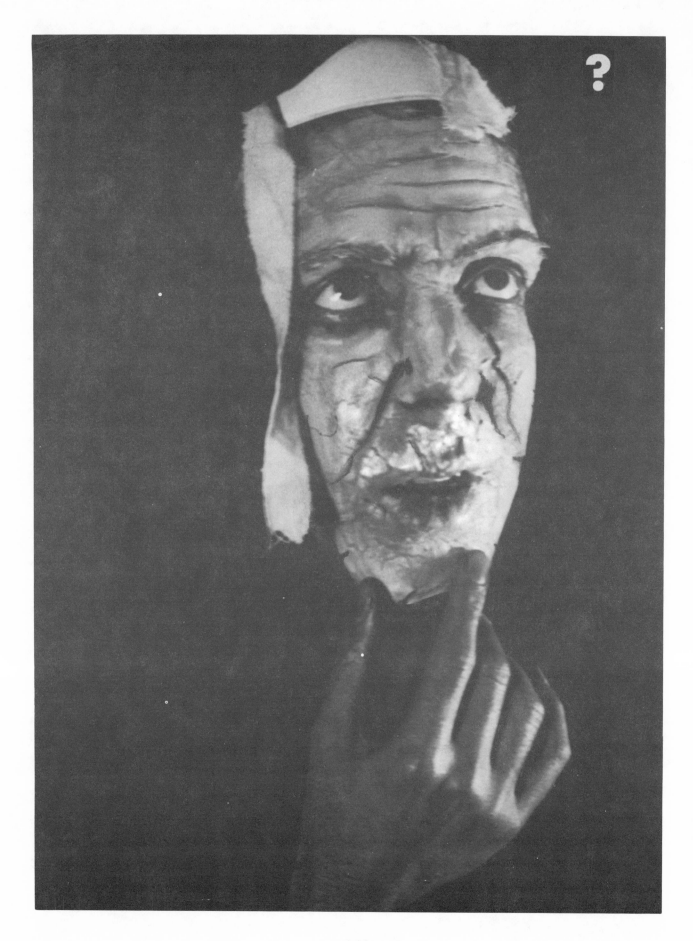

Dear Harold: June 5, 1937

By next Tuesday I will be on my way back and it will be all over. But I will return for good some day. That's a promise!

Jim Mooney and his friend, Lee, want me to bum on a freight with them down to Mexicali over the weekend. But I don't have the dough or the inclination. One of their friends did that and got a good six months in the can - won't be out until Halloween! So, much as I like the guys, who are hell-roarers after meh own heart, I refooz.

No more book-buying. The cash is low. If Herbie reads this, greetings you hammerhead! I may return by bus. It would cost $29.50 and the cheapest I could go in somebody's car would be $20, plus the auto-cabin rent and the meals. I can remember a dive near the Mohave Desert where we paid 35 cents for scrambled eggs and toast. Some gyp.

Henry introduced me to some marvelous pipe tobacco called Dream Castle, put up here at two-bits the ounce. Have you ever eaten East Indian curry? Mrs. Kuttner tried some on me, a hot, chop suey sort of dish with a delectable flavor and all kinds of gunk in it.

                                        Fatten up the calf and stand by ...

                                                                — Bob

Dear Fiddlestuffer: June 9, 1937

Today the Precision Process peetchas were returned from LAUGH Magazine and the rejection slip advises that I keep in touch. Ptheh! It would appear that our stuff is not slanted for LIFE or LOOK, either. What next?

It looks like Milt Gelman has the job at the Cambridge Library.

Today I went down to the depot, I t'ought dat I was hard, and there was Hoibie, filthy in a dining car apron and pants of a great white-lessness. (George Graham had a car in which we drove down to the yards).

We had a talk in the dining car as the engine moved us onto various tracks, Hoibie assuring us that we were not going anyplace. We played a few wickets of horseshoes, four-handed (with the chief cook). Graham has on a very light tsoot and has to be extra careful with the percheron oxfords lest he got all doidy. Who is this C/O Kuttner, a brother of Henry's?

                                                    A-a-a-a-a-a-aaa!

                                                                —Ha!

150

CLEFT IN DOUBLE
A FOLDING

It has been a long time since that first day that the Gauer Candy Store gave birth to chocolate covered nuts. Since 1920 Vernie's Candy Shop has been open on Saturdays, Sundays and all holidays with the possible exception of Good Friday from 12 to 3.

The Mag did spade and roll cremes and make all manner of candies under the aegis of Mammy Gauer and when times grew tender there was penny candy with slobbering bratties picking one-of-these and one-of-those and leaving sticky fingerprints on the glass. And the gas-fired popcorn machine and the ice-cream tank and the grim days when hardly any-body could afford the luxury of a little peanut brittle or chocolate-covered coconut shreds. Mammy Gauer cussing out the 'factory-mades' from Fanny Farmer and not buying broken pe-can when whole ones (halves) cost twice as much.

Uncle Gus at the batch-warmer, kneading molten hard candy.

But then the seventeen years mentioned by Thrasybulis came to an end and in the week of June 13, 1937, the venerable joint FOLDED! The premises were abandoned, Ruth's Hosiery Shop move in, and the Gauer family elbowed into the living quarters above. Jeepers!

The store window as Halloween approached.

151

Norman Gauer and Robert Bloch in front of the candy store
Mammy Gauer is dimly seen in the entrance

Earl Pierce, Jr.
Washington, D.C.

Monday June 7 1937

Dear Earl:

Thanx for the return of the New Dictionary etc., and the abnormal psychology stuff you sent is going back to you with this letter.

I am glad to note yr success with *Weird Tales*. I bought the July issue, seeing my name mentioned in Bro. Blo's story and also a letter from you to the editor. I haven't seen your *Dime Mystery* stuff yet, but I might rummage for back copies at a magazine exchange down the street. Apparently you don't know Bro. Blo. is in California visiting Henry Kuttner. He left this slab last May 15 and he's expected back soon, provided he does not catch on with something out there ...

I am glad to have your comment about *Dr. Arnoldi*. I had some doubts about Thayer's quality, but enjoyed it afterwards. It appears to be an idea that is too much for him, as he admits at the conclusion, being better suited to an H.G. Wells. If you like Cabell, The Lab now houses seven volumes in the plain, Kalki Edition, the last one being a gift from Awgie Derleth when he came to town a few months ago, *The High Place*.

Other recent acquisitions are O'Hara's *Appointment in Samara* and *Butterfield 8*, which I like despite the lending library scent. Gordon Sayer's *Mirage of Marriage* is cheap-looking item, but surprisingly thoughtful. Philosophy and humor abound. Don't buy *Mrs. Astor's Horse* unless you like mediocre accounts of stupid goings-on. Only the title is clever. Bloch sez he has bought Chas. Finney's *Circus of Dr. Lao, Cream of the Jest,* and Arthur Machen's *House of Souls*.

The picture magazines have not been kind to me, as I have tried unsuccessfully with an insane poolroom sequence, a weird affair in a dentist's chair, and I am now working on a more carefully considered series of photos in which a drunk climbs a rope to the top of a huge foot, and subsequently explores the female form, sighting mountains, wading thru a bellybutton full of water, etc and etc.

I do need a job. Which the taxi-pushing I quit last January is not! And Vernie's Candy Shop is no more. Sold. And I spend much time in The Lab.

Sell more *Dime Mysteries*, and pip pip

Vignette

The incredible interlude
at Koeller's gardens

UNCLE NATES said to Gauer: "Why don't you come down to Emil Koeller's on the Green Bay Road where I am playing in the band, and be a waiter?"

Mammy Gauer's brightness at the news faded a lot when it turned out to be just Saturday nights, not all week long. Young men took their dates to places like that on Saturday nights for beer and cheek-to-cheek dancing, with live music. Most of such places had male waiters.

One of them at Emil Koeller's would be H. Mag. in a nifty white shirt and black bow tie. You didn't need any experience, if you could walk without falling over your own feet, you could be a waiter.

The aforementioned took the streetcar to Green Bay and Keefe for a rendezvous with Artie Algoma, leader of the band. Artie had a car and was waiting for Uncle Nates, who stepped off the next street car. We got in with Algoma and asked if it was the bus to Koeller's Gardens. The guys laughed and hollered "What?" at each other, some kind of inside joke.

"Snatch", the cornettist came along in an ambience of halitosis modified with the piney scent of gin. He got in and passed around some marijuana cigarettes. Six for a dollar, they cost him, he said, and for best results we should keep the windows of the car closed. An outrageous idea on that hot June evening. We were supposed to suck air in with the smoke, "Snatch" proclaimed. He sucked noisily to illustrate. Gauer nodded, bug-eyed, realizing this was the fast life.

Everybody started hollering "What?". Artie caused the starting motor to whine, at first in high pitch, then gradually lower, with dying whinnies. Just before the battery went dead the vehicle let go with a pthisic, baboon-like coughing and night-howling, followed by an explosive fart and then a fusilade of them.

Artie worked something sticking out of his dashboard until the uproar steadied and we rolled out onto the highway like a fused bomb, and tooled along trailing wisps of marijuana smoke. The interior stank with a heavy, pungent aroma like cheap lavender perfume. "Although I grew dizzy from sucking air, I could detect nothing spectacular happening to me in the drug line," The Mag confessed later. Evidently imagination had something to do with it.

Either "Snatch" had cut-rate narcotics or he knew what he was talking about, both of those ideas striking the waiter-to-be as being equally improbable the moment he considered them.

The boys of the band all wore the same kind of jacket, a red and white creation of the sort seen on burlesque comics at the Gaiety. The place was almost deserted at that early hour. One door opened on the barroom another on the "ballroom". At one end was a rostrum skirted by a low brass railing hung with velvet drapes. Uncle Nates went to a locked cupboard for his drums.

The Mag. got three dollars from Emil Koeller and a note book for jotting tabs and was all set to start earning a living. The leader of the band was hangin a sign over the railing: *Nineteen dollars Given for 1914 Pennies.* He has a million of 'em. The boys started to warm up. Algoma pranced around the rostrum, then pounced on Uncle Nate's drums to club them frenziedly. Revelers started to trickle in.

The night wore on and "Snatch" had numerous gins during the first few hours, claiming the drunker he got the better he played, but Gauer could detect no improvement whatever in either his solo riffs or the work of the ensemble as they struggled to transmute base cacophony into two-four time.

Belly Snider was the pianist but he could also sing. He kept a box of crush hats under the piano, one funnier than the other, to embellish his song styling. When the sweating dancers retired to their ice cream chairs, Snider stepped forward with hands upraised against feeble applause to deliver popular ballads with ribald alterations.

"Take-offs", they were called. He sang *My First Piece*, with lewd gestures and heavy emphasis on labored double-entendres and got the audience guffawing heartily at each dirty part. Elbows dug ribs and knowing screams rent the stale air around Belly's head. He leered happily through a cascade of sweat at this tribute to his talent, like a gargoyle in a shower of melted lead.

At midnight sandwiches could be ordered. Entertainers and waiters could have one free sandwich during the evening. At one o'clock in the morning, the first of two "floor shows" started, preceded by an exchange of funny dialogue and comical stories between Artie Algoma and Belly Snider, underscored by muted burps from "Snatch's" cornet.

Algoma wore a disheveled red wig and Snider a German army pot-helmet (into which he pretended to urinate). While they were doing that, H. Mag. Gauer was clearing 40 cents in tips, but when some beer drinkers sneaked out the barroom entrance, he wound up 10 cents in the hole.

A lady resembling Texas Guinan, strapped into a sequined evening gown from which parts of her struggled to escape in all directions, advised everyone in a roaring basso that A Good Man Was Hard To Find, as the combo behind her shredded My Man into shrill strips of sound.

She raised both pink, bulging arms straight out from her sides as she sang, her head thrown back in ecstatic ululation. It looked as though she were in water to her armpits, yelling for a lifeguard.

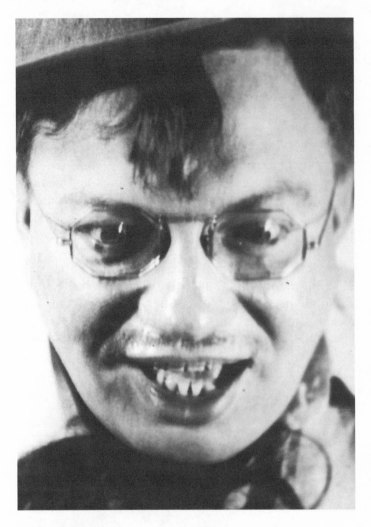
"Uncle Nates"

Dancing resumed for a while until a lady broke loose and began an impromptu belly dance. Uncle Nates started some rimshots to encourage her. She made a circuit of the floor leaning backward, shrugging her shoulders from side to side, making her ample bosoms plunge in what one of the waiters thought was a most entertaining fashion. Emil had to come running with hands upraised in cautionary semaphore against rioting on the premises.

Disappointment was widely expressed, some taking it as a personal loss. Youths were always expecting more revelation than they got - at the movies, in night spots, in books, and in real life. When you sent for those hot-ziggerty 'eight-pager' dirty cartoon books with title like *Maggie & Jiggs*, and *Confessions of a Traveling Salesman*, all you got was a page of stale, clean jokes, nothing like the ones Duh Beaver's friends in the National Guard had with the much-thumbed and dog-eared pages of graphic scenes with Tillie and Mac.

The shocker was to see these loveable, familiar and always proper folks - office workers in everyday situations - naked on a desk-top, with Tillie saying "Oh, Mac, what if Mr. Simpkins catches us!" Some of us never learn and are always suckers.

Among them, no doubt, the clientele at the road house. The young men were ordinary enough, clumsy and careless in their movements, laughing when there was nothing to laugh at, self-consciously, and they appeared terribly anxious to act out some role of what they imagined they could be, gleaned perhaps from the movies, bewildered by their failure to achieve that.

Nor were the young women particularly or basically attractive. They postured, they fooled around without dignity, they poked at their escorts and they giggled and grimaced, sometimes in derision of each other.

They were probably aware of their femaleness and the ardently sought treasures under their skirts, but they had no idea of how to dress, wearing anything that would fit even if it exposed shaven armpits or brassiere straps or hung down over their front without any emphasis at all. They worried about their hair, their nails, their jewelry, and were careful not to let the oafs scuff their pumps.

Unbaited traps!

Toward the end of the second floor show a girl (a known half-wit, according to Snider) appeared in a dancing costume, and with a paradiddle from Uncle Nates, the drummer, went into her act, during which she did several "splits". She scrubbed her posterior with a ribbon, whirled around a lot, ran with the ribbon trailing behind her, and then bifurcated, socking her crotch to the floor in a way that was cringe-making. The spectacle held everyone spellbound, because she was unable to arise from such a position.

If someone didn't help her up, she executed a maneuver that was like crawling out of a trench, her bottom blackened after the second of such disasters from contact with the dirty floor. Yet the poor thing shrugged away the shrieks of laughter to dance some more, no doubt convinced that she would be an artiste on some future stage in a better time ...

Her name was Josephine. Brother Gauer was eating his ham sandwich (it was his second, so he had to pay) when Josephine came into the kitchen for hers. There was some talk, briefly, until the band had finished playing the last set. It turns out Josephine and Madam Goose are good friends and that she was in the mob playing ball on the Pulaski Street playground.

With an extraordinary good sense that Bro. Gauer does not always exercise, he broke off the colloquy and sought out Artie Algoma and Belly Snider, who, even more stewed than the bartender, to whom Gauer had to give back his dollar of change-money, were heading for the car, his only transportation to the carline.

No attempt will be made to describe the effect of six hours on foot midst crashes, band-squeals and yelling, but whether it was worth $2.40, gross, to endure it or not is what one might call moot.

Vignette
Cloaking the clunium

It happened that Bro. Gauer was clamoring at the doors of the State Employment Bureau for a job as a photo technician, and got a card to a haberdashery store on Wells Street, the one with Richie Mitchell's Gym and punching studio on the second floor. On July 26th this happened. For the number of $15 feeblers per week. But on July 29th, the Boss decided he was passing out too many pickle covers and gave The Mag but $10.

After that, on July 31st, Bro Gauer is obliged to work at the magnificent stipend of per week the number of bucks $6. In order to experience get. And for an approx. 50 hours sold pants ... ties ... shorts ... shoes ... shirts ... socks ... suspenders ... garters ... overalls ... gloves ... sweaters ... fur-lined wind-breakers and caps.

Also the victim became an expert at altering clothing and shortening summer pants. A demon with the crotch-tape, a madman with the shoe-horn, and as one demented in the baking heat of the display windows.

It came to pass that on September 13 The Mag demanded and got the number of $15 blorks per week. But management then gave him a boot in the glute and he departed on Sept 18 1937, leaving the burden of sales on those who remained, including "The Fox", the Boss' son-in-law.

PERSONNEL CHANGES

Bro. Hoibie Williams, co-founder of The History, since his embrasure of the Railroad in 1936, and later when he began to work steadily thereon, mostly out of Green Bay, has become as one apart and not often seen on Brady Street anymore. A peripatetic gustafrication no doubt out of Bro. Hoibie's control.

MEANWHILE, several new figures have appeared, among them ROBERT K. VAIL, now employed in place of Milt Gelman at the Cambridge Rental Library.

Bro. Vail is a wearer of porkpie hats and suitings of an Esquire weaver and models clothes for a fashion photographer. Very dapper. He is an exponent of a cardboard baseball system of some kind, and was immediately offered a franchise in the Blue-Eye League.

This revived the League from the crushing blow resulting from the withdrawal of the Mighty Stugatchus. The VAIL HOMBURGS suited up a team, and the EIGHTH OFFICIAL SEASON got going on September 27 1937 and at this writing, Oct 5th, the First Quarter of play has

Bro. Hoibie

158

been completed. The Bloch Fungulas hold a commanding lead.

Very recently H Mag reconstructed the Precision Process pingpong table. Bros. Vail and Gelman joined in popularizing the basement jamborees. A glimpse was had of a fair pongist in the person of Lucky's friend "Nifty".

Other spear-bearers in the current opera have been Mert Koplin, Cousin Sherm, Paula Kovack, Mike Menos, Tom Jeffries, Joe Boysa, and Wallio. Also George Graham.

MONSTER IMPROVEMENTS

The Library has been tumescing. The first mentioned total of 55 volumes has more than doubled. Only a few factory throwouts remain on the east wall. The Thorne Smith collection has been completed. The James Branch Cabells have been augmented handsomely, and dozens of new purchases added.

Then The Mag. bought a monster ROLL-TOP DESK for $6. Only by removing the attic door casements and dismembering the desk could it be lugged into The Lab. A magnificent structure, with manys the drawers! And room for the ocean of filed material evicted when Uncle Nates knavishly reclaimed his steel filing cabinet.

Then Sister Alice contributed an enormous phonograph, which was carved down to its essentials to save space and it became a whooie-box for high-class wheels contributed by Bro. Bloch, such as *Danse Macabre*, and *In The Hall of the Mountain King*, etc. Improvements in time of flux . . .

Up to this time there was only an Edison Phonograph playing quarter-inch-thick bakelite pancakes (splitting apart in layers) affording such tuneful hits as *All I Have Are Sunny Weather Friends, On The Hoko Moko Isle,* and *The Whistler and His Dog,* plus *Valencia, Selections from Carmen,* and *Tales of Hoffman.* And maybe Alma Gluck singing *My Little Gray Home in the West!*

Bro. Bloch located his own fun-box in a music store for the laughable and absurd sum of three poops. A willing Bro. Gauer placed that crank-organ in the back of a taxicab he happened to be driving for the Checker Company, and whisked it into the Bloch establishment.

Then began a period of record-buying - at the Salvation Army and Goodwill secondhand stacks, which produced little of value - and then at Bradfords, Grams and Gunniss, the three moosic-houses downtown where repose the waxen tootings of Victor, Columbia and Brunswick plus an occasional Decca. Even Bro. Vail was caught up in the madness. Bloch was investing five peeplows into blast-platters every month, and did it for a year, buying mostly weird and oriental sounds.

Thus many hours were spent in listening booths and at in-the-dark sessions playing them. And a considerable number of hours trying to repair the damned machines!

Before the flux!

It was on May 10th 1937 that Bro. Bloch prepared to duck off to Cali-fricking-fornia. And it was on this eventful day also that Bro. Gauer decided to renovate the Lab. The social and economic reasons for this were puissant. However, this note will deal with the physical changes only.

The Lab was relieved of the entire stock of chemical equipment and supplies. The many rows of shelved reagents, salts and compounds and the apparatus connected with their employment, was all packed into barrels that supported the main experimental bench - and parked in the outer attic. The huge cabinet of empty wine and whiskey bottles was taken down, the couch shifted from its age-old positon next to the West wall. The old atmospheric stuff disappeared as a result of the insistent scrabbling of The Mag.

In the heat of those summer weeks a grave general omission was committed so far as the records for posterity were concerned. There were no photographs taken by the Precision Process of the OLD LAB - a circumstance now incredibly to be regretted. In order to rectify this horrible mistake as far as possible, and before memory fades, Bro. Gauer and Bro. Bloch hereby attempt to set down a written description of the Anteroom Previous to the Great Flux.

THE GREAT NORTH WALL

There rose from the floor on the north wall a pair of glucose barrels that still retained an inner hardened glaze of corn syrup. These barrels supported a long table, or workbench that extended from the west edge to within 3 feet of the East Wall. A linoleum covering fitted over the horizontal door, making the entire resistant to acids and other strong chemicals spilled thereon.

Ignoring the litter on the surface, and the tools and magazines stored underneath, the disinterested observer would note the shelves, green-painted, rising against the green wall, stocked with bottled chemicals. Four rows of shelves, with a fifth where the encroaching down-slanting ceiling allowed. Most of the containers were regular reagent bottles, with a few oddities.

An illuminating gas outlet pipe was fitted to the rear edge of the worktable. A rubber hose some fifty feet in length, carried gas from a downstairs bedroom, through the window.

Frequently, water collected in the outdoors section of the gas-line and froze, and repairs with glass tubing became necessary.

Several Bunsen burners were all connected, via "T" tubes, to the line.

Also on the workbench, stood ringstands, tripod stands, quart bottles of Nitric and Sulphuric acid. A reflux condenser sprouted its tubes there likewise and was supplied with cooling water for its jacket from a 4-gallon tank that had a head of compressed air pumped into it. This tank leaked slightly when pumped up and sizzled continuously when in operation as through threatening to bust. The working surface of the table was frequently moist with unknown fooze.

The line of shelving continued around the bend onto the West Wall for some 3-feet, bearing more chemicals, mostly in their original containers (dry reagents, as Potass. Nitrate etc.) There were three of these shelves, supported on the South End by brackets screwed to the first of the door-casings. At the East End of the North Wall where the workbench fell short, was a table with typewriter and pile of manuscripts and stuff of an assorted nature. Directly next to this table on the East wall, was a small cabinet of some of the rarer and more valuable chemicals in small glass-stoppered bottles (Mercury, Chloral Hydrate, Yellow Phosphorus, Trioxymethylene, and what.)

The reader will remember that the entire room was bedizened with unclean gribble. The boys were very careless about cigarette butts, crumpled typing paper and other discards. There was some spitting, too, and dribbling.

Well. A microscope rested on one of the shelves, as did several of the better florence and erhlenmeyer flasks. The atmosphere of the North Wall was distinctly scientific.

God, what a mess!

THE WESTERN FRONT

The appurtenances of The Lab rather fused and blended into one another in their effect, pushed together in the small space. But the West Wall was mostly couch, covered with heavy-duty colored, but doidy, sheets. Occasionally it collapsed to a lower level. It extended from the chemistry bench to the doorway about 7-feet away. The West Wall is interrupted by two doorways, the one nearest the workbench being nailed shut and never used. The couch is in front of it, and above the couch next to the ceiling there was nailed a large chest the width of the unused doorway, made of tin and wood, painted purple. The cover opened upward and outward. Inside there was plenty of empty bottles of infinite variety. All dead soldiers.

The doorway in use was more than a door - It bore the photo enlarger, an oversized apparatus, which swung out with the door, and into which the occasional visitor was wont to bang into with a guilty flush. It did, however, withstand all assaults and bangs. The door itself was fitted with a snappy Yale snaplock and entrance could be gained only by key - in the dark of night in the attic no small feat in itself.

AREA TO THE SOUTH

The south Wall is much the same as before, except that the photo apparatus and shelving was improved at the time of the Great Flux to better contain receptacles for photo papers, chemicals, developers, fixers, toners, bleaches and other minutiae. The photo printer is now sunk into the table. The space under the table, formerly congested with assorted bescrilched bottles, now is replaced by an undershelving ....

A pale red light was affixed over the photo table on a toilet seat hinge and another hung by a cord. A somewhat inferior switchboard clung to the wall also. This corner was very difficult to clean and the space next to it was occupied by a light-stand bearing two very heavy reflectors not originally designed for photographic purposes, which wobbled over the room benignly. It may be said about this department that it produced many of the fine and unusual pictures that graced its walls and the archives.

In many respects the Eastern Wall presented the most complex problem in arrangement and this was due largely to the presence of a pair of small steam radiators situated in the center of the area. An expansion tank, like a large bomb, hung over them. The effect was to split that side of the room into separate, unalterable dimensions. The windows on that side were formerly blocked out and painted black overall. Now the Southern one is adjustable to allow light and air to enter. A linoleum-topped table there supported a monster iron filing cabinet four feet in length. Very heavy. On top of that cabinet were more shelves carrying the large books, letter files and over-sized volumes, encyclopedias, dictionaries, etc. Also a card file of double-width, of wood. Nearly every paintable article in the room was a dark green, one remembers. Shelves, woodwork, plaster, everything was green. There were certain inaccessible places retaining the original slimy salmon pink.

A rare old photo from the old lab, showing a graphite crucible electric-arc furnace ablaze, in a carborundum experiment

The over-sized desk-table extended from the South Wall at one edge to the radiators to the north. At the point where the table touched the radiators the casing of the First Window rose in green splotches. The upper half of the window was covered with slabs of cardboard and wooden shelves to the number of three were fitted into the recesses. The reference books on chemistry and physics were held there, together with assorted camera parts, papers and supplies, such as the paper cutter.

The window extended almost to the floor below the table and was blocked up to prevent light from entering so that the room could be used photographically during the day. The table was supported by 2x4's. There always seemed to be a lot of gunk under this arrangement. The Monster Desk did not appear in this location until a few months after the flux and therefore the description deals with this area up to the arrival of the desk.

The second window was also blocked out with painted cardboard. A board on top of the radiators supported a lamp and a point-headed radio. The second window also had the shelves containing the burgeoning Goon Library. Various signs were posted conspicuously admonishing the prospective borrower no lending was permitted.

TO THE CEILING

The ceiling is lower than in most rooms, so that Bro. Bloch, being tall, frequently bopped his dome on a 200-watt bulb bulging from the central fixture at the time. The sole electric outlet for the room appeared in the center of the ceiling. Awkward. So The Mag screwed a conduit box into the plaster next to the original socket and from this connection fitted gas pipes as conduits which ran in all directions. One conduit branched to the West Wall over the door where it joined a flexible conduit and followed the wall to the photo department, where it sprouted onto the Switchboard for that area in a multitude of spaghetti-like strands.

Another pipe led northward, taking the rounded portion of the north wall in a graceful curve and belched another wire onto a porcelain receptacle screwed to the dormer beam that projected through the slanting ceiling at this point. A double socket was screwed in there, providing current at the chemistry bench and juice for the electric stove thereupon that heated certain flasks borne in the ringstands. Approximately half-way up along the north wall line there appeared a tee connection and still another pipe popped off there to the East. When it reached the East Wall it curved into flexible tubing and ran down the casing about three feet. There it branched into two exposed cords, one traveling to the other side of the radiators to supply the desk on the South with a triple socket outlet, and the one going north ran along the edge of one of the shelves to the other side of them where it fed a porcelain wall fixture commonly found in the better bathrooms. This outlet supplied alternately, the fan, the heater, and a lightbulb. The entire system of pipes was supported by an occasional strip of metal curved to fit the pipe and screwed into the plaster of the ceiling. Black paint covered them, making them look like genuine conduits.

Previous to this - long ago - the ceiling was webbed with unprotected wires of varying insulations, and gathered themselves at an asbestos-covered switchboard in a frenzied electrical bazoo.

A scientific and structural marvel, the Monster Photo Enlarger, a major item of Precision Process equipment

THE FLOOR

The Floor was invariably covered with gunk!

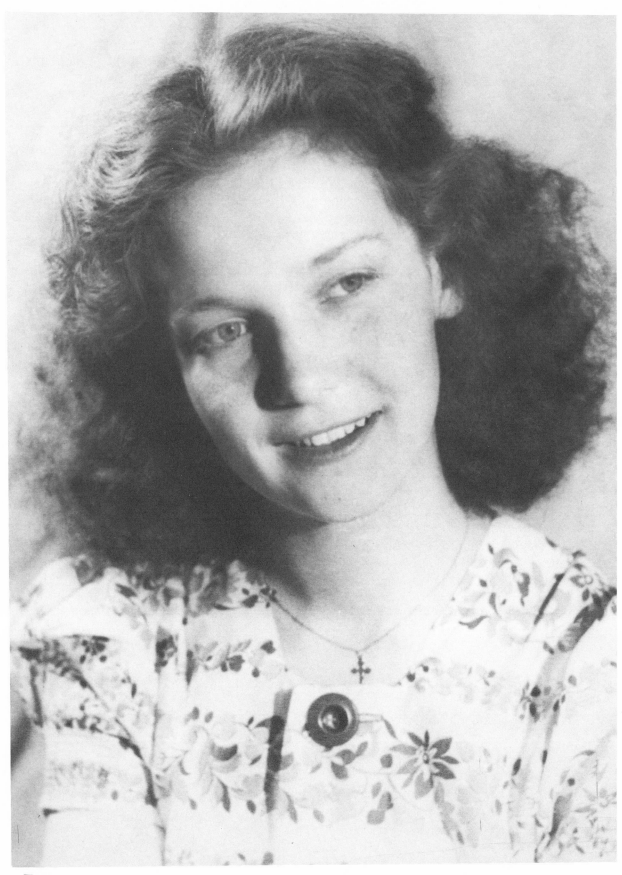

Trinket

THE COMING OF (AGE)

By rights this account should be written with a pen dipped in vitriol. Or better still a brown tongue dipped in the nebulous fooze of a blue-hackled hangover. But this isn't Huysmans.

Anyhow, about this birthday observance of Bro. Gnormie's coming of age on the 17th of October 1937, at 21 years, net. He and Duh Beaver and Mim Powell sat about for weeks contemplating the prospect, but nothing much happened until the night of the 16th, the time for the birching of the natal mongrel-hostelry.

Now take a big pot of chop suey and a monstrous white cake and a great cask of beer and an abundance of blackberry vino and a bunch of cigars. Insert celebrants, such as Madam Goose and one called Trinket, a flushed and incoherent by then Mim Powell, and a busted-out Col. named Warren. Nor was Duh Beaver on hand, probably because of an over-consumption of RETARDO.

Those on the premises proceeded to get stiff as four-by-four boards, realizing that this saturnalia bore little resemblance to the bold sweeping effect of events in the days of yore. Ora Pro Hubris!

THE CHRISTMAS BRINGERS OF JOY

There is an influx of much stuff. There are cigars to the number of bounty, with ciggies, cans of fine smoking shreds, all to be consumed in the cause of tabagism. Garcia panatellas at 2 for 5, some fine San Feclice at 5 cents a can of Beverly Blend of exquisite parts and exquisite moneys, Murads, Helmars, new smoking pipes and all like that.

At the Gauer's and Blochs, the festive yuletide and the beating of dead dogs. Christmas trees are mandatory, and presents. Plenty of plum puddin and the merry resounding of greetings.

Uncle Chappie and Aunt Louise are visiting Alice and Mammy Bedard. Aunt Gertrude is visiting the Blochs. UNCLE AL (Beck) a new character, and EDDIE BROPHY (another), paying court to Mammy Gauer and Aunt Annie, respectively, in the Gauer parlor, part of the Exodus picture ...

Doidy Hoibie came, out of the North, with presents for the people. And Bro. Blo. did from F.W. Wright a check to the number of considerable, get. And H. Mag., after working in shirts at the Boston Store, a cheap salary gleaned. And he could afford a new smoking pipe and a pouch. And there was a lot of gladness at the presentation of an exposure meter to the Precision Process by Alice. And cigars from Uncle Al.

And so the happy days, now past ...

1937

remembered

It would have been stimulating to present a spectacular sequel to the exit number of last year, 1936, a Pantomime (With Spoken Dialogue). It should have been produced under a permit issued by Neptune, Bringer of Old Age, with special flatulences issuing from a copse of bushes back-lighted with blue spots.

Scenes to have been included: The Cambridge Library (Well of Haggardness Number) ... A Night in California (Starring Kuttner & Mooney) ... Sprail & Vague, a combination offer ... The Emil Koeller Ballet Conducted by Artie Algoma with Uncle Nates on the drums ... Excerpts from the Johnny Walker suite, introducing "Mag, You Made The Pants Too Short" and "Haberdashery Blues" ... A new Williams·monologue ("I Been Workin' On The Goddam Railroad") ... a rehabilitation sequence, from The Lab Dance by Jazdejewski. And a monstrous finale on stage.

BUT

Circumstances conspired to ruin rehearsals and most of the costumes were not paid for, so the whole thing had to be abandoned as a Fake.

THE AUTHORS, however, are rumored to be hard at work on a forthcoming opus tentatively entitled "1938", which may turn out to be a light-hearted belly-buster in contrast to the somewhat tragic "37" effort ...

THE HISTORY
1938

BOOK 4

A FIRST NOVEL
IN THE LAND OF THE SKY-BLUE OINTMENTS

A Bloch-Gauer book collaboration burst on the cultural scene in January, 1938, in two typewritten copies. It was preceded by a 30-thousand word outline, an allotment of work, and many hours of nighttime toil since the early October days when the idea first came up. It was a chronicle to affright the eyes of Henry Kuttner, other Californiacs, and local aficionados of the esoteric.

The story revolves around Black Art, a wizard, who lives in a villa with some odd associates, including an unfrocked priest, an undone doctor and a cynical, educated loafer. These three pals persuade Black Art to hurl a weekend party as respite from his grueling necromantic labors.

The Wizard meets an array of guests - Omar Kyoebleh, a strange Persian, Phillipi Stringleborg, a mad greaser, Fiddlestuffer, a timid clerk, Lefty Feep the celebrated sportsman, the Colonel and the Major, militarists, The Little Guy speaking in a strange argot, Floyd Scrilch, Poopse W. Tewya musical conductor, F. Gregory Coprophalia the eccentric author, Mary Cadjadge, a. toots, Mlle Fustilaire lady perfumer, Charles Hovacoe and Doctor Stugatchu, and many others including a burlesque comic and a perverted gorilla.

In a drunken effort to prove his wizardry, Black Art holds a Black Mass and evokes an incubus who proves to be woefully undersexed. The assembled proposed writing a "Doidy Book" to inspire tentigo in the Fiend.

The volume deals with this search for material, including encounters with Fink the Doidy Book Man, Peeping Tom the Voyeur, the stories of Bobo Farblebleester, the strange tale of the Japanese spy, the saga of Waldo Gonad and the Sexaphone, the Little Guy's Story, the weird narrative of the Horse-Faced Man, an interview with Doc. Lessgland, and Coprophalia's Tale.

Black Art meets with The Sexual Congress, attends a Burlesque show where the comic, Marshall Mandrilljazz, suffers an overdose of musk. Mr. Stoof the unfortunate gentleman who lost his guts visits the party, as does Fiddlestuffer's Boss, who beats Fiddlestuffer. Hurrell W. Tchetch is the bulemic photographer and we meet the original Traveling Salesman. Thru the story run such figures as Lumpatsias Fudjumbrundis, Stanley Libido (The inventor of Sex) and dozens of women, bartenders, servants - and Caspar the Naked, a Familiar.

Interspersed in the narrative are erudite comments on a variety of themes, combined with notes on the mantic arts, gastronomical divertissement, horticulture, philosophy, architecture, music, and a wealth of stuff. Hubris is eschewed throughout and subtle understatement serves to place restraint on fantasy.

In no case has verisimilitude suffered, though artistic integrity remains paramount. Imagine if you can, a book combining the virtues of Finnley Wren, The Circus of Dr. Lao, and Thus Spake Zarathustra combined with the writings of Mencken, Joyce, Proust and Cabell. Imagine such a volume and you won't have any idea of what in hell In The Land of the Sky-Blue Ointments is all about!

F. Gregory Coprophalia

169

AKNOWLEDGEMENT OF PROPER NAMES

Hurrell W Tchetch
Chas Horsefinder
Basil Metabolism
Cerrulian Bollix
Toomer Omphalosz
Grabinger Leftwich
Graum T Pootznya
Havalook Ellis
Herman Hormone
Frank Buckalato
Yaddlesnotch Dreembugger
Hiawatha Donglepootzer
Bobo Farblebleester
Osgood Nascene Stercore
Nosblowe Foetibugger

Mylhoven Strimbleteep
Andrew Galatazemia
Eglantine Stench
Hungry Morriss
Rimbaltz Griblin
Percy Gleep
Fosco Screel
Waldo Gonad
Tom W Uzz
Mort Bonum
Max The Axe
Underbucket,
Ninnyhammer &
Slobberpocket

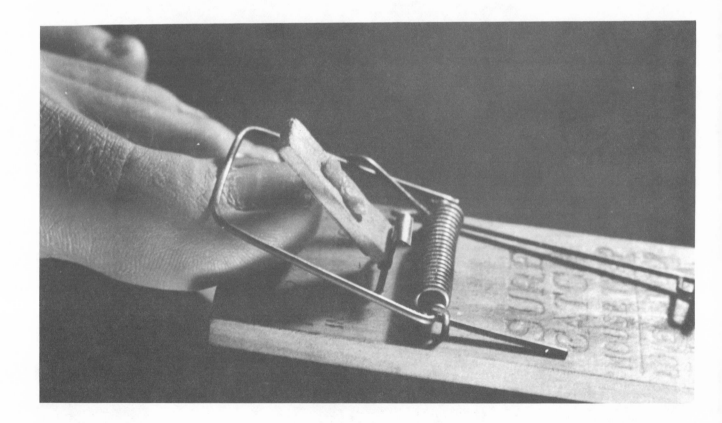

TheDottleknockers

OR, MAKING THE CAKE IN THE WOOD

Willimas and Gauer got started smoking pipes when Wallio showed up with a nifty apple-bowl briar which had a pipe cleaner in the shank for a filter. When it got filthy, you just put in a fresh cleaner. The pipe cost 50 cents and allowed a sweet, plain and gratifying taste. Dr. Grabow, Dr. Sur-Dri, Dr. Frank Medico, and the fabulous Dr. Cherrywood Extremis followed. The pipe photo around here somewhere is a Medico, which uses a filter insert.

Bloch favored a Sherlock Holmes style pipe shaped like a saxophone and Gauer came by a Kaywoodie (a big name in pipes), via Uncle Nates, but with a shamefully skinny bowl that smoked hotter nor a $2 pistol. He also had a tremendous toilet bowl of a pipe with a lozenge of calcium carbonate ($CaCO_2$). The top of the pipe unscrewed, you took out the begunked carbonate, roasted it over a gas flame to drive off the foulness, and replaced it. Much to Gauer's dismay that did not do a thing that a good flushing in a regular toilet wouldn't have done.

Union Leader was the favorite pipe tobacco, despite an incursion by Bro. Hoibie with Kentucky Club, for exchanges at holiday time. Bloch introduced a perfumed tobacco with sugar in it from California called Dream Castle, very exotique, and erupted with a diaphoretic known as Deer's Tongue - a combination of all of these, plus a pound of Papa Jazdejewski's cigar leaves, was kept in The Lab in a can with wet blotting paper and was widely admired as the best smoke in town.

Bloch got a good start smoking Seee-gars when he was waggling a rubber one doing an imitation of Robert Woolsey (of Wheeler & Woolsey, a comedy act). Schowalter's Drug Store has the dubious rum-soaked Crooke, recommended by Schowalter, Sr. himself, and the fellows also bought the 3 for 10 cents Cremos and the five cents straight King Edwards. But for solid comfort nothing can compare to the 15 cents straight Havana Brown, a truly great smoke!

A handsome cigar box has been provided for dead butts. Here the defunct smokes lie, waiting a rainy day. In it are many total yards of smokable butts and many foreshortened remnants of genuine five cent hemps, most of them with the bands still on them.

The cover must be kept closed at all times, lest the odor escape and wreak havoc. The problem with these lovely artifacts is to keep them moist against the day of resurrection.

The horrid stink of smouldering underwear in The Lab is only that of Bro. Bloch's nargileh, or water pipe, which, like the Hookah and the Hubble-bubble, have sucked from them a gas permeated with tidings of a street in Calcutta after an elephant had exploded in the gutter, an especially poignant experience if the misguided sensation-lover is using Turkish tobacco...

March 25, 1938

SCREAM A WHILE WITH
The
HAPPINESS BOYS

The Club (or Colla's Tap as it is sometimes called) is a barn-like tavern but a stone's throw from Bro Bloch's apartment, vis, at the cor. of Jackson & Knapp St. SE. The floor is covered with tables, conveniently placed amidst the litter of butts which are being forever spawned by fertile cigar-smokers. The tables in turn are covered by beers, and the chairs about them are covered by the pygas of the customers. There is a mechanical phonograph shooting great blaaaaawping sound waves through the smoke.

General procedure is to enter the dive, take a table, and wait for the appearance of the waitresses, consisting of Snow White and the Seven Dwortches. Upon rubbing a beer glass these elfin sprites appear and for the small sum of one-fifth of a twobits they fill said goblet to the rim with a combination of urine and a purgative which is jokingly referred to as a "beeeer". The liquid is consumed immediately and another is called for, together with a hard-boiled egg. Texas Hamburgers may also be procured. And a basket of "shoes" — a mess of shoestring potatoes. The phonograph grinds out a horrible noise, and there is gay banter exchanged from table to table, viz:

WAAAAAs THE SCORE, HEY? .... UPPYA YAH!!! ...ANUDDER BEEEEER! SEZTA HIM HA .... WAIT UP HAY ..... THE SCORE !! WAAAAHHHH! ! HOOOOOOOORRSECOLLAR ! ... HEY KELLY HELOO GANG HERE'S KELLY. .... AAAAAH, LUCKY .... MARCELLA GEDDSNUDDERBEER, HEY ...... MIGYIA! .... WHATSASCORE ??? ... HAHAHAHAHAH HESINNA CAN ..... GETSANUDDERBEER AND A HOOOOOOH !!

And some guy comes in selling newspapers and an old bugger walks around and a guy gets sick, and night after night, there is no score.

The scene is duplicated at *Scotty's Igloo*, where the Eskimos howl and Bro. Vic is to be found and where Orry is the bartender, and if you wait long enough, Vail will show up ......

By visiting these two places, Bro. Bloch learned: That Lucky is leaving penuriously for New York, where he is going to seek his fortune. So Bloch lent Lucky five bucks for cakes.

He stopped feeling good about that when Lucky was seen in his old haunts two days later. He never went to New York and never paid back the loan, either.

A TRAP WITHIN
A TRAP

WHAT'S THIS NOW ! ! ! cried H. Mag. Gauer in an aggrieved voice as he well might, for another uzzing by the Fickle Finger of Fate had been committed.

Somehow Mammy Gauer knew. She didn't know what, but she knew something, and good old Doctor Hardy to Brady Street came. He pressed a spoon handle on The Mag's tongue, peered into the cavern of snaggled crags that represented his candy-ravaged teeth and found **bad news** deep in the hole. He clucked some. He went "N-n-n-oing" through his nose and fingered his black bag.

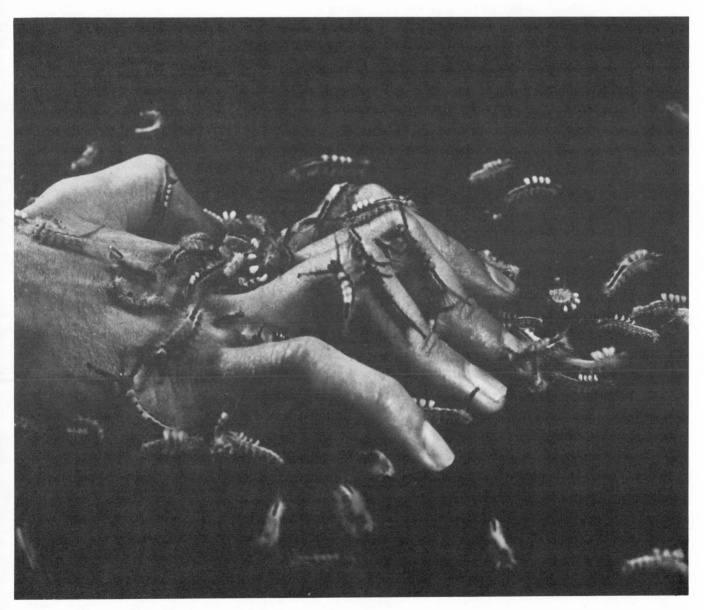

He viewed Gauer's bared chest, discovered his sensitivity to light and declared the patient had a typical scarlet fever rash. He grabbed a swab and a bottle in order to paint The Mag's neck with what the latter confidently identified as AG2NO3, or silver nitrate. Dr. Hardy allowed to Mammy Gauer that she certainly had a young genius on her hands who would be a great scientist one day, and called for the Honey Wagon.

The enormity of it was dazing. Somebody thrust a jar into his hands with words etched in the glass: "Urine Specimen Bottle, S.F.I." Science Fiction Institute? Stale Fat Inside? Not quite: *Scarlet Fever Isolation.* Limbo!

The receiving ward was paved with small tiles, alternately blue and white, like a natatorium. The walls were a desolate brown like porkchop gravy. Odors of carbolic and boiled cabbage permeated the air and woodwork in a deep-seated, determined way. Somewhere a horse was coughing its lungs out. There was a steady "wockle-wockle" of crockery being washed in a kitchen.

In The Mag's cell a youth lay in a bed at the choice location next to the window. He let go a gob of phlegm into a paper bag on the floor.

"Young ducks 19, old ducks 15, young tom turkesy 21 1/2, old tom turkeys 17 - may lard 3 and 5 3/4 bid," claimed a radio in a worried voice.

From Bro. Gauer's bed, four feet off the floor, he could see outside. A row of cottages, lawns coated with manure, aimless tree branches and clots of brush growing out of the hospital grounds. In the distance a church steeple raised a cautioning finger in a greenish mist.

There was a certain discomfort to be found in the rubber-filled pillow and sheets like aluminum foil. There was a par-boiled copy of Redbook magazine on a table, still moist from the sterilizer. Nurse came in to cry Lights Out before its pages could be separated, and the lump in the other bed acknowledged that with a frightful farting and after that, loud snoring, The Mag. turned off his radio for him and fell into a disease-free slumber.

The mound in the other bed awakened at six, long enough to turn on its radio. lift a leg and from the ankle attached strip off a few areas of dead flesh. Then it fell back among the sheets while The Mag. had to listen to the first hour of a Three-Hour-All Request-Early-Risers-Club-Program-With Jolly-Bob.

The face poking from the sheets was an ashen pulp, like thrown oatmeal, dotted with pustulating gobs of acne. That disaster was fitted to a beefy body which, at about seven, when breakfast arrived, heaved to a sitting position. A crack in the oatmeal effect broke open and a voice announced that the ensemble was called Boleslaus (Balzy) Bolda, age 18, under a two-week's sentence.

He had scarlet fever all over and spent a lot of time in hot water in the bath tub. He retired within himself, sitting cross-legged in the manner of a scorbutic Buddha in endless contemplation of his peeling feet. (his navel was O.K.)

Balzy's radio programming became an increasing abomination as he tuned it zealously and then didn't listen to it.

"Every dance orchestra I ever heard of burst into our sterile cubicle with such offensive outbursts as I Double-Dare Yew (to Sit Ovah Heah) and The Dippsy-Doodle (Will Get In Your Hair). I was invited to swing and sway with Sammy Kaye and to be captivated by the sensational rhythms of Gordy Gench and his orchestra, and I was beginning to lose my sense of proportion," Gauer wrote to the Keeper of the History in his absence.

"It was like a heartburn in my chest," he said in a report that was dispatched to the autoclave for boiling and sanitary delivery by post," ... and now for Barbara, requested by her father, and for Alice, Ange, Mary-Jo, Emma Mark, Keith, Corky, Lefty, Stinky and Butch, and for Eddie Goldman and Ed Whitney and all the lads at the Acme Body Shop, Louis Armstrong plays I Double-Dare Yew! And Armstrong would give forth with fervent "Hot Mommuhs" and his drummer would devote himself to a merciless belaborment of the skins."

When Gnormie and Bro. Blo came for a visit to the outer desk they snuk The Mag. a handful of cigars - big succulent, corona-size Havana Browns. There would never be a cigar like that again! And The Mag. would smoke them after midnight lolling in a bathtub full of hot water.

A complimentary copy of the Morning Sentinel newspaper came. Gauer would read about somebody like Seyss-Inquart and hand Balzy the sports section. There was a war brewing in Europe, and being fought only in the headlines at this end for now, but it meant no more to the scarlet fever boys than a clash of Kurds in the Khyber Pass.

The really important news was on Balzy's radio, saying it would upchuck a double onslaught of Thanks For The Memory, and You're A Sweetheart, and for encore, as Balzy wrenched the dial, You're a Sweetheart again.

Nurse would bustle into the toilet to empty several quart jars of some horrid liquid into the bowl. With the door to the suite open, the elevator could be seen to break its cable and begin a free fall to the basement with a screaming moan. In the kitchen someone was trying to corner a frightened moose in the crockery department.

Gauer figured he still had some life left to live and that this too would pass. But would the balance of the boon be spent in a prison like this one, or with a limb shredded in some awful war somewhere, or on a hospital cot beggin for morphine, or gassed, trying to pump with a rotten lung? He'd probably have to kill himself, as an act of mercy.

The brooding would be interrupted by a voice with idiotic cheerfulness saying: ...and now for Ockie, Shortie and Cazzie, and for Mrs. Brixius and her son, Peewee, who is eight years old today (congratulations, Peewee!) Emma and Norb, I Can't Give You Anthing But Love, (Baby!).

When night fell with a soundless crash, Balzy would drop senseless to his mattress and begin a broadcast of his own, talking in his sleep. A conducted tour of Boldian dreamland.. The Mag. is terrified of sleep-talkers, as he was terrified of the insane. And the fellow revealed another revolting aspect of his personality - he could break wind in his sleep.

The other-worldly caterwauling could probably have been interpreted by Bro. Blo., but that and the awesome farting was enough to uncage the animal in H. Mag. It was as though a nameless evil was forcing his hand. He got out of the kip and crept with infinite stealth (with apologies to Bro. Bloch's Creeper In the Crypt) through the darkness, scarcely breathing, with but a single idea in focus.

In the next room a child was choking to death, doctors were administering oxygen and calling out, but The Mag. ignored all that, his hands clasping and unclasping nervously as he approached his quarry, mayhem in prospect.

Prying a rube from its socket (prudently unplugging the set beforehand) he took it out and hammered it sturdily on the floor of the bathroom to scramble its insides. Then, with a fiendish grimace he sneaked back and pronged it back in the set.

His disappointment and disbelief were understandably acute in the morning on being snatched to wakefulness by the announcement that Somewhere A Voice Is Calling would be rent by Alma Gluck and the Victor Concert Ensemble, especially for Mose John, O.G. Gilbert, Ray Crout, Coach Carroll, Ray Tiernan, and for all the paint guys at the Seaman Body Plant!

The Senior Author had to be brainy about it, leave no clues. Instead of throwing the whole accursed birdhouse in the toilet or out the window. Before he could dip deeper into the occult, breakfast arrived, followed by the noon snack, four o'clock crackers and milk, and then supper. And to fill in, the music of Lou Breeze, Ace Brigode, Freddy Martin, Orrin Tucker, Sammy Kaye, Ted Weems, Red Roberts, News W. Report, Bob Crosby, Ted FioRito, Caspar Reda, Leighton Noble, Isham Jones, Henry Gendron, Cab Calloway and his orchestra, Livestock W. Report, and the rippling rhythm of whoinhell ever did that.

Followed by Nurse and three other worthies responding to cries of FIRE ! ! !

And sure enuf, a wad of crumpled newspaper was ablaze in Balzy's birdhouse!

As the cone of the loudspeaker caught fire the polka music of Heinie and his Grenadiers went to a ragged screech, Nurse threw water from a bottle, somebody grabbed the remains by its cord and jerked it into the hallway and a crowd gathered. Balzy slept through the whole thing.

His ability to separate himself from reality was phenomenal. Gauer told him what happened over milk and farinah, likening it to The Holocaust at Peshtigo. After that Nurse brought clothes. It was discharge time!

And not a day too soon, either. Gauer was on his way to being a hardened criminal and fiend. Or, as Balzy put it, a lousy arsonist!

A BULEMIC NEED TO EAT PEANUTS

The evening in The Lab was something of a trap. As usual there was someone there to flush it. Enter, 'midst a flourish of hautboys and shofars - Madame Goose and a certain Josephine (Josephine The Dog, from Koeller's Gardens, yet!) Get in closer, folks, all new stuff...

They are looking for Duh Beaver and Gnormie. Soon all four are merrily shaking dice and futzing around. Then the radio is an excuse for interpretive dancing led by Josephine The Dog. Various pantomimes were had which might have brought eye trouble to a scoptophiliac. The laughing, blobbering nymphs sportively clutch and howl. They shriek out ribald stories, make advances, resulting in acrobatics and contortions., all culminating in a monster melee during which Bro. Blo. is seen to climb on the phonograph to escape, followed by Josepheen and they both fall off.

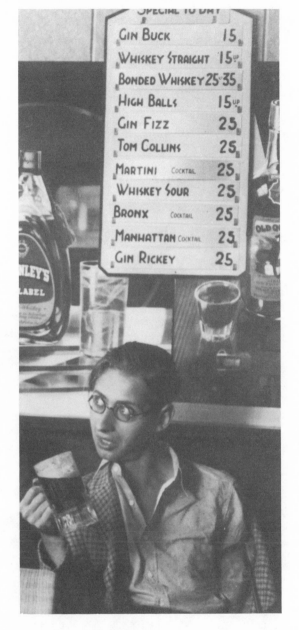

Bro. Gauer looks pained and aggrieved at the unauthorized programming of all that soupmeat. After a time, all exit, laughing and scratching.

After that, ennui drove local citizens to THE CLUB. They goof beers there. Bro. Gauer relates to a circle of spellbound his experiences in the Health Hotel imitating the Scarlet Fevered Pimpernell. Fortunate (Lucky), comes in. Bros. Gelman and Warren follow. Beers to the number of bock for same. A Mose John enters, and Jack Waldheim. A great hooting results, with the pushing together of tables, banquet fashion. There are energetic pantomimes, imaginary poker games, very elaborate and fantastique. An imaginary shell game run by Vince Emanuele in which everybody loses. Bro. Vail tells of a job he has modeling clothes. Bro. Gauer, grown weary of boiled eggs, pops.

Others follow to the exit. Soon only Bros. Bloch, Vail and Vic Ehr remain. But not for long! Oh, no! Lucky comes back, and Kelly (who sits at the McKinley tennis courts with a stringless racquet, very effete). Knee deep on the floor lie dead remains of steak sandwiches and egg placenta. There is a lot of gibbering. Bloch sees the room reeling and pictures blur of Vail, Vonier, Shinners, Gelman Jose (Mijo,

as his last name turns out to be, the worst poker player on the planet), Ehr, Baehr, Warren, Vince, Lucky, Kelly, Mme. Goose, Josephine the Dog, Waldheim, and Colla's daughter, Catherine.

He leaves by back door before it is too late to do anything.

WHAT'S THE SCORE, ANYHOW?

Paul Kovack and Lucky, with Sprague Vonier, were gathered around his Phonograph listening to Pierne and Borodin until Gauer and Bedard arrived, followed by Lucky. That made the entrance of Gnormie and Trinket less improbable, but the whole contingent then got out of the small apartment and went a block down Knapp to THE CLUB (Colla's Tap), where each round of stuff came close to one buck. ($1). and the frycook started to heat up the shoestring potatos.

H. Mag. Gauer, affiliated with the Precision Process, had his Voightlander camera, cut-film, tripod and flash with him. He focused in the dimness on lit matches held by the clubmembers.

He removed a slide from a film-holder and shot 15 cents to hell by popping off a flashbulb and that subsequently resulted in the club portrait appended to this account.

Bro. Gauer is never in many of these historically significant documentaries because he is always on the other end of the stick, camera-wise...

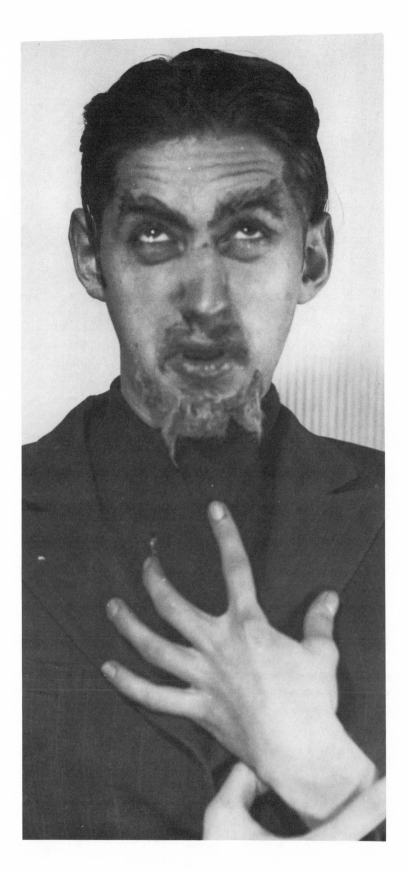

Count Laver D'Fotch

181

Under April Skies

Berto Warren took Thursday off from his taxi driving calendar for the avowed purpose of playing his favorite pastime with the Mag., vis: tennis. But at the appointed hour (bulletin) Warren failed to appear.

Whereupon H. Mag. tried to get Milt Gelman on the phone but Milt had started work at Leeds Shoe Store downtown, part time. It might be mentioned that Vonier and Lucky also fit the ladies with slippers at that location off and on (pun).

Vail, who works at the Cambridge Rental Library has Thursday off, and responded to The Mag's call with news that Victor J. Ehr (who drives an elegant LaSalle as Chauffeur for an east side dowager) may have the vehicle and they could play some Golf!

Williams has been 'bumped' off the road for an indefinite number of days and had offered to "trow duh ball around" in a manner customary as hell in days of the past. But the workout was abandoned when Hoibie decided instead to spend some time with his old girl friend.

Bro. Vique snorts up in the big green car at The Lab. With him is a lad named Sid Derry, whose sister is married to Ehr's brother, Hank. H. Mag provides the contingent with mashies and putters, plus a wood-shaft brassie and driver they could pass around as the need arose. A mess of golf balls from the Economy Boys, some with severe cuts and bruises, are given out to the needy and deserving, and Brother Gauer brings his spavined golf bag, which had been run over by a car in a long-forgotten parking lot, and his collection of ball-axes, broken tees and rags. It is noted by the not too ungrateful recipients that the brassie's wooden shaft has a distinct warp in it, but they are undaunted. H. Mag's 67 topped the eighteen hole shoot-out at the Brown Deer course the County provided for their pleasure.

Before giving up the day entirely, the ensemble repaired to the Bellview Pharmacy at Belleview & Downer for monster chocolate malted milks and topped those with some fine Chicago Motor Club panatella cigars. Doing the honors behind the cool of the marble soda fountain were two zanies, Larry LaBorde, and Art Toppel, who did not stint in filling the huge glass shakers with the swoon-making semi-liquid.

* * *

AND NOW ... on another full day in the sun, with a smell of the lake in the air, Bro. Vail suggests a little tennis and he and Bro. Gauer retire to the Juneau Park courts for their first game of the season. (The Mag. had been proclaiming for weeks that he "smelled spring" but this was the first day he actually could. Only no nets were up. They played without a net. Kelly came along (former president of The Club). Sure enuf he had his stringless racket with him. He sat and watched.

A plan arose to eat downtown. Bro. Gauer refreshed his toilette, carved over to Bro. Vail's, they carve off to Bro. Blo's and Bro. Williams is there to join them. The entire tribe foots it down to State Street, to KING YEN LO's which has a common entrance with a Chinese Laundry, home of the finest suey in town.

The gourmands are provided with mounds of suey on chow mein with copious dishes of egg foo young on the side, they being gobby rafts of placenta submerged in a brown gunk. Oolong tea in mugs lubricates the ingestion. Bro. Gauer, who experienced distinct seismological disturbances on a previous engulfment, had to "watch himself". The usual Havana Brown cigars tied it all up.

Tangling the Lines

NOW GAUER comes to 620 E. Knapp to call Vail on Bro. Blo's telephone. He uses a mongreloid dialect, which puts Vail into fits at the Cambridge Library where a lot of funny calls come in anyway, and he has to deal with them.

The phony caller may be somebody protesting that one of the books he returned was "dirty". Or with a finger up his nose, The Mag. can do a fussy lady wanting an obscure book Vail doesn't stock or never heard of..

On taking off the vocal whiskers, Bro. Gauer stirs Bro. Vail to such a maniacal frenzy of rage that things got broken or tipped over in the latter's vicinity and endangered the telephone he used as a gesticulator.

Came Good Friday. An Anglican voice, very unctuous: "Allo theah ... this is the Reverend Dakin ... yaws ... yaws Undahstand, young man, you are keeping yuah establishment open this awftahnoon ... commercial establishments close on Good Friday, dontchaknow ... yaws ... what's that, you ah not the proprietah?" Vail, unwilling to risk the chance the call might not be ligit, hems and haws.

"Veddy well. But it would be impious. Impious, aw, yaws, ahem." And more of the same as the stricken Vail tries to cope with the crappy imposter. Then Bloch and Gauer dash over to the Cambridge Library to hear the story of how some old rooster of a cleric wanted Vail to close up shop. They die laughing and Vail realizes it is the same crumby old gag again. He puts on a really masterful performance of high dungeon and outrage, probably getting more satisfaction out of his histrionics than the perpetrators got out of goading him.

A few used books were purchased, Vail kept the establishment open and the unemployed duo departed. They had a date with Milt Gelman in a pool parlor to enact a series of pictures Gauer wanted to make in order to give photography a bad name ...

In The Next Shot, Gelman Gets The Eight Ball
Right In The Mouth, Symbolizing "Man's Fate in '38"

SPORTS
We Do 'Em

Sports are often done. Golf is a fine sport. It is played by Vail. Sister Alice plays it. Bro. Bloch plays it with a putter only. Bro Gauer plays and keeps a stock of clubs in The Lab for the others. These folk are wont to gambol on the Lake Park pitch-and-putt course where all holes are par three.

The greens cause cursing. They are too fast, Too slow, have gunk spread on them. The players have lousy luck. They top the accursed ball, they duff, they hit it in the middle with the knife-edge of their mashie. It is not a simple game.

Of late (in April) these games have been rather frequent, and a taxi is usually employed to ride up to Park Place and afterwards, walk back. Engaging sidelight: Bro. Vail's passion for buying a bag of eclairs from Merlin The Magic Baker and eating them in The Lab after a game and listening to the Brewer ball game on radio.

Baseball, we do it

A taxicab supplied by Bro. Vail takes The Mag and himself to the Bellview Pharmacy, near the Downer Theater, hangout of friends and pious companions of Bro. Victor J. Ehr, otherwise known as The Scorekeeper. Bro. Vic is plenty red in the puss, a side effect of being very enthusiastic about everything.

A mob of louts and friends of the Scorekeeper are capering in a lot across the street behind the popcorn wagon. Half an hour later approx. sixteen of said hooligans are assembled on the Lake Park football oval on the lakefront for a little game of baseball.

The younger Emanuelli, Veach, was among them. He pitched a few innings. H. Mag played third base and handled such chances as came his way with precision and despatch. Though he let himself get caught off first base in the second game. The Scorekeeper scampered and capered with enthusiasm throughout the first game. "MAG!" he would scream as he got a batted ball and slammed it over to Gauer's position with great vehemence, narrowly missing taking Bro. Veach's head off in the pitcher's box.

* * *

185

The Last Poker of the Season

A poker session was had in the Precision Process Laboratories one evening. Bro. Vail was present with his friend, Victor Ehr and Carl Baehr. It was had at one-cent-settle-for-half under the title 'penny ante' and proved to be popular.

Vail's dining room was also used at frequent intervals, mostly on Thursday nights with an occasional Sunday afternoon or Monday night thrown in. The game was always 'dealer's choice', which meant the dealer had the right to call his own game, which could be a wild-card proposition, rather than straight draw or stud. A noisemaker was lowest of the three hole cards wild. That made it possible for the holder of a royal flush to be greeted by the cry of NO GOOD! and to see five of a kind.

As winter waned and spring ripened, the exercise fell into disuse and then suddenly it was born anew with a monster game at The Scorekeeper's home on Frederick Ave. Bros. Vail, Baehr, Bloch and Gauer joined Ehr around a kitchen table in that fine, big residence occupied by Mammy and Pappy Ehr, five brothers and two sisters, with a nice pie truck and a landscaping truck parked on the side lawn with a passenger vehicle being dismembered by the younger Ehr youths, Tom and Nick, Jr.

That affair was followed a week or more later by an invitation from Mert Koplin to a game in his sumptuous quarters in the Park Lane Apartments on Prospect Ave.

Bro. Mert had extended himself and a green felt covered a large dining room table, with seats and ashtrays for all. Everyone came well-dressed.

Bro. Koplin had committed a grave error in inviting too many jimokes. Ten players were a ridiculous number for poker, as there were not enuf cards in the deck to accommodate that many hands. To shuffle discards only led to chaos and strife. There, hideous things happened to (reading from left to right): 1 - Koplin, 2 - Ehr, 3 - The Spanish Flyer (Jose), 4 - Vonier, 5 - Gelman, 6 - Lucky, 7 - Vail, 8 - Warren, 9 - Bloch, and 10 - Gauer.

This gathering constituted the last poker game of the season ...

Mert Koplin, Robert Bloch, Harold Gauer, bearing trophies won in an S.O.L. Derby. Bro. Gauer is wearing his Linclon High School letterman's sweater, but the actual chamberpot won by Bro. Bloch was not available, so a bedpan was substituted. (From the Precision Process collection, Historical Section.)

TWILIGHT MEN

We dint do nothin, officer! We weren't even neeeeer the place, we wasn't even neeeeer it even! Honest we wasn't. Not us, hey, not us hey! Gnormie wasn't around. Gelman wasn't either. Bloch? No, no. Vonier? We aint never even HERD of the guy! Madame who? We don't know no Goose dame. I'm tellin ya, officer, we don't know nuthin'. We don't know anythin' ABOUT it!

What? Somebody jumps outa the car and turns in a FIRE ALARM? Don't give us none o dat. Onna south side with the car? Sattidy night? The hell we were ... we was not. We can prove it. We got witnesses! We dint ... no, we ain't arguing. We're just telling ya, see? The five of us was NOWHERES NEAR no fire alarm box on no south' side, and we dint see nobody pull no alarm. And we dint hop in no car and scram, of course not. HEY, WHERE ARE YOU TAKING US? HEY, YOU CAN'T LOCK US UP! OPEN THA DOOR! -- OPEN UP! TAKE OFF THE LEG CHAINS! WE WANT OUT !!!

188

On the Astor Hotel Roof

An Informal Spring In May

Certain locals were intent on hurling a Spring Dance that fruited in May as a gala affair in the Astor Hotel ballroom.

Bro. Bloch, that genial menial, escorted Gertie Kranas and Bro. Gnormie came with Trinket. That ensemble went in Bro. Gnormie's battered car first to the Highway Inn for rye & soda and some vivid dancing. Refreshed by that they pounded down a half gallon of beer and rushed to the Astor Hotel lobby and thence to the penthouse.

Vonier was there in a white coat and Gelman in a brown one, and Lucky had a 12-piece band that played sarabande and fandango. There was much dancing. Bloch & Kranas were favorably compared to Velez & Yolanda. Those such as Dolores Green with Berto Warren ('Promoter' of the affair), Virginia Smith, Vonier, Emily Mosey and Paula Kovack, left to go dancing out on the Blue Mound Road at Corny's "The Ship". It was one of the smart places to go.

Bro. Gauer tarried with his equipment to take a picture of the band.

Lucky (in mufti, lower right) with band and canary

189

The Affair of the Shrifted Shorts

MAMMY LEAVES -- Mammy Gauer and her sister, Annie, left for Pulaski (Wis), abandoning the Brady Street property to the mercy of merry-makers.

FIGHTS WITH FLESH -- Bloch and Vail and Gauer and Bedard gathered in the Mammy Parlor to discuss a method of blowing the ears off so fine an evening.

So Alice and Bob ran out to buy olives and cheeses. A pony of beer was ordered from the East Side Beer Depot. The Mag. had a beer pump and it fit nicely on the keg. The three men put out six bits a piece and the delivery man prepared to depart.

But when he got as far as the door of the kitchen, he had to fight his way through a wall of human flesh ...

HORDE FALLS DOWN -- The flesh consisted of Gelman in the lead, followed by Jose, Lucky, Sprague and Koplin. Lucky paid three dollars to Gauer for the band photos and the horde fell down. The spigot was opened and streams of orange foam spilled forth, and the bladder after that heaved gouts of the bland bewilderizer for all.

BLOATED BY BEER -- As if that were not enough, Bro. Warren, taxihat on, in came and beers had. Then he hove out into the night again and there was more consumption of the Beer bloat.

There was a bottle of old and rare wine fermented in a notorious Brady Street cellar but a few weeks previously and the more intrepid sampled that cautiously. It had been spiked pretty good.

All this while Bro. Vail was being instructed in the proper application of the expression "Mixoscopic Zooerasty" which he had been misusing, until a time came when the pony began to sound hollow to the bangers thereon and it was deemed empty. Bro. Vail showed signs of fatigue.

VAIL SLUMBERS -- Presently he donned a dressing gown belonging to the Gauer Bros and took his ease upon the sofa. The humidity caused him to remove his pants (His shirt having already been dispensed with) and he soon fell into a slumber. Bros. Bloch and Gauer and Sister Alice came in and kicked the snoozer brutally, but he failed to awaken.

SOMNOLENCE -- At this point Bro. Bloch was constrained to place an artificial flower in the braidized Vail's hand, tenderly.

BEARS CHERUBIC EXPRESSION -- Vail turned slightly toward the wall, his face bore a cherubic expression of contentment. He held the posy on a trip through dreamland.

ONLOOKERS CONVULSED -- Sister Alice, feeling the situation warranted a bit of risque, carefully stripped the dressing gown from the body, exposing it in a pair of natty shorts with a Boston Store label. The spectacle as he snored clutching his wire bloom, smiling in satisfaction with his lot, served to convulse onlookers. They collapsed to the carpet, groveling and heaving out manys the boisterous ha ha. They went to the kitchen for another drink and to relax their strained throats.

Sister Alice
(One of the suspects)

FEELS TOUCH OF BOOT -- They returned to the scene fully expecting to see the slumberer at least partly awakened by the draft upon his shanks. But nay, he snoozed. Heavily, as though hypnotized. Someone touched him with the heavy boot, but he gave no heed.

CUTS OFF SHORTS -- A member of the party, perhaps as barrel-dizzy as any present, procured a pair of shears and approached shaking with laughter. And inserted the shears under a leg of the shorts. And impulsively cut the material. Including the waistband. The trunks fell away from the denuded figure. That caused all to scream hoarsely with mirth and they crawled away.

COVERS BODY -- Frequently after that, sadists crept back to view the figure turned to the wall, collapsed in amusement, and went away again. This continued until Bro. Gnormie was summoned from his attic den to view the remains, and he charitably covered Vail with a blanket.

THRUSTS FUTILY WITH LEG -- Members of the cast then temporarily took their leave. Sister Alice was taken home. Bro. Bloch went up in the attic to sleep in The Lab because his Aunt Lil from Chicago was visiting his apartment. And The Mag. went into his bedroom in the back of the flat.

About six in the morning, Bro. Vail threw off the effects of his indulgence and his blanket and regained consciousness. He thrust in vain with his leg, he reported later, attempting to put on his shorts that were but a mere tatter of violated broadcloth. He went home. Silently he crept away, crushed and broken, while the ignorant perpetrators righteously slept.

MAKES FULL RECOVERY -- Later in the morning, or about ten-thirty, Bro. Vail was back.

Bro. Bloch had risen out of the attic and Bro. Gauer had stirred out of his back bedroom. Alice came. The doughty quartet caught up golf sticks and set out for Lake Park on foot.

During that long walk the parties of the second part told Vail the foul deed was perpetrated by a pack of uranists inadvertently sponsored by Gelman. Which was a damned lie.

* * *

192

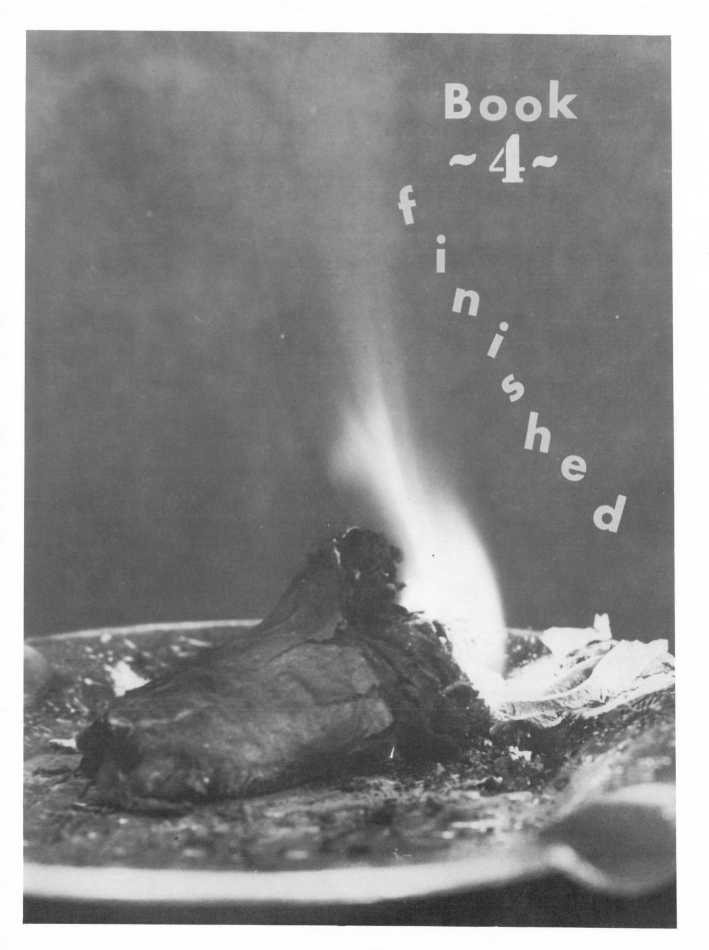

Book
~4~
finished

Santo Cementhead
At Age 22

THE HISTORY BOOK

5

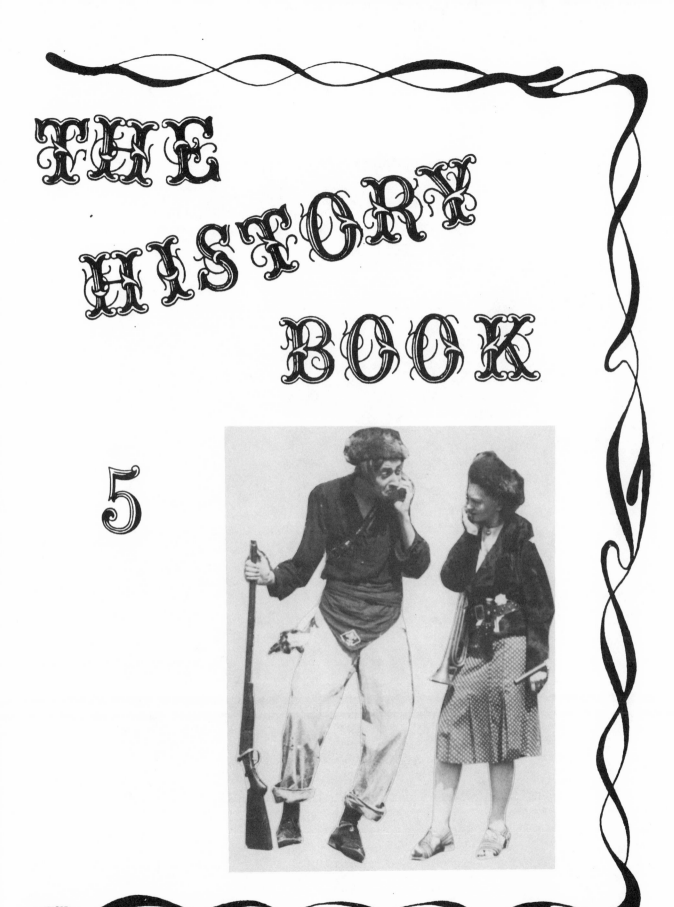

Minor Notes of a Minor Notary

June 1938

Down the Stairs
And Out the Door

NORMAN GAUER, a boxer of the fisticuffs school, was on the card at the Riverview Rink and Ballroom on Thursday night, and after that he decided he was good for a few more rounds on Friday - said rounds consisting of champagne and scotch - for which he provided the pickleskins. Bro. Bloch was invited to partake of the slaughter-water and also Bro. Vail and Madame Goose. They gathered in Norman's Den to do what they could.

LAUGHTER and gaiety prevailed as the partakers became cham-pained. Then a merry gallop on the White Horse Scotch, and the clop of hooves rang thru Vail's stomach: he began to belch the Light Cavalry Overture - out the window!

Some are kind to call Vail folksy when he speechifies, but others find him upchuckly when he heavifies. His exterior decoration did not meet the approval of art critics.

Nor did his toboggan slide down the attic stairs. When he got to the landing, there was Mammy Gauer! Vail said, politely, "Hello!" and continued banging his fundament down the stairs to the street, where he changed more or less to foot-power . . .

And to the Barndance, Away

On the next night, or Saturday, Mike Menos tooled up in his roadster and was ready to take Norman and Trinket, Bro. Bloch and Gertie to a silver wedding in Germantown. The celebrants were related to Trinket Schwerm.

They arrived at the brawl-hall in a haze and heard the rustic musicians whooping up as barn dance. Couples pounded the flooring with their feet. There was a bar and behind it loomed a Little Guy and an Old Bugger, serving beer like mad.

Both were at least Cardinals in the Drunk-as-a-Pope Division and loudly urged all comers to haveanudder beer! They watched eagerly as the beverage was downed, snatched the empty glass to substitute a full one with great enthusiasm. Trinket's brotz and a guy named Spats greeted the visitors.

A member of the orchestra had a cat caught in the pleats of his squeeze-box and ruptured it. Another passed gas into a clarinet and then abused a mandolin while still another grabbed the piano by its tusks. His fingers brushed the boar-fangs in popular ditties.

The only way to stand it was to drink more beer. Spats ran around trying not to explode. Bro. Bloch finally took a deep breath and swung Gertie into the swarm of battling barn dancers. Papa Schwerm cried out to the orchestra, "Play Only A Shanty In Old Shanty Town!" Which it did, spraying it all over.

When the food came the youths went to a dark spot across the railroad tracks behind the depot. The girls brought heaps of provender which they devoured in a private party out of sight but not out of sound of The bacchanal. Then back to the hall for more dervish work on the dancefloor. It was dawn when the girls were conducted to the Schwerm residence. The folks were not back yet, so Norman had to jimmy open a window so the girls could get in.

After which it was homeward unbound.

* * *

The Three Day Saga Of
The Second Coming Of
Henry Kuttner

Now in June, 1938, Bro. Henry Kuttner wheeled his Plymouth across country from Los Angeles. In no time at all he was in the Brady Street Lab, going through the archives, the Stuff, and doing the funny peetchas routine.

A Sac Prairie Saga

Because Kuttner was enfoolished and somewhat dismelieued by cross-country driving, Gauer took the wheel on Sunday and drove with him and Bloch toward Sauk City, home of author August Derleth.

The fabulous Sauk City Sage came to the door to admit the trio in person. An electric phonograph stood in a corner stocked with Mozart, Brahms and the other tone poem boys and also a few compositions of Debussy and Franck. The host played the latter's D Minor while a delicious scent of clover swept through the house from the open windows.

BRO. DERLETH, wide of chin and shaggy of brow, wore a blue polo shirt and gray trousers and sported a mild manner and friendly attitude.

He led the visitors to a restaurant in the heart of downtown Sauk City, and summoned a waitress he called "Honey". After a repast of quite edible foostachi, the party went to one of Derleth's favorite haunts, Ye Olde Harness Shop where the air was heavy with the peculiarly pungent smell of old wood and oiled leather. Horsecollars decorated the scene and the host pointed out the saddles, boots and snake whips.

Then it was back to the house and hippity hop up to Derleth's den. There was a photo of Derleth signing copies of his Wind Over Wisconsin, currently in the bookstores. He opened cupboard after cupboard of stuff - books to be reviewed, books to be read, collected and bound copies of magazines in which his stuff had been printed, a bound collection of one-frame cartoons featuring The Terrible Tempered Mr. Bang, and some more or less obscene volumes he did not display.

Then he got out a board-bound book the size of the newspaper funny pages, which contained in consecutive order since 1922, the work of Windsor McKay - Little Nemo in Slumberland. These cartoons of the Prince and a green-faced jimoke and the shifting into unreality and breakdown of normalcy in them, forgotten since childhood, suddenly came back clearly as the pages unfolded under Derleth's loving hands.

Then another field trip was started, Derleth first affording his charges, Bloch, Kuttner and Gauer, ice cream at the drug store - huge strawberry beslobbered sundaes - followed by a march along the Wisconsin River, over hill and marshland, to the place on the cliff where Derleth, on a summer day, would lounge with a good book.

He pointed out Dead Dog Hole and other places mentioned in his writings, and the men viewed the mighty panorama below. The sunlight had by then assumed a pronounced slant, and Bro. Gauer, with a cloud-filter on his trusty Voightlander, slipped many's the slide holder into it, pointing and focusing, and Derleth, with his miniature, flopped about on is belly in a frenzy of candid picture-taking.

After a nice dinner in town there was more outdoor exercise featuring a foot-powered expedition to the Old Railroad Bridge accompanied by a brigade of mosquitos as twilight settled in. Derleth described the swiftly moving night hawk (listen for the whoosh of its wings after a power-dive!)

The boys had to see the pea-cannery in which Derleth spent 11 summers measuring out sugar and salt and lounging about reading and writing stuff..

It was in full operation, belts whopping, cans dinkling down chutes and steam twirzing out of giant cookers. Derleth pounded upstairs in double time, waved an arm toward pipes purring with shelled peas, indicated graders, revolving drums, and glued all eyes to the spot where pipes disappeared into the floor.

Photo by writer Derleth of photographer Gauer taking photo of writers.

Then the gang bolted downstairs again to take up the journey of the dinky vegetable. They were washed, scalded, jazzed thru more pipes, then the thrilling climax where the brine, cans and peas all came together in one roaring bazoo of moaning iron, and ZUT! Tins defecated into bales hung on trolleys for sweating localry to push out toward the waiting trucks.

Derleth then had to address the Board of School Directors and there was a lot of hand-shaking and fond farewells as three exhausted lummoxes with mosquito bites big as warts blew Sauk City.

What's the Score Anyhow?

History When and if it Happens

A BACKSTAGES BACKACHE OF JUNE 30, marked the end of the fiscal year and Alice's birthday, an occasion that called for celebration and wild abandon. The Bedard wench was deluged with presents from hundreds of admirers and friends and fireworks were shot off on playgrounds and in public parks.

Privately, a little peach wine was shot off in The Lab. Gelman stumbled upon the scene escorting a fugitive from the Steppes of Central Asia, but then quit the birthday score for one in Gnormies' den, where there was card-playing and ballad-singing.

The parlor of the Gauer establishment in the flat below was peopled by Mammy Gauer, Aunt Annie, and Aunt Annie's boyfriend, who bears a striking resemblance to the movie's Eddie Brophy. By Saturday the Backache was resumed after Mammy Gauer and party had departed.

Bro. Bloch and Bro. Gauer provided spaghetti, onions, cheeses, sauces, spices, soups, with which to construct a monster and super tube-tingling evening repast. A bot. of claret in the light of a candle further observed Alice's birthday. They hammered that down with a little more peach wine and ...

Part Two of the Backache

Loaded to the gunnels with food & drink the banqueteers tooled a few blocks down Brady Street to the apartment of Bro. Robert K. Vail whose folks were likewise absent.

The place was a shambles of wretched jimokes. A shirtless Bro. Vic Ehr opened the door, very red in the puss. Bro. Vail was flopping around like a badly-chloroformed biological experiment with his white jacket hanging sweatily and beerily from his tired frame. Bro. Veach Emmanuele, a dapper figure, and Gelman, bereft, and a couple of cases of bottled beer completed the uncleasing picture.

"The Mob" had just left. Veach grabbed Bloch and got him into a fake poker game with blazing speed. Theis amusing fellow performed feats of legerdemain with the deuces, such as concealing them in the back of his neck, and in other ways conducted himself in a distinctly killing manner.

Witnesses attested the performance was extremely funny. His cigar had long since gone out after only an inch remained, but he continued to clench it in his teeth. It began to fall apart, but he retained the shreds, still smoldering, to the last bitter flake. Guys like Veach didn't give up any of life's pleasures easily ....

Beers were had and Bro. Vic claimed attention by laying on the floor in a drunken manner and calling for a taxicab. Meanwhile the bathtub was being filled with cold water and Vail had fallen asleep on the sofa. An attempt to carry Vail into the bathroom failed, as he was not so paazed as in the shorts-cutting incident.

Then began a hideous series of pantomimes and violent struggles in which anybody could have been thrown into the tub.

202

"O.K." cried Veach with a horrendous leer and graphic gestures, "Let's carry Vic to the taxi!" and Vic, not knowing whether to resist or indulge the fantasy, finally decided he could walk, and Veach accompanied him placidly.

Passing the door to the bathroom changed all that, and Veach was transformed into a human merry-go-round. Arms and legs tangled in a furious assault upon Bro. Vic, but he could not be forced down into the water. So he went home. The rest followed in ragged disarray.

Part Three of the Backache

Sunday was Virile Day for outdoor sports, so a ball team assembled in The Lab consisting of Gauer, Bloch, Vail, Baehr, Gelman and Madam Goose in a robust outfit burst down to the Pulaski Street playground. A certain Eleanor and Josephine the Dog were supposed to be there but weren't. A fake game began. Lucky came riding on a bicycle, Western Union style. He joined the fumbling throng chasing Bro. Gauer's clouts. After the aforesaid clouts were soaked with human dew, the trek homeward began, baaaaping, hooting and screaming, tossing the ball and blobbering.

Finally Madame Goose grabbed the ball, howled, and in a Mandrill-like motion hurled the spheroid smash-damn through a neon sign over an establishment labeled EATS, causing it to read E-tzzz! in a tinkle-tankle of broken glass and gutted dangle. Two moose stuck agitated muzzles out of the raped diner and stared in aggrieved accusation as Madame Goose, Vail, Baehr and Gelman disappeared in a forward tap-dance at great speed.

Home was safely reached, however. That night the remains of the spaghetti was demolished and over the ensuing Fourth of July the celebrants decided to give their backs a rest.

* * *

Date	Name	1	2	3	4	5	6	7	8	9	OUT	10	11	12	13	14	15	16	17	18	IN	OUT	—
1937 AUGUST 4TH	BLOCH BEDARD GAUER																						
1937 AUG 22	BLOCH BEDARD																						
1937 AUGUST 29TH	BLOCH BEDARD GAUER																						
1937 SEPT 5TH	BLOCH BEDARD GAUER																						
1938 APRIL 5TH	LUCKY BLOCH GAUER																						
1938 APRIL 12TH	VIC EHR BLOCH SID VAIL GAUER																						
APRIL 14TH	BLOCH VAIL GAUER																						
APRIL 18	BLOCH GAUER																						
APRIL 26	WILLIAMS BLOCH GAUER																						
APRIL 29	VAIL GAUER																						
MAY 1ST	BLOCH BEDARD GAUER																						
MAY 29	BLOCH BEDARD VAIL GAUER																						
JUNE 2ND	BLOCH GAUER																						
JUNE 5TH	BEDARD GAUER																						

Date	Name
JUNE 26th 1938	C. DAVIS
	B. VAIL
	BEDARD
	GAUER
July 13th	GELMAN
	VAIL
	BLOCH
	GAUER
July 14th	GELMAN
	VAIL
	GAUER
July 21	GELMAN
	GAUER
July 23n	BAEHR
	GELMAN
	VAIL
	GAUER
July 26	VAIL
	GAUER
July 24	BEDARD
	VAIL
	GAUER
July 27	Bloch
	GAUER
July 31	BEDARD
	GAUER
August 3	Bloch
	GAUER
August 7th	VAIL
	GAUER
August 9th	Bloch
	GAUER
Aug 9th 2nd Round	Bloch
	GAUER
AUGUST 14th	BEDARD
	GAUER
August 18th	BLOCH
	GAUER
August 21st 1938	DEMOS
	BLOCH
	GAUER

205

Tennis is mostly Shagging the Ball

You held the tennis ball overhead and let it drop. If it bounced as high as your waist, it was O.K. If it was still white and had hair, so much the better. A good four-dollar racquet with the handle-tape unravelling and one or more strings of gut coming loose - perhaps the frame a little warped for lack of a press - put you on the court in good shape. You wore a pair of Keds-type sneakers over your street socks, and were ready for instant gratification.

Repairs to the "uproar stick" were made by knotting the end of a length of gut, pulling it through one of the holes on the rim of the racquet with a pair of pliers, and anchoring it on the other side with an ice pick to keep the tension, and so forth. Until the wood finally split, you had what you needed.

The Milwaukee Park System provided cement or asphalt-paved courts in chain-link fence enclosures, three courts abreast. The chain-link also served as a sturdy canvas-hemmed 'net'. The Brady Street sports lover could find a playing surface at Lake Park, where a nice, high fence of rusting chicken wire kept the balls from flying down the ravine, and at McKinley Park across from the lakeshore. Another was further south along the lake near the Northwestern Road depot. There was also a nice clay court with a net of vegetable matter in Riverside Park near the high school.

Tennis was not all hitting winners across court. It was mostly shagging the ball after you hit it, because it went into the other courts where players had to stop at cries of "t'row the ball, hay!" and hurl it back. It was an irksome proposition all around, particularly when a blackened clunker rolled back instead of one of the three new ones you had in play.

There was also a lot of running around behind the courts to track down maniacal swats by novices playing in their street shoes or, more usually, never able to hit the ball at all, except with the rim of their racquet. It did little good to hook your fingers into the chain-link and ask the little kid out there to toss the ball back. He couldn't throw it high enough, it would bounce back, and eventually, you had to leg it over to the gate, circle around, and hope one of the ball-eating dogs roaming the area - a certain breed fed on tennis balls in the grass - hadn't devoured it.

Score was kept by yelling it. All close calls were in favor of the player on that side of the net. After an exhausting two-set match, it was off to the Bellview Pharmacy for a tremendous milk shake sludge and to light up a fine Havana Brown cigar, and then it was home to sleep for the rest of the afternoon.

* * *

Summer Sausage and Baloney Sliced Plenty Thin

Throughout May and June young Gnormie Gauer had been polishing his guns and cleaning his hip-boots and talking about a camping trip to Wautoma. And In July, having been assured of a welcome (royal) from Trinket - who spends the summers at a cottage in those parts - Gnormie and Bloch - who learned that Sister Gertie would also be there - decided to get packed. Mammy Gauer gave lavishly of her eggs and fruit and the two hit the road (in National Guard Uniforms).

To the depot with footlocker, duffle bag, suitcase, the future buddy bar salesmen boarded a train and found the smoker. There Norman fell asleep and Bloch watched a poker game by four rustics hunched over a bunch of silver with cards held in horny hands. Change cars at Fond du Lac for Wautoma. One of them might well have served as a presidential washroom for a campaign train during Grant's first term. There is a stink peculiar to old railroad cars, a cloying scent of urine. The Iron Horsecollar pulls out of the station, its steel guts vocally pleading for Tums, and onto a spur line single track. Gazing out the rear platform is pleasant, the boys watch darkness fall as the sun yields and bows its bloody head.

The conductor lights gas jets. Then the lights go out and the train runs backward. A hummingbird flies in through an open window, defacating freely. After a long time, or at 9:30, a weary conductor bawls WAAAAh-toma. Out onto a dark platform, bag and baggage. The freight man says the depot is closed, as no trains are expected on Sunday,, and nobody can leave no baggage there overnight, see?.

So the baggage is parked beside the deserted station and Norm leads Bro. Blo by the hand into town - a long street with six taverns, a movie palace, and a double-deck ice cream dive. Every long-eared farmer in Waushara County is on the streets this Saturday night. Not buying, not drinking, just watching and gazing at the electric lights.

Thumb a ride 2 1/2 miles to the Trinket Schwerm cottage at the lake. A hello and a piece of pie from Mammy Schwerm. And thru a terrible mistake, Gertie is to come up here the following week, O God. Then another hitch, back to town, and a tent is pitched in the dark, with cursing, next to the water tank on the R.R. tracks. Mosquitos come for blood transfusions. Troubled sleep in the canvas doghouse as drunks out howl the dogs down the road in the darkness.

After breakfast in a hashery, a genial filling station attendant carted all the baggage up the line to the Waushara Tourist Camp - for free.

The Waushara Tourist Camp is across the road from a pavilion and dance hall and adjacent to a gold course and a beach. 25 cents a day,, trailers, tents and cottages. In the back is semi-solitude near a swamp, and it is there that the efficient Norman erected his poles and set up camp. Wood is chopped. Cooking utensils - coffee pot, two cups, two canteen cups, one canteen, one mess-plate, one tin plate - come from the duffle bag. The food - two cans of beans, one tomato - likewise. A fire is lit. Lunch. Then off to Trinket's.

Rifle-shooting at tin cans. Sodapop at the Pavilion. The pump-water stinks. Locate the outhouses. Learn the roads. A swim, a wash, purchase of more food. Happy farmers gladly drive the boys the two miles into town.

On Saturday, Gertie arrives. She and Lucille swim in the lake for four hours without touching land. Young Gauer and Bloch accompany them via a rowboat, Bloch rowing back and forth for miles between the mermaids in the satin suits.

Evening and into town for a monster bazoo that ended with Bloch reeling oafishly about camp in the darkness, chuckling as he lurched. How jolly, to be sure.

Sunday is fun day and more good clean stuff. The girls bring food. They buy things. Norman is grateful enough to attend church with them. An electrical storm in the evening, magnificent in the dark, comes up. Rain falls, but the boys have broken camp and sleep in the Schwerm car. Up at four A.M. for a walk in the dawn about the lake. It all comes to an end with Pappy Schwern driving the boys with their stuff back to Milwaukee . . .

The East Side Louts Lose Again!

Player	Pos	1	2	3	4	5	6	7	8	9	AB	H
S. Bussalachi	lf	1-1	1		0	0	E⁰	0	0		7	3
A. Emmanuelli	ss	Hr-1	1		0		E-HR	HR	HR		7	6
T. Purpero	3b	1-1	wO		0		1-1		E	1	7	5
J. Emmanuelli	P	W-1	0			E	w·w		2	0	5	2
W. Lee	cf	2-1	1			0	3·0		0	1	8	5
W. Wirth	scf	1-0		0		W	E	HR	1	0	6	3
Victor J. Ehr	1b	1-1		0		1	W	WW	2		5	4
V. Emmanuelli	c	0-0		1		E	E	1	E	W	4	2
Hank Ehr	rf	2	1	2	1	0		1°	0	0	8	5
C. Emmanuelli	2b	1	0	0	0	2		0	W		6	2
B E L L V I E W		14	2	1	0	4	10	3	5	2	**41**	63	37
EAST SIDE LOUTS		3	0	3	5	0	1	0	1	4	**17**	42	18
M. Ehlke	3b	1		1	1°	0		0		1	6	4
J. Levine	c	1		1	W	0			0	1	5	3
C. Baehr	ss	0		1	E	0		E	3		4	2
H. Gauer	P	1		0	E	2		0	E		4	2
N. Gauer	rf	1		1	0	E		E	E		3	2
N. Demos	lf	0		1	E	0					3	1
W. Mickey	scf	0		0	0			W	0		4	0
F. Demos	cf		0								1	0
W. Albert	1b		0		1	E	0				3	1
M. Gelman	cf			0		1		0	0	0	5	1
G. Ehlke	2b		0		1	2		W		W	3	2
B. Vail	rf							0		W	1	0

More beer was spootzed down the drain on August 21, 1938 as the result of the Louts dropping another ball game and the barrel. Unfortunate circumstances dogged the contest: Bro. Bloch arrived late, and when he took over the scoring duties, the first five innings were hopelessly nutzed up. Many errors had been scored as hits. (The East Side Louts committed at least twenty errors!) Spectators hung to the sidelines throughout, spellbound.

H. Mag Gauer pitched the first (Arrrgh) inning and the last three. Of note is the presence of FOUR Emmanuellis on the Bellview team, a new record.

It should be said here that Bro. Victor J. Ehr plays first base with terrific verve and plenty histrionics, so that pretty soon everybody is having a big fun time. Brother Hank Ehr is good hit, but lousy field. H. Mag hit one a good clout, far back in right-center field, a sure homer .... but Hank kept stumbling backward, both hands stretched hopelessly skyward, staggering rearwards crazily, and he finally CAUGHT it ! All the other fly balls out there, he dropped!

— THE LAST GAME of the SEASON —

TONY EMMANUELLI ALICE MADAM GOOSE BRO. VAIL LUCKY

		1	2	3	4	5	6	7	8	9	AB	HIT
T. McGovern	lf	1		2	0		0	hr			6	3
R. Hobart	ss	0		0	1		0	1	1		6	3
Carl Baehr	2b	1		0	1		2	1	0		6	4
H Mag Gauer	P	0		1	0		1	3	2		6	4
Norman T Gauer	1b-C		w	2		0	2	1	0		5	3
C. Blake	cf		1	0		w	2	0		0	5	2
Robert Vail	rf		0		1	0	1	0		0	6	2
M. Ehlke	3b		2		2	w	0		w	0	4	2
C. Emmanuelli	c		1		0	1		w	0		4	2
D. Washburn	scf		0		0	w		2	1		4	2
BLUE-EYE LEAGUE ALL STARS		1	3	1	4	1	3	5	4	0 **22**	52	27
BELLVIEW PHARMACY		5	6	0	2	2	0	1	6	1 **23**	52	29
S. Busalachi	cf	3	0		0			0			5	1
J Emmanuelli	lf	1	3	0		hr		w			5	4
T Purpero	3b	2	w	0		0		1			6	3
A Emmanuelli	ss	1	2	0		1		2			5	4
Ben Coughlin	P	3	2		1	3		1			6	6
Sid Derry	1b	1	2		0	0		0			6	2
Ben Koenig	2b	1	1		0	0			0		5	3
Victor J Ehr	rf	2	w		1		0		0		5	3
V Emmanuelli	c	0	w		w		0		2		3	0
P Purpero	scf		0		1		0		1		5	3

Aug 28th 1938. Official Scorer - Alice Bedard. Note presence of 2 Ehlkes, 2 Gauers, 2 Purps, 2 Ehrs, 2 Demos .....
and <u>4</u> Emmanuellis. Closest game yet - lost in the ninth.

Screwballs as big as Watermelons
A Summary

WILLIAMS is standing on a street corner. He is wearing a boater-type straw hat, very dapper indeed. He is talking to a guy. The guy has a dog. Williams reaches down to pet the dog. The dog, taking offense at the skimmer, bites Williams on the hand.

A group is walking down Maryland Ave. on a Sunday, headed for some sandlot baseball. Bloch, Gauer, Vail, Baehr, Alice Bedard and others. Baehr and Vail and another jimoke are throwing the ball back and forth and Bro. Baehr, visions of Mme. Goose dancing in his head, stretches out his arms like a gibbon in heat and hurls the ball smash-damn into a neon sign over a garage on Prospect Ave. The sign reads Wunderlicht & Prepelitza, but Carl changed that with a tinkle of smashed glass and a grate of twisted coiling.

Baehr and his cohorts take to their heels and gain an easy two-block lead on The Mag, Alice and Bro. Blo. Some people never see anything like that happen in a lifetime. Already, Alice and the Bros. Bloch & Gauer have seen it twice!

Bro. Jerry C. Lehr brings his wife and child to the Brady Street Lab to visit Bro. Bloch and The Mag. The kid drizzles into its pants, onto Lehr's pants, onto his wife's dress, and leaves a hideous blue spot on the couch.

Bro. Baehr has a permanent wash line strung across his apartment on Franklin Place. On it he hangs the diapers of his 3-week-old child and anybody who visits has to paw a way through these festooned urine hankies.

Williams and the Hat he got bit in.

Victor J. Ehr, with chums, makes a furious round of debauchery - Lindy's, Scalers, Scotty's The Leiderekrantz, and Collas. Heaves out the window of a yellow cab traveling at thirty miles an hour.

Alice and Bro. Blo get paazed on 'Koombacher' beer in a tavern while Bro. Gauer is allowing 17 runs in one inning in the ball game.

Bloch & Gauer, walking in the damp night air of summertime on Franklin place, meet Carol Davis near the Bobby Burns statue in Dog's Park and get from her all the latest dope on birth control. She has been attending a lecture on the subject downtown and is walking all the way back home.

Bro. Gelman, finding the atmosphere of The Lab oppressive, takes a walk with Bro. Gnormie into the night. Beneath the window of a Knickerbocker Hotel apartment, Gelman whistles, furtively. He is signaling for his "ginch". There is no answer.

Bros. Bloch & Gauer go into the Sanders Bros Drug Store and Dispensary of good malts and one of the Sanders boys sez: "Hay, I got here 2 rolls of film some guy brought in of doidy peetchas! Nooooods! I can't send 'em to Cook's Photo Service. You develop 'em!

So Gauer develops the films and only one frame turns out at all, and that was taken by a guy with scrivener's palsy, of some wavy lines with blurs in them. Disappointment was expressed all around. Gauer demanded and got a chocolate malted milk made with butter pecan ice cream and with an egg in it for himself and Bro. Blo.

Philippi Stringleborg

The Inscrutable Work of Time
Pappy Bedard Dies

Late in September, 1938, Pappy Daniel D. Bedard died. The effect of that was fierce. Mammy (Alvina) Bedard and Alice were thrown into dire straits. Sister Alice took a week off from work to attend to the bewildering detail and did that with aplomb.

The Mag and Bro. Blo. moved the household goods in the family's 1930 Model A Ford. Cousins and other relatives were transported to the railroad station and the cemetery, and errands were run. The vehicle took people to the funeral, to burial in Wisc. Memorial Park, and it was used to help Alice search for new living quarters.

After twelve days, Alice returned to work at the Dime Store. Bros. Gauer & Bloch toted thousands of wooden crates and cardboard boxers down to the car, rode hunched over in the crush, and lugged said goods upstairs again into two rooms on the second floor rear at 1657 N Astor St., where Mammy Bedard and Alice now reside.

The stuff that didn't fit was sold. The Mag parked the automobile in a lot each night late and retrieved it early next morning thus avoiding a parking fee. As Alice settled down in her new nest there was an attempt to estimate the score, which eluded tabulation.

How to dispose of the nickel-plated Ivor-Johnson '32 revolver? What market for the unhappy stuff left behind by uprootment? Wrenches, hammers, saws, a notary seal, a hole-punch, a bottle of brown gunk, Alice's typewriter, glassware, dishes, Xmas ornaments, Pappy Bedard's sewing machine repair parts, a pencil shar-

Daniel Bedard and his daughter, Alice.

pener, a nickel-plated twin-blade razor sharpener, and a considerable other excram.

Alice's bed, her dishes, some of her stuff, were carried into the Brady Street attic. On the 20th day, the third Monday, Alice, Bob & Harold climbed into the oil-burner for the last time. They found a used car dealer at 27th & Kilbourn who uttered a czech in the amt. of fifty aplombs in exchange for the decrepit equippage, and thus did the scene shift. . .

Members of the Proletariat -
With Some Exceptions

Saturday evenings are sometimes very difficult to kill. The Sat Eve of Nov 5th was particularly hardy. But Bro. Blo's name had been plucked like a gob of fuzz from a blanket by a prominent Milwaukee bookseller who invited him to a *gathering*.

It was a very long and frequently transferred streetcar ride with The Mag and Sister Alice to a place where a large clutch of jimokae had assembled - about 35 dowdy, bewildered and assorted lunks and lunkim, swallowing beer, pretzel sticks, sandwiches, and doughnuts, milling about and whapping conversational doghouses.

A beffy fellow without a tie, a scar on his mug and a general air of disrepute hung about who was thought to be somebody's old man, but he turned out to be Jack Conroy, author of *The Disinherited*. He stepped to the middle of the parlor and gave out for several minutes on the subject of the now defunct *Anvil*, an amateur preletariat magazine "For The People". He and other blowouts wanted to start it anew . . .

He retired then and was seen no more. The bookseller, in a soft shirt,, huge knotted tie and the general appearance of Count Bruga, could be seen through a rift in the crowd whacking home the handle of a beer-pump. After that exercise he introduced a Milwaukee poet. The poet held up a copy of *The Disinherited* for auction. Progressive bidding was had and more grub brought in. That was embellished by officious bustling by some part-time librarians, Chicago stooges and local hungadunghas. Then The Milwaukee Poet again, who would read selections from *The Last Parade*, a vanity-published book of piffle written by himself. His voice vibrated with gassy fulminations of a proletariat nature. His face burst into a toothy bazoo and he walked out backwards.

By now the curtains were hanging in loose gobs. The trays were mired in bubbly beer-slop. Half-filled ganders of stale beer stood around, the carbon monoxide increased ten-told, somnolizing the melee-ites. Sandwich crusts lay in dumps, two kinds of wax paper lay in desolate heaps in the corners of the seats. Napkins lay crushed on end tables.

Here and there on the carpet a dropped and squashed pistachio nut. A lady's foot pressed the floor, tapping, looking very much like the latticed crust on a blueberry pie. Fat legs like a forest of baseball bats. Magazines laying around - *Mother Church* and *The Shout*, having the appearance of stuff floating in the water near the disposal plant. Puckered lips and thin, pink jowls and blue, bushy-haired and glossy-skulled, square keisters and oblong ...

The visiting trio hastily made its escape.

215

Tender was the Summer Night
Life With "Mother"

Bros. Gauer and Bloch, keepers of *The History*, sat in the summer night on the front stoop of the candy store. Small moths and a lot of tiny green bugs fluttered into the light from the plate glass window The Mag was not on store-watching duty. Mammy Gauer and Mr. Jazdewjewski were *klatching* in the back room.

The Bros. smoked their pipes, moodily, and spat across the sidewalk still radiating the heat of day. Three blocks east a streetcar made the turn from Farwell onto Brady Street, iron wheels screeching on ungreased rails. Then it thundered past with a deafening roar, all windows raised, the warm light streaming out through the gratings. There was only one passenger in it, who stared, open-shirted, into the rushing wind. The sound died out and they could again hear the whicker of nighthawks chasing bugs in the air around the firehouse hose-tower.

Presently they noticed a shiny yellow automobile moving westward through the gloom. It stopped, and in the driver's seat was a big, handsome woman with a hello sucker smile, wearing a big, flowered hat. Her boisterous voice, muffled because the windows were up, floated out to the two loafers on the stoop.

"Hey!" cried the frowsed virago, rolling down the window. Hanging to the wheel with one hand, she leaned over to point directly at Bro. Bloch. The Mag. arose and advanced into the street close enough to address the occupant.

"What?" he enquired, squinting uncertainly.

The vehicle jerked and went dead.

"Listen, I want to find Scotty's Igloo, you know where that is, bright eyes?"

"What?" the Mag. said again.

The conversation continued to sparkle until both of the front stoop loafers were crammed into the car next to the lady and The Mag. was driving it to the Igloo. The vehicle docked at a space in front of the tavern and the lady got out.

She stood taller than either of her companions though a good deal less steadily,, a stunning, Junoesque, movie-star kind of celebrity. She had magnificent, long, fat-calf legs, full-bellied thighs and her girdle must have had the strength of The Brighton Strangler, for it modified a truly steatopygous fundament. And there was no doubt about the quality of her brassiere - the objects it fought to contain were copious indeed!

Bro. Blo's eyes bulged. A course of drool caught in the corner of H. Mag's mouth and started down his chops. Bro. Blo. couldn't get over the big hat and figured an over-ripe exotic like that on the loose had to be more than merely boozed up. She had to be, like, weird!

She led the procession into the Igloo and the group ranged in impressive array along the bar, engaging it in a matey grip. Orrey, the bartender, suffered a seizure during which his eyes revolved like the sun in the sky during the vision of Fatima and a deeply agonized Bro. Vail stepped up to get the score...

He was carrying a book he had just bought, Jules Romain's *The Boys in the Back Room* and the lady viewed that and Vail with displeasure.

"Whaddya mean, coming around here with filthy books? You could be arrested for selling nasty crap like that!" There was howling and Vail retired in bafflement as deep as that he had brought to the affray.

216

"Jeeeeez!" Orrey breathed at recovery time, advancing with a rotary motion of his slop rag. It would be dark beers all around with the Great Lady doing all the paying and all the talking, too, as she cased the house with a keen and mascara'd eye. It turned out her name was Elfrieda. Elfrieda something nobody could catch.

Her burden was sorrow, now half-drowned, on the way to total immersion, with friends she could count on, namely Bros. Blo and Gauer, and Duh Beaver, who happened to be standing by trying to look her in the eye. Nothing light-hearted about "Mother."

Duh Beaver had taken to calling her that, cautiously at first, and when she did not take out a pearl-handled Derringer and shoot him dead, more boldly. All concerned drank more bock beer that was good for them, and as for The Mag. he had trouble deciding if he was paddling a canoe upstream or charging on horseback. Bro. Bloch was laughing hysterically at gags he was silently telling himself.

"Mother" then shouted in a voice that could be heard in the last row of the balcony that "everybody" was invited to her place for sandwiches. She included Orrey the bartender in the bargain offer. "I got a big ham", she said.

"You sure have, 'Mother'," quipped Orrey, which he should not have quipped, because she gave a wobbly toss of the flowered hat that cut him off without a cent. She blew more blasts on the vocal trombone, and like the Valkirie, she led the worthy from the Igloo - Bros. Bloch, Gauer and Goose.

Duh Beaver had pumped so many beers into his tank that he walked bent over as he dragged his beflabbed body into the waiting carriage. He got in back, Bro. Blo got in front with Elfrieda, and The Mag. again took the wheel. He noticed a certain pounding in his head but felt otherwise quite sober. His companions on the other hand appeared quite far gone, indeed, chloroformed. He concentrated on getting the address right, having had extensive taxicab experience, and then piloting the craft in the right direction. Unfortunately the car would not start.

"You gotta turn on the ignition, sweetheart! "Mother" warbled. It was true. He did that. The motor brayed a shuddering moose-call. Mother said "Take it easy, honey!" and then everyone seemed to disappear into the upholstery. It was only that The Mag. had let the clutch out rather suddenly.

During the uneventful (to the driver) ride, "Mother" told about her school days at Smith College, her dramatic roles in radio productions, her marriage to the notorious gambler and associate of Louie Simon, Augie Krahn.

Bro. Bloch made bold to enquire if Mrs. Krahn's gambler husband was at home presently.

"Hell, no, Sonny!" she exploded, detonating the words sharply. "He's off and running in Miami-frigging-Beach and for all I know he's diddling every whipsnading bitch on the boardwalk, and I don't care, blast it!"

"You mean Atlantic City? They got a boardwalk in ..."

"I know where there's a board-snortin'-walk and I don't give a whistle-toot if he puts the blocks to the whole Atlantic seaboard, you hear that?" She lapsed into a broody silence but Duh Beaver suffered a laughing fit in the back seat where he knotted himself into spasms.

"Stop by the river and we can throw him in" she complained bitterly. "He's no better than a jazz-happy mandril, he isn't!" She wrestled around to gaze at the struggling Beaver behind her. "I bet you got a blue bottom, haven't you, you little baboon?" She attempted to poke him, but he simply continued to scream and flog the cushions with flying limbs.

217

The Mag. hoped a cop would not stop them, but they reached the Krahn residence in the respectable suburb of Lake Bluff without incident. The driver gave prayerful thanks to the tender stars winking out of the cool summer night.

"I don't give a damn how late it is, boys," the hostess bellowed under the neighbors windows as they sashayed up the flagstone walk, "We gotta have a slice of that ham!"

The door was unlocked and all the lights were on. The party barged in and whacked the door shut again with such a jarring concussion that it scared the daylights out of a little bulldog that had been sleeping in the kitchen. It tore from its box all a-yap and slobbered saliva on the solicitous Danny Goose between shrill barks.

It's name was "Mama's Little Tootsie" and was supposed to go back under the sink where it belonged. It finally did that, voiding yellowly on the dining room rug, first.

"Don't mess up the place, now," the lady cautioned her guests. "If Augie got wind of you guys hanging around, I'd hate to think of what would happen."

The Mag. looked at Bro. Blo. and whitened. It was hard to tell if she was just jawboning or what.

"Augie's the kind of guy, he wouldn't hurt you, but he's got gorillas on call you wouldn't believe, you know, so take it easy, you know what I mean, bright eyes?" She gave The Mag. a vigorous slap on the backside and a throaty chuckle and a wink and took off her hat.

"Hey, I seen one of them, now, Goodyear balloons" Duh Beaver cried as the big hat sailed past him and into the dark of the bedroom. He had rent the fabric of reality and was gazing into the private world of his own fancy that called for a lot of loose-lipped chuckling and he did not hear the part about vengeful goons lurking in the background.

There was a big ham in the kitchen, studded with cloves, covered with sugary rings of baked pineapple, wallowing in a brown sugar and beer sauce. The celebrants made coffee, found pickles, toasted bread, and had a midnight feast. Bro. Gauer took over cutting the ham just as he had slipped into the role of cruise director. Next he would be advising the lady on how to invest her income and what to squirt on her hair. A future leader of men.

"It's a fact," said "Mother" Krahn suddenly, gnawing gristle and pointing the knife at Bro. Blo., you're a dead ringer for my husband, Augie W., the sonofabitch!"

Duh Beaver disagreed, though he had obviously never seen the vagrant Krahn pere. The Mag was afraid his friend was getting out of hand and might rip off his clothes and exhibit muscles or violate other proprieties, but he had all he could handle just to sit upright and excrete his burden of suds.

"My cousin used to work for him!" he exclaimed.

"Mother" lifted the one eyebrow that remained mobile on her forehead.

"I knew it! You're a pack of degenerates, the whole shifty-eyed pack of you! You should be ashamed of yourself!"

It was easy to see 'Mother' was not amateur at throwing the bull either. "What are trying to do, kid me? I seen better than you on a meat counter!"

Duh Beaver studied the faces H. Mag was making at him over her shoulder and he finally got he message. He began to tell diversionary anecdotes about his life in the National Guard. Some of the chill rolled off.

"There was this one guy," Danny related, "we called him Eagle Beak, see? And this here Eagle Beak and us guys was horsing around and like that because it was this Eagle Beak's birthday! We got this here chocolate cake with the maraschino cherries all over in the icing and the first thing we know, all the guys are betting Eagle Beak a two-bits each he can't eat the whole cake, see?"

Duh Beaver was a great one for telling eating stories.

"So this here Eagle Beak says O.K. and starts to eat up the whole cake. Well, we see him going to maybe get away with it, finally, so we start telling him jokes, like, and funny stories, you know, and hollering and pushing him around because nobody wanted to lose no two-bits apiece.

"Eagle Beak is just cramming the last hunk of his cherry-studded cake in his mouth when the funny stuff gets to him and he starts laffing, see, and he heaves up and down and starts to strangle and all, and he turns red in the neck!

"Then he sort of shudders and two cherries come out — one out of each nostril!

Bro. Blo. fell out of his chair and The Mag started to crawl around under the table, thinking that was pretty funny and Duh Beaver programmed a lot of screams in a high-pitched and beer-sodden voice. But "Mother" was abjectly searching Duh Beaver's contorted muzzle for some clue to what was so funny, her mouth drawn down in stupefaction. That made it all the funnier.

It was close to puking time for somebody. The Mag. didn't want it to be a Precision Process Program. He eyed Duh Beaver closely but the latter was for the moment captain of his guts.

"We'd better get going!" he proclaimed, nodding agreement with himself as he had seen Neil Hamilton do in the movies, "it's getting late ..."

"Mother" agreed. "That's right, bright eyes, before the truant officer finds your friend here" - she indicated Duh Beaver, who nodded with foggy geniality - "and locks him up for life." She laughed hollowly, mockingly, at her own words, giving out with the veteran trouper biz and smoothing her generous curves with her hands and she quitted the festive board.

"Wait until I let some of the air out of my tires!"

She headed unsteadily for the bedroom, evidently enroute to the toilet, switched on the bedroom light, and then let go with a terrifying up-and-down scream of bloody murder. Bro. Blo. blenched and Bro. Gauer blanched as Duh Beaver shook off his mantle of bemusement and sprang to the alert, and "mother" staggered in a half-circle and hung to the bed post with disbelief drawing haggard lines on her face.

There was a man more or less propped up against the headboard, bleeding. His fine duds were all wrinkled and dirty, his face was a bluish green and swollen from what was obviously a fierce beating, probably in the alley behind the house and he was no doubt and probably the notorious gambler, Augie Krahn, right then and there just coming out of a swoon.

"Aub uld zahg percomorphum" (or words to that effect), he groaned, kicking out spasmodically with his legs, wrecking the bedspread still further. He had one eye in working order and tried to focus it on the disorganized visiting parties, saying "I don't think those are the guys ...!" He flopped backward, calling for the ceiling light to be extinguished, and "Mother" wearily exhibited a jigging thumb aimed doorwards.

"Mother's" new-found chums beat a hasty retreat to the veranda and the cool of the tender summer night for some air, but it didn't do any good. The younger member of the expedition "went" into the funkia and the authors of The History fought their gorge.

Then they started walking. It was a long way.

219

OH GREETINGS !

And Summary of the Ninth Blue-Eye League Season

THE SEASON just passed and concluded on Nov 7th, 1938, had some interesting aspects. The Fungulas have now won more seasons than any other team. This season, The Mags finished runner-up, only one full game behind the leader, and The Hammers and The Homburgs finished in a tie for third.

The season was marked by the withdrawal of Bro. Baehr from the league at half season. In his stead came Bro. Ehr, who took over certain of the Baehr Kiester players and finished out the schedule. With a certain pride and turgidity the Blue-Eye League presents the averages and statistics herewith:

FINAL STANDINGS, TEAMS

FUNGULAS	29-21
MAGS	28-22
HOMBURGS	24-26
HAMMERS	24-26

TOTAL RUNS SCORED

MAGS	380
FUNGULAS	367
HOMBURGS	367
HAMMERS	181
KIESTERS	136

Home Runs, MELEFIGHT, (Mags) 19
Triples, DOOGE, (Hombs) 16
Doubles, SHAPIRO, (Fungs) 15
RBIs, BUSTAGUT, (HAMMERS) 15
At Bat, LAPIDUS, (Fungs) 225

Robert Bloch, Mgr. Fungulas
H. Mag Gauer, Mgr. Mags
Robert Vail Mgr Homburgs
Victor J Ehr Mgr. Hammers

The Fungulas beat the Mags 7 times. The Mags beat the Fungulas 10 times. The Fungulas beat the Homburgs 11 times. The Homburgs beat the Fungulas 6 times. The Mags beat the Homburgs 8 times. The Homburgs beat the Mags 8 times. The Fungulas beat the Kiesters 7 times. The Kiesters beat the Fungulas zero times. The Fungulas beat the Hammers 4 times. The Hammers beat the Mags 4 times. The Mags beat the Kiesters 5 times. The Kiesters beat the Mags 3 times. Homburgs beat Hammers 5 times. Hammers beat Homburgs 4 times. Homburgs beat Kiesters 4 times. Kiesters beat Homburgs 3 times.

INDIVIDUAL BATTING

	T	AB	H	HR	3B	2B	RBI	Pct.
Fracas W MELEFIGHT	M	191	70	19	10	13	49	.366
Pos F WASSERMAN	F	191	69	14	9	13	48	.361
Hungry MORRISS	F	197	70	15	8	9	48	.355
Tubal SCROTUS	M	185	65	13	13	10	47	.340
Dom SNATCHATCHA	M	100	34	4	8	5	19	.340
Wally WANGER·	H	189	64	7	12	12	31	.3386
I SCOTTY	V	68	23	6	2	1	12	.33817
P G STAFOONGE	M	207	70	11	8	11	35	.33816
Potsy KOOMBACHER	H	210	71	13	8	12	40	.33800
Black TOM	V	170	57	10	11	9	37	.335
Joe BUSTAGUT	V	198	66	13	10	12	51	.333
Rookie Joe VET	H	200	66	9	15	7	47	.330
Shorty DOOGE	V	187	61	6	16	11	28	.326
Buster BLADDER	V	191	62	10	10	8	26	.324
Bargain SMALLHOUSE	V	106	34	4	5	6	14	.320
LIVERLIPS	V	191	61	10	14	6	27	.318
Stabber FITZNOODLE	M	213	67	13	13	12	39	.314
C L d'FOTCH	F	192	60	8	13	11	39	.312
Sam LAPIDUS	F	225	70	10	11	11	28	.311
F W WRIGHT	H	196	60	11	11	12	43	.306
Billy MINSKY	H	187	56	7	6	11	29	.299
Toomer OMPHALOSZ	M	101	30	7	4	6	22	.297
Hotfoot O.OUCH	M	207	61	14	5	13	35	.2946
DREEMBUGGER	F	217	64	12	11	7	42	.2944
Bishop SHAPIRO	F	205	60	6	9	15	32	.292
Studs NOOKY	H	206	60	10	13	13	25	.291
H L SHAWOWSKY	F	157	45	5	7	5	27	.2865
Tad ODD	H	213	61	15	6	10	35	.2863
Feckless FURDY	H	207	58	10	10	9	30	.2800
Milt T BIGSCORE	V	107	30	9	5	6	21	.2800
Max The AXE	F	179	49	7	10	7	27	.273
Fosco The RUPTURED	M	104	28	5	6	3	22	.269
Frank FLUMEY	V	81	19	3	4	4	9	.234

UTILITY

	T	AB	H	HR	3B	2B	RBI	Pct.
B'whp SLAVELASHER	F	4	1	1	0	0	2	.250
Tom W UZZ	M	9	2	0	1	0	1	.222
A FUMBLEKIESTER	F	20	3	0	0	2	4	.150
Elmer BLIRCH	M	1	0	0	0	0	0	.000
E DOESIT	V	1	0	0	0	0	0	.000

Sylvester W. Skadietndapmn
COMMISIONER of Blue Eye League Baseball

NINTH SEASON PITCHING

	T	W	L	IP		T	W	L	IP
Lou LATRINE	F	6	1	89	H W STRUGGLE	M	3	3	79
COPROPHALIA	F	10	3	94	H UPJOHN	H	10	10	117
F ORGAZZ	H	4	1	62	MANDR'JAZZ	H	3	4	99
C NAKED	M	7	2	77	S T VENDER	V	3	4	79
LUNCHAUSEN	V	5	2	46	TCHETCH	M	3	5	62
RASKALNIKOV	M	5	2	85	F GROIN	M	5	8	78
SKIKADILLIA	V	2	1	15	W GONAD	F	2	4	56
Luke The PUKE	F	4	3	69	M JERGOFFER	H	1	2	53
Regus PATOFF	M	4	2	60	S S SLOTH	H	1	5	59
C HORSEFINGER	F	6	3	83	SCHLAPPERM'N	F	1	6	56
L O'TOOLE	V	5	2	34	S LASHER	V	0	2	27
F P ANDERER	H	4	4	75	B CUE	V	0	2	25

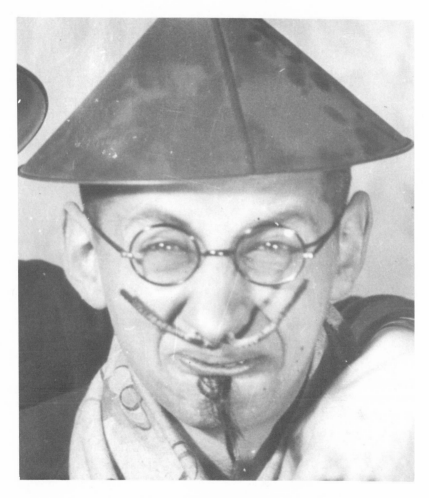

Jack FuGroin
(Traded by the Mags in mid-season to the Fungulas for
Raskalnikov and two minor league outfielders).

A LISTING OF ALL KNOWN BASEBALL PLAYERS APPEARING IN THE BLUE EYE LEAGUE ROSTERS DURING ITS EXISTENCE AS A LEAGUE
Dated September 28, 1938

Adolph S
Black Art M
Adamowitz M
J Aardvark F
Max The Axe F
Abe Addlepratz F
F P Anderer H
Bass Ackwards F
Ernie Agony F
Slaplap Barndancer
Art Blossom F
Al Bino F
Milt Bigscore V
Buster Bladder M
Joe Bustagut V
Master Bates M
Bell E Bandoski H
Wun Dum Bumm S
The Brain S
St Don Bosco S
Wm Dobsha S
Elmer Blirch M
Petey the Beep M
Benny S
F. Belch P
Abe Bortion F
Bunghole Benny F
The Bugger F
Gast. Belch F
C. Bollox F
Chas Brutch M
Clem Cloaca M
F G Coprophalia
Scottsb. Case F
Dangle Cuelga
F B Cokolayvitch
Y Dreembugger
Ct L d'Fotch
C. Drizzledraw's
Shorty Dooge V
Easy Doesit V
Joe S Duck S
Dave the Dude S
Ortho P Dick S

Busy Ditch F
E Didimus P
C Dopplegaenger
H Donglepootzer
Anton Dirp M
Havalook Ellis
Trans Elmer M
A Fumblekiester
Lefty Feep M
Gnu Face M
Fallopius M
Fellatio M
Little Fungula
Ferd Futz F
Smiling Feces P
Pratt Fall F
B Farblebleestr
Nos Foetibugger
Osb Freebish F
Fr. Fundament F
Eb Fooch F
Stabb Fitznoodl
E N Foop
Feckless Furdy
Frank Flumey K
Jack FuGroin M
Fastball Floogie
Sam Goniff S
The General S
Percy Gleep M
Rimb Griblin M
Col Ginsberg F
Geo Ghunk F
A Groinberg F
Waldo Gonad F
Little Guy F
Hairless Harry
Chas Hovacoe M
Cloven W Hoof
Hothorse Herbie
Chas Horsefinger
Herman Hormone
Jazdejewski M
Stan Jeeper M

Jimoke F
Joe Jazz M
Max Jergoffer H
Blind Jake
Fadder Kaufman
O Kyoebleh F
P. Koombacher H
S. Krotchbinder K
Liverlips S
Sam Lapidus F
Grab Leftwich M
Lou Latrine F
Prof. Laxis F
Manuel Labor F
Doc Lessgland M
Tiger Lipschultz F
M Mandrilljazz M
Maharajah F
Hungry Morriss F
Al Mink P
Basil Metabolism F
F.W. Meleefight M
Billy Minsky H
Norb Nuzzbaum F
Caspar the Naked M
Fake W Nogo M
P W Notmuchleft M
Studs Nooky H
Overanious P
Toomer Omphalosz M
Frenchy Orgazz H
Tadd Odd H
Limpy O'Toole K
Hotfoot O Ouch M
Potzkopff M
Milton Phipp M
Luke the Puke F
Jake the Plomber F
Falstaff Prezz F
Popo F
Grizzley Pazz F
Herman Phrodite F
H. Public P
Pulaski F

Regus Patoff M
Pedro Pheel M
Raskalnikov M
H. Redeemer F
Sex Roamer F
Fosco the Ruptured M
Dr. Stugatchu S
I Sneakafelia S
Schlapermann S
Anton Steuquepukchu
The Snuffer F
X.T. See H
Stoopnagle M
Floyd Scrilch M
Sid Snirzz M
Jno Semipopo M
Fred Steenk M
Gil Spooldripper M
Tubal Scrotus M
Skikadillia M
Straminkia M

M. Strimbleteep M
Sol Sloom M
Cecil Slotcch M
Dominic Snatchatcha
Jeffrey Snartch F
Burt Sturred F
Livid W Sensuallips F
Stunguloo M
S. Sputum P
Tommy Salami F
Emmanual Stinch F
Snuffy Smith S
Hoyle W. Struggle M
The Stiff S
Steeplejack F
Philippi Stringleborgh
A Salvo H
Reamer Steamcleaner H.
Sudden Sam Sloth H
Percy G. Stafoonge M
P. Threepwood M

Unnatural Tom M
Hurrell W Tchetch M
Nameless Urge F
Hardy Upjohn H
Tom W. Uzz M
Merde Vous F
Rooky Joe Vet H
Jurgen Wagstaff F
Pos. Wasserman F
Wally Wanger H
Doggy Whapsaddle M
Fielding Yocshamosh M
Antsmosh Strandnagel
Edgar Cadapa
Cerulean Bolloxx F
N Drogyne

Sylvester W. Skadietndapmn

225

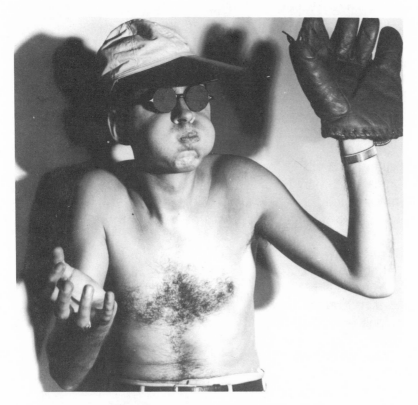

Osgood Nascene
Stercore - outfield,
2nd base, Fungulas.

Meritorius Performances, Ninth Season

FUNGULAS:
Four-hit game (Coprophalia, Puke). Shutout (LaTrine). Stercore (Struck out 4 times as pinch hitter)

HOMBURGS:
Three home runs in a row (Nooky, off FuGroin) Three home runs in 1 game (Tadd Odd, off Naked)

HAMMERS:
Three-hit game (Lunchhausen, Cue - a shutout) Five-hit game Three homers in a row (Bigscore, off Horsefinger) Three doubles in a row (Bigscore, off Raskalnikov)

MAGS:
Two-hit game (No walks, balks, errors, FuCroin, Struggle, a shut-out). All-time league record. Three-hit game (5 pitchers used) Four-hit game (Patoff, Tchetch, Naked).

(*) The BAEHR KIESTERS were granted a franchise, but could not field a team to play enough games to qualify in the official statistics. This was also the last season for the EHR HAMMERS.

Most of the players in the line-up of the Mighty STUGATCHUS, since the retirement of Manager Williams, have disappeared and none are now playing in the Blue-Eye League.

SPORTS, WE DO 'EM

The Downhill at McKinley Park is an easy one near the road, and there is a sidewalk to come back up on. The steeper part is more of a challenge since it heads into a grove of trees at the bottom.

Skis are something of a rarity here, as the custom is mostly snotty kids sliding on sheets of tin and flattened cardboard cartons. The few toboggans are brought by groups of scrambling "rich kids" who should really be someplace else.

So too for the panting juveniles in knitted wool scarves and tassel caps operating sleds with wooden front runners that can be turned to steer, watched anxiously by parents in big cars parked nearby.

Flexible Flyers abound, however, since they are not only used for sport, but for all-purpose lugging of goods, bundled babies and by the daredevils who hitch to passing trucks.

Barrel staves, when they can be found, are not much use as skis since there is no good way to strap them on.

The remarkable thing is the number of people willing to freeze to death and get sopping wet simply for an extremely uncomfortable bang and jounce downhill.

Alice and Gauer pause at the gate to the areaway between the candy store and the tavern after some downhill work on the slopes at McKinley Park overlooking the beach.

THE WAD IS SHOT
written at the conclusion of the now deceased 1938

DISEASE ... In February, 1938, they carried the stiff body of H. Mag off to the diseasery with a dose of scarlet fever, and he emerged a month later, very morbid.

THE CLUB ... An era of scoring it at Collas was in vogue during February, and many shillings decomposed into beers.

MUSICALE ... Friday afternoons at the U W Extension were when recordings bellowed on an electric phonograph and louts in the halls cried out: "Whadda they playin' in there ... symphoneeeeeees ???"

NORMAN'S CAR ... Norman's car lived a short life, and died.

SCISSORING ... Memorial Day saw the cutting of Vail's shorts.

SECOND COMING ... On the 19th of June, Bro. Kuttner came and fell up to his elbows in Koplin's bathtub, Bro. Augie Derleth's fat kiester was photographed and Chicago visited.

FOREIGN OBJECT ... Alice's birthday, a party at Vail's, and they almost got Bro. Vic thrown in the bathtub.

A RURAL TEN DAYS ... Bro. Bloch and Gnormie in Wautoma.

BOSTON STORE ... The Mag worked week-ends at the Boston Store almost continuously.

BALL GAMES ... Sunday live baseball at the Maryland Ave playground, in both English and Italian.

DEATH ... Alice's pappy died in late September.

LIFE ... With "Mother", her car, beers, and problems.

PROLETARIAT ... communists, neo-poops, and pains.

THE PASSAGE OF TIME ... An item more important that those foregoing was the slow passage through the time tunnel, without benefit of profit or honor.

FUSEL OIL ... the first, top ounce of whiskey in the bottle, according to Vails' Uncle Frank Flumey, an authority on Art, Literature, photography, chess, foreign policy and community life. Also dog-breeding, Poker, Music and Religion .....

SIGNIFICANT BOOK ... "In The Land of the Sky-Blue Ointments"

BOOK 6

THE HISTORY

In Gay, Carnival New Orleans

ROBERT BLOCH and H MAG GAUER decided, one day in January, 1939, to carve off to New Orleans (La.), there to write a new and different kind of rabelaisian novel, blending fantasy and reality into a unique literary fudge.

To this end a Yale lock was screwed into the door of The Lab. Dust was wiped from cardboard suitcases. There was a horrid rumor of onanism at the bank, with Bro. Blo. extracting the most generous portion.

Items to be taken along were a framed photograph of a foot, a pair of pliers and a screwdriver, Ferde Grofe's *Mississippi Suite* on Victor black label, and the notes for the proposed book, NOBODY ELSE LAUGHED.

Abandoning work on *The Dictionary*, the Precision Process Annual Inventory, and the forthcoming issue of *Brutal*, the custodians thereof capered onto a Greyhound and in 24 hours they had galloped through Champaign, Effingham, Paducah, Dyersburg, Memphis, Jackson and on into New Orleans. On the way they saw sharecroppers living in what looked like corn cribs, a chain gang toiling along the highway, swampy bayous, and signs like "Colored Waiting Room", all new material.

It was a soft, rainy night with a warm, strange aroma in the air as the parties took up at the Brown Roach Hotel, which turned out to be in the French Quarter. After a hearty breakfast of chicory coffee and a mess o' grits, they looked thru the *States-Times-Picayune* want-ads for room- and-board. They lugged their luggage out to the Will-O, at 1511 Louisiana Avenue.

The Authors unpacked a lot of pictures and hung them on the walls and unlimbered their gear. They called a typewriter rental agency and ordered two typewriters delivered for the total sum of $5.25 and popped out to examine the city:

From the Will-O it was 30 blocks to the center of town at Canal and St. Charles. The streetcars, for such they were called, went up one street and returned by another street and in the narrow passages of the French Quarter they took up almost all of the room, causing newcomers to cringe against the buildings in fear of the gnashing wheels.

The doors to the cars slid open sideways and the windows were always open, with someone hanging out to buy newspapers or food from vendors reaching up from the street. The fare was 7 cents. There was a motorman in front and a conductor in back dinging on a totalizer.

The travelers noted the high prices for liquors, such as $3.98 for a bottle of scotch, a 4 cent tax on ciggies, making them 18 cents a pack and causing pockets to bulge with foolish aluminum slugs called 'tokens'.

The purchase of a second-hand Model T turned out to be impractical. The inquirers were astounded and aggrieved to learn that a wretched specimen on a lot was selling for $95. The same lowly equipage in Milwaukee would have brought $20 top. Sorrowfully the idea of having a car for the stay was abandoned.

The visitors were urged very emphatically in local advertising to consume *Jax, Dixie, Union City*, and *Regal* beer. And *Royal Crown Cola*. Trying these out, the Authors found them to be liquids most annoying to the kidneys. Bladders cried for mercy and tongues called out "Ptchehhh!"

They settled down to their typewriters. They shook the fleas from their piles of manuscript pages and notes. In nine days a complete book, NOBODY ELSE LAUGHED, went into the mail to Bro. Henry Kuttner, Californiac, who would agent it.

By night, walking was the thing - through the dark streets toward the center of town. The routes varied, through places where there was no sidewalk, where tree roots stuck out all over, hunks of iron grille spanned ditches. Street names were laid out in blue tile at intersections. Front stoops encroached on sidewalks. Mighty trees arched the street and hung down in yards on the opposite side. Wrought iron fences guarded stately mansions.

There was a damp, indefinable, aromatic, earthy smell . . . uncovered garbage cans at guttter-side predicted a rich stink for the days to come. Boxes of oyster shells flexed their putrid muscles in anticipation of the Mardi Gras.

The room at the Will-O boarding house possessed double beds, a gas-plate, a private bath, and a fine porch overlooking the street by Prytania, on the west by Louisiana, the east by Toledano, and the north by Saint Charles, the artery leading downtown toward the French Quarter, and upon which the streetcars teemed numerously.

SOME ADVICE
From An Old Hand

DEAR BOYS   Jan 14, 1939

So you are in New Orleans! Stand at the corner of St. Peter and Royal. Take off your shoes or something, for that is holy ground. I mean 704 St. Peter, where I quarreled bitterly with my first wife, wrote *Girl From Samarkand* and entertained Robert S. Carr in regal splendor. Then pause before 305 Royal Street. It was there I began my career as a professional fictioneer, entertained H P Lovecraft, Kirk Washburn and other pious and learned persons. I also brewed excellent beer in 5-case lots and made synthetic sherry from raisins in a 15-gallon barrel.

Go to the French Market Coffee Stand where there are tables under an awning. See if a very lovely brunette is on the night shift. It's been 10 years since I was dazzled by her creole beauty. Go further, through the Market to the Po Boy Sandwich Stand where the mightiest glutton in history succeeded in eating only two of them at 10 cents a piece.

Do not go into Antoine's on St. Louis St., Galatoires on Bourbon, nor yet to ... hell, I can't think of the place. But if you can rake up $10 or $15, a light luncheon with wines is an experience never to be forgotten. Also patronize the Gem Oyster Bar on Royal, Name Your Drink 15 cents. Try a Ramos Fizz and a Sazerac. They are unique even if you don't like them. (See my article on New Orleans in the 1938 June issue of FOR MEN)

Then in Exchange Alley there are old-fashioned saloons where women are not admitted, not even the lewd ones. The crawfish ala creole are princely at 10 cents per plate. Then on St. Claude, very inaccessible, is *The Original Poor Boy*. Ponderous sandwiches. "Original" is a New Orleans catch-word. There are at least seven "original" absinthe houses, etc.

The Green Mint Patio on Gov. Nichole St. is admirable for coffee and doughnuts, and for creole wenches and African music. Visit the Napoleon House on Chartres, wines 5 cents. I cite from my 1935 visit en route from Mexico City. Beware of homemade or synthetic absinthe and of liquor that was smuggled from a ship. Both seem to be pumped from the bilges.

Having given you a few rough bits of advice, I conclude by saying forget the boarding house - get a cheap attic studio some as low at $10 a month, furnished or semi-furnished, eat po boy sandwiches, mingle with the denizens of the Vieux Carre and peace be unto you.

— E HOFFMAN PRICE

MINGLING WITH THE LOCALS AT THE WILL-O

Having lived in the excellent rums provided by the Will-O for two weeks, the men ran into havy trouble when Mammy Oberling wanted to move them from their second story suite to the first floor. She had a cruddy day bed brought in to supplement the single bed. But The Mag grabbed her by the t'roat until lather bubbled from her blueing lips, and presently the double beds from upstairs were brought down, thus affording the lectular comfort to which the occupants had been accustomed.

Enjoying a half-gallon of grappa
and a bowl of goldfish
with the boarders at the Will-O

However, this arrangement featured a shared bathroom with an ancient pair, Mr. and Mrs. Woonzy. The old lady played on her private piano in the middle of the night. The old geez wore a green eyeshade, even under his hat and put three spoonsful of sugar in his drinking water at every meal. The old parties doddered everywhere and both suffered a double rupture the night H. Mag. locked their access to the bathroom and forgot to unlatch it again so they could get in. It was in the blackest part of the night and the roaring and pounding was enough to strip the rind from a leather watermelon.

Bro. Blo. regularly engulfed oyster sangriches, while Bro. Gauer guttily enfolded po boys, consisting more or less of an entire loaf of french bread cut lengthwise and begunked with certain meats and/or mystery substances. Sauce was flotched on that and the bread scrounged together with a horny hand. They were variously, 5 cents, 10 cents and 15 cents. The 5 cent ones were pretty good, the 10 cent ones still gooder, and the 15 cent ones were never tried at all.

There was the time Bro. Blo went to a movie and the Oberlings and Williams' took H. Mag. gambling. They went through the streaming night to the JAI ALAI CLUB out near the softly stinking Mississippi River. It resembled the Riverview Roller Rink in its spacious splendor. Everything was wide open, as on bingo Night at St. Hedwig's on Brady Street.

Big green tables with croupiers spinning roulette wheels and wielding crooked sticks. Mooches frantically placed mauve and yellow-colored chips on the boards. Mixtures and assortments from every station gathered here for the big score.

H. Mag, on account of he was nearly thrown in jail for toying in the same manner with pennies on a Ping-pong table, took a shot at the goddess of spots and dropped half a buck. Perhaps it was unwise to double three passes in a row on account of the fourth shot was phooey!

The group then went across the street to the CLUB ARABI where Pappy Oberling got into a 50 cents crap game and it took quite a while before he could throw himself out of it again without too much harm. Hundreds of slot machines lined the walls and the gamblers could also play racehorse games, Kino, Roulette, or just gawk. The Mag. manipulated some slot machines and managed to shake the iron arms for about $2 worth of greetings. Mammy Oberling hit a jackpot and purchased manhattans for all. Hot milk and doughnuts at the French Market completed the festival.

The boarding house food, when not confounded with broccoli, tizzy umbragio, or carrot greens, was double OK - crawfish bisque, buttered yams, belly-style gumbo, and all kinds of Creole ingestibles and also oyster stews and seafood combination offers, all of which could be enjoyed at the Will-O family-style round table.

In the Metarie Cemetary, a former swamp, the folks are stored above ground for sanitary reasons, in these huts.

235

Eating in other places, such as the fabled ones in Exchange Alley, was also good for the people. Pickled pig's feet stood there in huge jars (The Mag's favorite) on the bar, and large pickles, too, with monster mugs of 5 cents beer.

In the back room at the GEM OYSTER BAR they were playing poker all day long and a man was hollering "Just one more seat at this here table, folks, just one more open!" They were playing 5-card stud and the house dealt, taking a chip out of each pot and putting it in a drawer.

Out front at THE GEM, attendants were splitting oysters, cold off the ice and laying them in a row on the marble bar for the customers, who were standing. The latter plucked the oysters from their shells with thumb and forefinger and goofed them. The more fastidious used a fork.

THE POLICE, it was observed, were forever hopping out of their squad cars to frisk black people. And finding stuff. One guy got nailed with a bulging pocketful of tokens. The cops themselves were borderline ridiculous.

One policeman was smoking heavily as he coasted by on a motorcycle. Another, wretchedly sub-standard in height, wore a checkered coat with a black fur collar over his uniform and had a ginch on either arm. Another's coat came down almost to his heels, had a million buttons on it, and a high-waisted belt. Still another officer affected a long cigarette holder sticking out of his chops at a jaunty angle.

In the NAPOLEON HOUSE on Dauphine Street, excellent wine was had in huge glasses for a dime. And there was the time H. Mag. and Bro Blo. stepped in out of the dark night into a bar on Magazine Street and there partook of a great mound of fresh-boiled crayfish dumped onto a sheet of newspaper. Incredibly good, accompanied with a bottle of newish red wine, the small tails became a casual but vividly recalled delight.

AND THEN - at just about Mardi Gras time The authors consulted their ex-stinking-chequers and decided they were penniless. It was goodbye to the Will-O with one last round of poker and the packing up of the novel NOBODY ELSE LAUGHED (which had not sold), and off to the bus depot on the morning of Mardi Gras, figuratively weaving between the parade floats en route.

Only one night had warranted the wearing of top-coats. For about $125 each, including postage, typewriter rental, book-buying and po boys, etc., The Authors had spent, using the term loosely, an interlude in a semi-tropical paradise.

Just how lucky they were was fully impressed on them when The Hound hit Champaign (Ill.) - for they were again in the land of snow and ice. A blizzard raged in Chicago ...

Reactionary, Post-New Orleans Brady Street
The Hysteria Following The Return of Gauer & Bloch

During The Author's six week bazoo in The South, a dearth of activity had transpired. But Bro. vic had found himself a ginch - her name was Jean - and Bro. Vail acquired the acquaintance of one named Jane. Both had come into orbit as a consequence of their being associated with the Cathedral Players, and amateur group of stage actors performing in theatrical entertainments.

A GLASS OF TEA was performed by the workshop of the Players. Both Ehr and Vail were involved in spreading the playlet on the boards and under the lights, as was Jane, the new girl friend.

Its performance was attended by not only H. Mag and Alice, but also Jean and Bro. Hank Ehr and attached Ted Derry (female) and a sprinkling of dew drops from the nearby Protestant Home for the Aged. Plus a scattering of Others.

The production came off without any sore skin, but a post-performance outburst by the Director was enuf to move the bowels of a constipated water buffalo.

It was a tall, skinny, poorly-articulated, ill-informed and halt-voiced bimbo who stalked to the fore in an exhibitionistic display of fofomania.

Her declarations were obviously copped from some freshman text on the drama, and cackled forth uncontrollably for an interminable time. A thin wisp of white, reticulated fooze squirted from The Mag's either ear during the ordeal and there was wonder how the boys endured these self-styled "Directors", who wanted the players to be like tubes of Pazo Ointment or strings of firecrackers.

Suddenly she busted open.

And everybody left.

ROBERT K. VAIL, bookseller and raconteur, took advantage of Bloch and Gauer being out of town to buy a lot of recorded music, which he fed into his newly acquired Monster Phonograft. He invested in a well-right-now Le Coq d Or, Le Oieseu de Feu, Prelude a l'apres-midi d'un Faune, Gaspard de la Nuit, and some fantasiestueckes. He goaded his instrument with them.

Being stage actors as well as music lovers, the Bros. Vail and Ehr bathed themselves in recordings like Maurice Evans reciting Shakespeare, which they supplemented with their own yelling and posturing and groping for lost lines. Post New Orleans Brady Street nurtured a period in which the most eventful evening entertainment consisted of laying on the floor in the dark en mass, listening to music. Many swooned.

It was a significant change for some of the locals who had formerly seen merit in tunes like Little Sir Echo, Tippi Tin, The Hut Sut Song, Three Little Fishes, and the big Slam Stewart hit, Flat Foot Floogie (With a Floy Floy).

Bro. Victor Ehr, devotee of Shakespearean theatre, amateur carnival barker and expert on the subject of low hole poker.

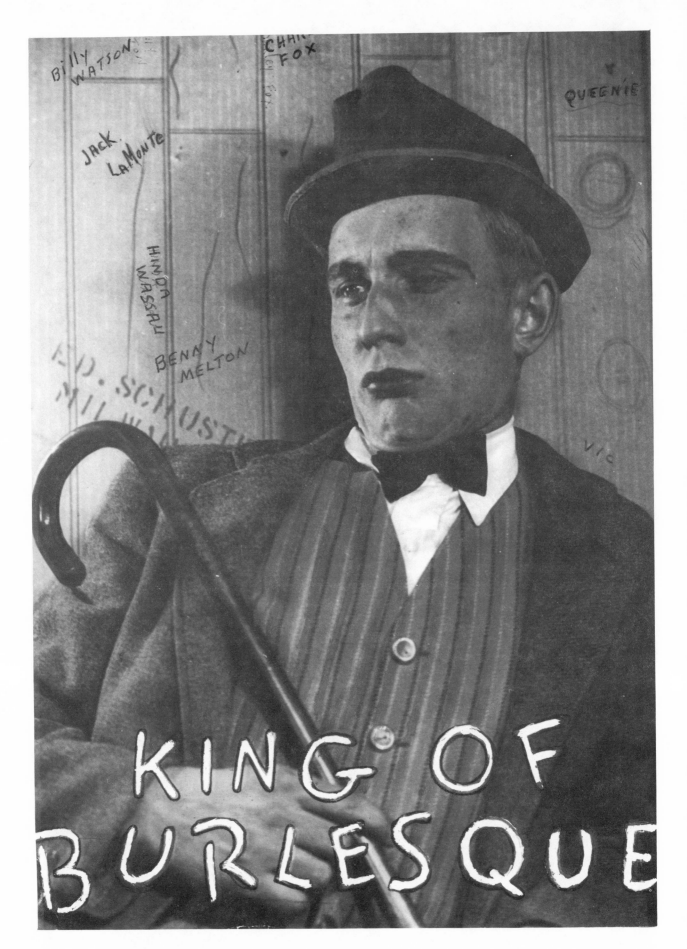

Alan Jones singing The Donkey Serenade was not altogether out of favor either, but the pioneering of Bro. Bloch and the carry-through by Bro. Vail and to some extent that of Bro. Gauer is having its effect.

The fellows enter telephone-like booths in the downtown record stores to audition new releases and to be captivated by the two-dollar Victor and Columbia offerings. It is a good idea to check the shellac dishes for gouges, needle scrapes, oily thumb prints or cracks before taking anything home.

It is no cinch to play them either. You have to hop up to start a new side every three minutes or so with the 12-inchers and even more frequently with the 10-inchers. That kind of attention to detail makes listening significant and commands close attention.

Bro. Vail is a devotee of The Peter Gray cactus needle. He has a gizzer that grasps the little green spine in its jaws and twirls it over a circle of sandpaper. There is a trick to getting the proper point, and as the needle grows shorter and shorter, Vail finds the set screw in his tone arm can no longer grab it and the cursing begins. He keeps a 20 cents box of steel needles on hand just in case. Ever since the crank-up machines in the Cohen On the Telephone days it was a matter of setting steel needles in shellac grooves. There was hissing, popping and wowing and when the sound deteriorated to a muffled squawk it was time to change needles.

Bro. Sprague Vonier gets along quite well with a plain electric turntable with a wire running from it to a cheap portable radio. The big revolution came when Bro. Vail invested in a new automatic changer and it was not long before the uproar boxes on Knapp Street and in the Brady Street Lab were fitted with changer/players also. They had faults, however, that the single play system did not.

The new-fangled deee-vices nudge the bottom record off a stack piled on a spindle so it will drop down onto the turntable while the others remain wobbling precariously above. Then a tone arm swings into playing position by a complicated set of greased gears and sliding levers being restrained by coiled springs, and the music starts.

The machine is kicked into its change cycle when the needle rides to the center and hits an eccentric center groove. Then the tone arm quickly ducks out of the way, another platter comes crashing down and the tone arm returns and plays that.

Some of Gauer's records do not have an eccentric center kick-back groove - some folks are kind enuf to call his stuff eclectic - and that eventually drove his changer insane. The needle just stayed at the end of the music, mumbling and ticking until its enraged master did what the accursed machine was supposed to do.

Then it went into tantrums and refused to play the music all the way across the record, going into its change cycle prematurely in a kind of pre-menstrual cycle. Then it started flopping two shellac pancakes at one time. Finally, in a fit of utter pique, it started putting the needle down an inch beyond the starting groove, playing a few bars, then jerking off on a new adventure in schizophrenia. The poor thing was obviously terminal and Bro. Gauer kindly took it out and buried it.

The old Edison console phonograph in the Gauer living room over the candy store represents his earliest musical influence. Mammy Gauer wouldn't part with it for anything, though she never played it. Bro. Gauer's cousin, Herbie Sipe, has an exact duplicate at his house, with a drawer in its belly containing the same assortment of records. People started out their marriages like that in the old days, with furniture that would last forever and pictures from the furniture store that would remain on the walls in the same places until the end of time and the big upright black and ornamental Edison phonograph would last a lifetime too, except the quarter-inch thick lamination of the discs were beginning to split apart and curl. And the

For those who desire a high quality Cactus point:
THE RCA VICTOR CACTUS NEEDLE
List Price 35 cents per package of 12

241

music - - All I have are sunny-weather friends ... The Whistler and His Dog ... Barcarole from Tales of Hoffman ... Sousa marches, operatic arias, selections by Enrico Caruso on the tonsils.

" *...sunny-weather friends, sunny-weather friends. They're all good fellows while the sun shines. But when clouds appear ... they are nowhere near - - Oh, give me a pal like father's only gal, who'll share the stormy days without a frown - - Oh, all I have are ... (Ouch!)*

I anyone wants to, they can go down into the Gauer flat and play *On The Hoko Moko Isle*, but nobody does.

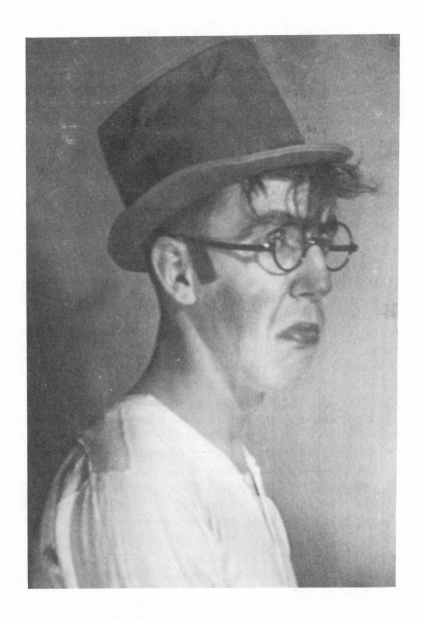

THE KEEPER OF THE SCORE - H. Mag. Gauer - ambled up Brady Street in the direction the Fickle Finger of Fate was pointing and was approached thereon by the mother of **Hoibie Williams**. She keened to him that Williams was <u>married</u>! Into wedlock, already! He had gone and done it without a word to his former boom companions!

Blork! Good old Wms, no doubt worn and boggled of spirit, but independent as hell, wearily climbing aboard the flying diner, railroading himself into a jailhouse of discontent, alas poor victimized, fickle-fingered Bro. Hoibie!

Uneasy and bereaved by the second-hand announcement, and by the Stugatchu Manager's self-imposed exile, his former intimates knew not.

A View From The Attic

A fool and his curtain are soon parted
—from the wisdom of Uncle Nates

LOOKING AT 1939 THRU A KNOTHOLE did little to convince habitues of the Brady Street Lab that Life was boundless opportunity wrapped up in the Future.

Present Time, they figured, had little historical value. The pointless striving was endurable at all only because they were too young to die.

A WAR rumbling in Europe added a new feeling, one of apprehension and the realization that if there was a draft they were old enough to have their legs blown off in it. If the National Guard was Federalized, Danny Goose and Norman and Col. Warren and Bro. Hoibie and all the frequenters of the Richards Street Armory who t'ought that they waz hard would be off in the stinking mud somewhere excreting into slit trenches, feeding belts into machine guns and getting their guts hung up on barbed wire, their heads filled with tunes like "A Trisket, A Trasket", "Chiquita Banana" and "This Can't Be Love."

Bros. Gelman and Koplin were going to the U. of Wisc. in Madison, seeking the academic life, where goldfish swallowing was all the rage, and around the country a week would not pass that some waterhead was not mailing you a chain letter. Bro. Lucky is on the coast, Berto Warren is working on the lake boats, smashing baggage. And Vail's Grandma Hassmann is reading 'hot books' from the Cambridge Rental Library entrepot.

There was a more innocent time when The Younger Crowd - Norman, Bert Warren, Jerry Schmidt and other members of the graduating class of 1934 school of thought had cherry picking of their minds. It involved hitch-hiking to Lake Michigan's Door County peninsula for a couple of weeks harvesting the sour cherry crop.

One could loaf in a recreational manner, (paying $1 per nite to recline in double-decker bunks in a barracks at Goldman's Camp Sturgeon and pay for the meals - in the orchards at noon it was usually kool-aid and peanut butter sandwiches) or work the trees, earning about 8 cents per pail.

Brother Norman earned something extra as a bugler. He could play only three selections, reveille, mess call and taps. There were entertainments at nite, including boxing. Bro. Norman won all of the bouts in which he was entered.

The elder Gauer was not a hitch-hiker. Neither was Bro. Bloch, and neither had anything to do with guns, but young Gauer and Duh Beaver and Mike Menos among others for whom shooting was a passion, spent a lot of time cleaning weapons and finding places to blow off bullets.

There was a good deal of target practice in the basement on Brady Street where the bricks of the south wall near the coal furnace finally got so shot away they had to be replaced by Papa Jazdewewski's stone mason from the faraway hills, followed by the serving of severe bawlings-out to the miscreants. However, the band of gunpowder stinkmakers managed to find a quarry or an open field where they could demolish tin cans and shatter bottles until their ammo ran out.

On one occasion, according to a participant in the exercise, they bought a couple of cheap shotguns from a pawn shop - 12-gauge, one-barrel, one-shot, very worn and used, for about $9. They took them by streetcar in torn and stained canvas carrying bags to the edge of town and then hiked into farm fields where they cleared the air of pigeons.

They took the pigeon harvest - hung about their necks, and their weapons on the streetcar to Duh Beaver's place and prepared a squab banquet. From a relative in the Greek Restaurant business they obtained a pitcher of gravy, which lent a rich flavor to Duh Beaver's culinary endeavors, much appreciated by their girl friends, who were invited in.

The nimrods could also shoot pheasants, and did so in season and out. Their tales of intrigue were many. An example cited was when only cock pheasants could be taken, and they had shot hens, so they put one in each of the four hubcaps on the old Buick they had and thus avoided search and seizure by any game wardens who might have regarded their expedition with distrust. They shot a lot of rabbits also, which found ready acceptance on the tables of their relatives and friends.

One of their friends, known only as "Hoagy", was from a small town nearby where he took them hunting one brisk fall afternoon. After jumping up and down on brush piles to flush cottontails, they decided to break into the local firehouse on the outskirts and take a rest. It was locked, since there was only a volunteer group that came running only on alarm signal, with a key. They broke in and came across band instruments stored there by the chowder and marching society. "Hoagy" decided the best thing to do was excrete into the tuba and thereafter to die laffing.

The rural authorities suspected "Hoagy" from the start, kept him all day in the jailhouse with a pad and pencil, but he refused to sign a confession and they had to let him go ...

The Entertainment Picture

It was at the Murray Theatre that J.C. Lehr got his first job, which was sweeping popcorn bags out from under the seats after Saturday matinees. (His brother, who could skate backwards, got his first job at about the same time, as a bouncer at the Riverview Roller Rink.)

The Astor Theatre (taking its name from the remarkable coincidence of its being on Brady Street at Astor), could be sneaked into by the side emergency exit and sometimes thru the window of the toilet in back if the grille was loose. Opening the side door in daylight let in a blazing blast of light, much to the annoyance of the patrons whose irises were open to F 4.5 in the darkness of their seance with the likes of Blondie, Tom Mix and Charlie Chan.

In the old days the Astor stage had a curtain and spotlights and painted flats with advertising. And a velvet-curtained alcove down front with a player piano in it. A theatrical troup, *Schultz & Bozo*, would play there and it was always a big thrill to watch them coming out after the show with their costumes and make-up on and get into two touring cars parked on the Brady Street side. They would be going to their next stop on the wheel, probably the Jackson, and then the Garfield, maybe the Uptown.

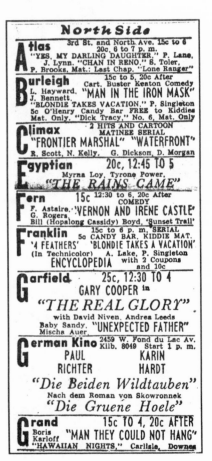

246

Saturday afternoon at the Astor was a guy on a motorcycle tearing up an incline as a bridge was opening. There was an impossible gap over the river as the episode ended. The next week in the serial he was tearing up the incline again. This time the gap was more leapable, and he made it across.

Bro. Bloch went all over town by streetcar to see movies like *Phantom of the Opera* and *West of Zanzibar* and his favorites were as diverse as Von Stroheim and Buster Keaton. Bro. Gauer and Alice ventured to outlying points too - they liked *The Thin Man*, the Marx Brothers, and old celluloid like *The Green Goddess* with George Arliss. It was prudent to check playing times in order to avoid such plagues as Bingo, Double-Dish Nite, grocery nite, and the other half of double-features that were no good.

* * *

THE CULTURAL SCENE, as THE HISTORY surveys the waning months of the decade, seems less than panoramic. Jiggs still wants to sneak out to Dinty Moore's for corned beef and cabbage, but Maggie wants to shed their shanty Irish origins and aspires to the society life. She catches Jiggs (who squints, wears a top hat and morning coat), swings him thru the air by the collar in back with two fingers, so he gets a black eye and cross-patches of tape on his head. Maggie secretly likes corned beef and cabbage too, and even Lester dePyster, a society simpleton is found eating it, to Maggie's red-faced embarrassment.

Other influences on current thought are Tillie the Toiler and Mac, office workers, Boob McNutt, the Terrible-tempered Mr. Bang, Major Hoople and the boarding house gang, Harold Teen, Ella Cinders, Moon Mullins, Winnie Winkle, The Toonerville trolley with Powerful Katrinka, Andy Gump and Freckles and his friends.

Freckles McGoosey, his young brother Tagalong and bumbling young friend Oscar Pletzenbaum do the juvenile growing-up act, like Skeezix does with Uncle Walt in Gasoline Alley. Der Katzen - jammer Kids don't do much more than put large firecrackers under the stool Der Captain is sitting on and get walloped on their behinds (their names are Hans & Fritz) for stealing pies cooling on the window sill of the kitchen. You have to get the Sunday Chicago Tribune for Gasoline Alley and to see Krazy Kat get brained with a brick thrown by a mouse.

* * *

Somewhat more advanced fare than that of the newspaper funnies can be rented for 3 cents a day from a drugstore rental stand.

Samples:

RED HOT — Carmine Mitchell of the glorious red hair evolves a cynical philosophy which clothes her in furs and jewels. But even the hardest armor is not proof against the shafts of awakened love, and Carmine is miserable in the midst of splendor.

SHE WAS A TRAMP — After resisting seduction by patrons of her adopted father's diner, pretty Evelyn James ran away and became one of those girl tramps of the road. There were plenty of men in her life after that.

PASSION PREFERRED — Paula Craig became infatuated with Gayno Lampry only to discover it was a passing fancy with him. The dramatic story of a woman who wanted more than passion.

DOCTOR'S OFFICE — Dr. Jeff Worden's private medical practice gave him a splendid opportunity to study human nature. But when Dora Drummond suggested he provide her with a mate for a eugenic baby, even the resourceful practitioner was baffled.

WATERFRONT WAITRESS — Regina Simmons, beauty-prize winner, comes to New York but is forced to find work as a waitress in a waterfront dive. But the men she waits on want her services after hours.

MARRIAGE FOR THREE — Clyde Aldrich tells Doris that marriage among moderns is an affair for three - husband, wife and mistress. Doris bets her husband is faithful - her honor against a diamond bracelet. She loses - bet, honor and husband.

CARELESS HUSSY — Black-haired Madonna-eyed Judy Wallis seems doomed to be the victim of men crazed by her beauty. Three men leave their mark on her soul. Pete, a human beast, Judge Goomer, who reaches out a helping hand, and Kim Bradley, a brilliant young lawyer.

BEDROOM AND BATH — Lovely Val Hendon and her husband Peter were very much in love until sloe-eyed Marta Stokes lied and told Val she had an affair with Peter. For revenge, Val decided to spend a weekend with attractive Donald Raeburn.

With kaflooie like that, and titles like *Swamp Hoyden* and *High Yaller* on the market, R.K. Vail and S.B. Vonier figured it was time for them to set up a 'fiction factory' and turn out some titles of their own. The whole thing will be in lower case, since that's the only way Vonier types . . .

* * *

248

Of News To Scientists

Doctor C.F. Hardy, just before he died, gave The Mag his microscope, a nifty three-power instrument including an oil-immersion lens and tilting stage, made by the Gundlach Optical Company of Rochester, N.Y. It came in a nice wooden case with a lock on it. The doc would want it back if there was a germ warfare or an outbreak of the Black Plague. Otherwise it was The Mag's to keep.

Thus, there were swamp waters to collect and scrutinize, bacteria and diatomacious earths to check, identify and catalogue. There were stab-cultures in agar, molds bred in petri dishes, and Gauer dreamed of buying an autoclave and a centrifuge..

With the scope came a box of Dr. Hardy's prepared slides that he had stained himself while at Johns Hopkins, of disease cells in various poses with human tissue in rich magentas and carmines. Mammy Gauer refused to permit them in the house for a time on the grounds they might be contagious.

The Mag charged 50 cents to examine sperm.

The client got a test tube plugged with a pledget of cotton and was instructed to produce a recent specimen, keep it at body heat, and deliver it to The Lab without delay.

Through the microscope a corps of little organisms could be seen flagellating with long tails through a glycerin-like seminal fluid. All the samples examined demonstrated this activity. For whatever that evidence was worth, namely that they had not died in transit, they earned an official Precision Process Certificate of "Motility" Proof of 'manhood'.

None of the clients were worried about moral questions or 'getting caught', (getting a girl in a family way) - your basic disaster situation. They wanted to be assured they were potent and that they could be a regular Cyranno de Bergerac.

The 50 cents fee included a souvenir microscope slide with the specimen stained gentian violet and with a little round cover glass cemented on for art's sake. A label gave the subject's name and date.

Recipients preserved it carefully, sometimes holding it to the light in a vain hope of seeing the little buggers with the naked eye.

Among the early applicants was a certain physical culture enthusiast in the Bro. Gnormie crowd who showed up with a half-gallon bottle containing an unlikely quantity of fluid.

The Mag and Bro. Gnormie attempted to eject him from the attic while he cried out in protest, with name-calling. He insisted it was his prodigious output and that The Mag should at least give him a decent break and look at the stuff under the microscope. And then, during the struggle with him the bottle broke and it was what the Gauer Bros suspected all along, namely urine, which Mammy Gauer forced him to clean up before it leaked through to the kitchen ceiling below.

The Mag went on to synthesize oil of wintergreen (methyl salicylate), essence of pine-apple (butyric ether), and essence of apply (amyl valerianate), which, being in her former line of work in the candy kitchen, Mammy Gauer could appreciate, not without some distrust, of course, about the purity of the product.

Making industrial diamonds was something else. An electric arc furnace roared in The Lab for a while, consisting of a graphitae cruicible and a carbon rod, which buzzed and snorted, gave off pink and white flame and a lot of oniony ozone smell. The resident scientist had neither the talent nor the money to build a high-voltage transformer, a circumstance to which he probably owed his life, since he suffered enough 110-volt jolts to convince him of his limited capacity to absorb more.

The furnace produced some carbide and a few grains of carborundum, but it fell far short of being a diamond mine. Nor was it a gold mine. The electric bill shot up alarmingly. His plans to construct a roentgen tube to produce X-rays also broke down, again fortunately in view of his cavalier attitude toward shielding himself behind lead. His lack of a pump to produce a vacuum and the dubious uses to which X-rays might be put combined to kibosh the project.

Making neutral grain spirits (ethyl alcohol) was a much more practical activity and met with approval all around. Every fall Mammy Gauer made grape wine in the basement with Mr. Jazdejewski. Not all of it was potable, so The Mag was at liberty to distill some of it to a delicious brandy, hardly realizing with what disfavor the Federal chaps would have looked on the procedure.

With his ethers and esters he transmuted that distillate into "cordials" and "liquers" of various colors and flavors. It took the best part of a day to make a bottle of Precision Process 130-proof artificial applejack (guaranteed free of fuel oil).

It's Springtime!

MEMORIAL DAY was always a period of rejoicing and spring-like capering and the 1939 one was no exception as Sister Alice and The Mag toured the environs, the latter hung with his trusty Voightlander, which did not hinder the jumping up and down and running in the sunshine.

At noon Bro. Vail decided to chloroform himself, with the help of Bro. Blo., Madame Goose and Josephine the Dog. They performed a rabbinical ceremony on some beer bottles and drained off 12 of them. Another doz. were procured and by the time Gauer and Bedard arrived they were prone in front of Vail's phonograph as an uncaged Firebird (Le Oieseu de Feu) had flapped out and was raising hell with the acoustics, Stravinski hot after it with a baton.

During the week warm winds bathed the Brady Street cement and rich stinks came from awakening Nature, but the arrival of spring coincided with the arrival of Capacity Days. The Boston Store said that because Bro. Gauer went to New Orleans with Bro. Bloch, he had technically quit. There was some consultation with the Industrial Commission, and H. Mag worked again. He replenished to a small measure his exhausted pockets.

On his first day off Bros. Ehr and Vail roused a work-weary H. Mag at eight in the morning by arriving in Bro. Hank Ehr's elegant automobile. Bro. Vic, with a catch in his voice as he stuck his head out the window, hollered "Golf!"

Gauer hustled up into the attic to get his spavined bag and supply of surplus clubs and it was a reckless caper onto the Lincoln Park nine-holer to test the dirt. To make a foursome, a grizzled conscript of the war of 1812 joined the trio. He had a stiff back, took a snatchy half-swing at his shiny new ball, and the group was off down the fairway.

Upon return, Bro. Bloch punched in, which made it a foursome again that moved swiftly toward the Bellview Pharmacy, known colloquially as 'The Finkery' Larry LaBorde, who was anything but fink-like, was called Larry Fink anyhow, for the convenience of calling the place

The Finkery, and it was he who was responsible for providing the finest of fountain drinkables.

Bro. LaBorde unravelled super-extra-fine, out-sized, double good Monster Malts, from which the folks sucked eagerly. They were excruciatingly good!

The Finkery was buzzing with talk of a picnic. Who was going, where, and just why, was muffled in an advanced state of apocrypha, but for a week afterward, seekers of the scooped ichor were advised to be at Bro. Vic's early on Sunday. A heated show of indifference developed. Sunday nevertheless dawned.

* * *

Bro. Vail tooled rapidly toward 1210 E. Brady Street and returned with H. Mag and curtly ordered him to produce Sister Alice while he rallied Bro. Bloch. All went to Adam's Tap & Chile parlor to await the coming of the host.

Soon Vin Konig and Margie Tchetch drove up in a Blue Streak. Lawrence A. LaBorde and Mary came in another vehicle, followed by one containing Phil Kestin and Irene, Bro. Dick Ehr and Bro. Wirth in the rumble. Ben Coughlin in a Super Eight also had a cadre of Bellview Rangers including Bro. Vic Ehr and Jean.

Gauer, Bloch, Bedard and Vail piled in where they could and it was off to Whitnall Park.

There was a ball game, then food was got out, supplemented with stuff from the park clubhouse two miles away. The party had split into two camps, the Upper East Siders on the hilltop and the Brady Street contingent down the slope. Bros. Vail and Bloch made a second trip to the clubhouse, 8 miles away.

On the hilltop, Coughlin, in a beautiful popular-tune voice crooned melodies. The people with the swell cars opened their turtles and rumbles and brought forth chilled cokes, sandwiches and cake. Bros. Vail & Bloch made a third trip to the clubhouse, some 12 miles distant.

A car-full at the apex left and was replaced by one driven by Bro. Hank Ehr with his ginch, Ted. Then Bro. Vic, with brown-eyed Jean, came running down the hill to where the Lower East Side Louts were encamped. A card game started. Bro. Gauer started a little fire. The smoke mortally confused the players, notably South, who couldn't see at all. It had also grown overcast and cold.

In Bro. Hank Ehr's car another trip was made to the clubhouse, 22 miles over the horizon, and after that the Afternoon of a Faun (Apres-midt d'un Fink) was over. The group on the hill writhed under blankets. The lower group huddled around a second campfire started by The Mag until a park fire-laddie approached and ordered it extinguished in the name of Chas. Whitnall, Founder of the park.

There was a general exodus. Potato-salad was left behind. The wind whistled, flatulently, as did the HOMEWARD BOUNDERS ...

* * *

Bro. Vic

The Far Pastures
Of July 1939

Madame Goose has moved to the east side and is now a farmilar figure, dropping in at the Cambridge Rental Library to see Bro. Vail, into Bro. Blo's apartment to see Bloch, and into The Lab with charm school graduate Josephine the Dog, to lend variety to the mix.

On Saturday afternoon in the Brady Street Lab (Apres-midi d'un Lab) they were emboldened to drink a half-pint of a beverage distilled five years earlier by H. Mag. from molasses, with results that did little to enhance the reputation of The Thunderbutt Family, holders of the original recipe.

Among the conversation topics developed were (a) How to boil a cardboard ringbaloney, (b) The advantages of hanging a trapeze in the attic, (c) How to play poker without chips, (d) How to shoot craps without dice, and (e) Rabelasian jests and bawdy gossip.

* * *

Mary Louise Bell in the Cambridge Library back room.

Mert Koplin is going to New York to seek his fortune there. He dropped in for a last game of poker and to say goodby. Milt Gelman, also loose because college days were in recess, announced he would become an instructor in athletics at a boy's camp and teach the little snots to pick leeches from between their nasty little toes. Berto Warren will hitch-hike to Door County to pick cherries out of Camp Naked, Shinners Herb will pluck bugs in an entymological bazoo for the Works Progress Administration (WPA) at $90 per dip. Sprague Vonier will be looking into work at the morning newspaper. Bob Vail will continue to prepare books for drug store rental shelves out of the Cambridge Library headquarters on Juneau Avenue.

Marge Christnacht's marriage was attended by Bro. Bloch. She joins the Lohengrinning faces of Clarence Lehr, Robert Blake, Joe Boysa, Carol Davis, and Frank Leibert, wedded blissters of yore.

How The Mag Dammed The Gully Washes
A Tale of Yesteryear

A certain Wayne Dowd, who in 1933 wore a pea-whistle and blew it a lot as the squad leader of Camp Gilmanton when Gauer was a member of the Civilian Conservation Corps (CCC) in the reign of the New Deal, wanted The Mag to attend a Reunion! (o God!) at the Cudworth American Legion Post.

It was not The Mag's inclination to do that and he begged off, but he was put in mind of the Good Old Days when a dollar-a-day-and-all-you-could-eat sounded (at least to Mammy Gauer and Papa Jazdejewski) like a bargain offer.

The Mag did therefore, suffer to be signed up, took "basic training" in a World War army get-up, chopping stumps out of the ground for two weeks

Gauer is toward the left in the 4th row. The Camp Commander is in tan britches in front flanked by two regular army shavetails. Behind them (in white) are the cooks, and at the right end of the front row is Dowd.
Camp Gilmanton. CCC Company 650. July 14, 1933

weeks and then rolled into northwestern Wisconsin to the site of an enormously eroded gullywash along the brink of which Army tents with room for eight army cots were pitched. They were playing *Stormy Weather* a lot then, a tune which still identifies the nighttime lantern-lit company street for the nostalgia-minded Gauer.

CAMP GILMANTON personnel wore U.S. Army fatigues and clodhopper shoes and bounced out in the back of a truck with shovels and axes to deal with farmland erosion. they

did that by constructing concrete retaining dams across gullies the County Surveyor indicated could be saved from eroding further.

That meant hammering together a lot of boards to make forms, anointing them with oil, laying and tying together reinforcing rods, and arranging to flush slops of concrete down sluices.

Gauer participated in that body-building toil until he thought his backside would fall off, and followed that with unrewarding hours of pounding the back-fill with a heavy iron tamper.

6 ACCROSS THE RAVINE IS CAMP GILMANTON

2 COMPANY STREET—CAMP GILMANTON

How he found strength to partake of hardball on the company baseball diamond was not known to sociologists of the era, but he got his share of stolen bases and extra-base hits, did not rupture himself, and ate reconstituted dried eggs, and learned to drink coffee. Up to then The Mag was a milk drinker.

The inmates slept on army folding cots lain with a bag stuffed with straw. Each week there was a parade to the straw pile for new stuffage. The Red Cross provided magazines and each cot had Reader's Digests and Red Books - some had doidy cartoon books -stashed underneath in lumps.

There were eight chaps to the tent, which had a center pole from which pended the owner's barracks bags laden with their personal gear. Side flaps could be rolled up and let down and regular policing of tent ropes and tent stakes was required, as was the area around the tents and the company street. As in the army or in a prison exercise yard, cigarette smokers learned not to discard their butts, but to split the paper off, scatter the grains and roll the paper into a tiny ball.

Goldbricking was something of an art, even in the CCC. The Mag got himself attached to the surveyor's office and went out to hold a stick upright among nettles while his companion peeked at it through a transit. The rest of the time he loafed in an office in the city hall tracing lines with india ink and doing lettering with his formerly shovel-horny hands. The only toilet in the barn-like city hall was a privy at the rear of a dance floor on the second level. Employing that convenience, with its twenty-foot drop, noted Gauer, was awesome.

Along about the time when the army-issue stoves were brought into the tents in preparation for the rigors of winter, The Mag declared himself for discharge, an honorable one was uttered, and he went home, taking along his green army poncho, khaki monkey-jacket, khaki shirt, his good work boots, his black dress tie and his underwear. (The clothes on his back).

HAVING RECOVERED from his reminiscences of the CCC and returned to Present Time, The Mag was confronted with something like the rupturing of a polish sausage in a pot of boiling water - employment with the SCS ! ! ! Or Soil Conservation Service, a dug pendant from the underbelly of the U.S. Dept of Agriculture.

The Federals had their Lab. on the Port Washington Rd. and sucked up river water for use in their photo darkrooms. This was very easy employment for the Precision Process photographer, although the photographic enlargements were made on huge enlargers operated on chain hoists, and the bromide paper exposed was the size of bed sheets, dragged through titanic vats of developer and fixer, One of the Mag's important assignments was to see that the grain of the enlarging paper remained in one direction on all exposures, and that they were fed into the gargantuan pants-pressing arrangement called a print-drying machine with the paper grain in mind.

That was to ensure that the distortion was evenly distributed on those aerial surveys, which draughtsmen would later bedizen with contour lines, elevation marks and other arcane symbolism. (These items would later be used by the air force in the invasion of Normandy.)

The Brady Street scientist earned $5 per day, with full pay for Saturday half-days, at 7 and one half hours per diem, and this was eminently pleasing to the fellow. The boon started on June 8th and ended on July 7th, netting $120 as the fiscal year ended.

FALLING BACK THEN, on his own flourishing business - the Precision Process - The Mag took photos of W. T. Grant Dime Store show windows, of Lucky's orchestra, Milt Gelman & partners on-the-street photo developing, and for Papa Jazdejewski's real estate business, photographed some 75 building and made three prints of each for $18.75 net, a real bargain for The Overlord.

New York Madness

Brother Hank Ehr addressed Bro. Bloch in this fashion: "How about going to New York with me in a month or so?" He was crying out in accents wild over the windshield of his car, which closely resembled that used by Jack LaMonte in blackout sketches at the burlesque, which was made out of cardboard. Then Hank disappeared into Scaler's New York Cabaret for tourist information and was next heard from at the Bellview Finkery. "Ready for New York?" cried Hank. "Well ..." said Bro. Bloch, and it was a deal.

Brother Vail kindly postponed his vacation and cancelled his tennis dates, Hank located New York on a map, pointing out that it lay to the east. That took care of the plans. The car was a 1939 Oldsmobile, which was build in 1929. It was painted a dead red, got 13 miles to the gallon, was easy on the oil, had four good tires ... and its convertible top had been circumcised so thoroughly there was none left.

*WHAT D'YA MEAN,
IT'S CLOSIN' TIME?*

At ten in the morning on Sunday, Hank drove up to Bloch's apartment on Knapp Street in his magnificent vehicle. Brother Bloch emerged resplendent in black riding boots and breeches and a black shirt. Vail arrived in equally natty getup. Hank was nifty in white and sported a yachting cap. Bloch and Vail affected jocky type beaky-caps. Gauer showed up to take the picture and retired again, as he was not going.

The knights Ehr-ant sailed down the street and out onto Hwy 41 in the blazing sun. On the road the idea came up that they should hole up in Chicago for two weeks, send postcards to N.Y. which Bloch's agent would mail to folks in Milwaukee an they would thus be saved all the harm of travel. But Hank stubbornly refused to go along with the scheme and kept driving, in spite of the news that Phil LaBorde, former owner of the Oldsmobile, had laid bets of 5 to 1 that it would never make it to the Illinois state line. They made it as far as Lima Ohio for a tourist stop, and to Uniontown, Pa for another.

Third day. Out of Uniontown, the Cumbersome Mountains, 2000 feet. A flat in Pennsylvania under the broiling sun, causing a woozy feeling in Bro. Bloch. But they made it to Maryland where at Frederic the house of Barbara Frietohie stands. But it had no toilet. By twilight, Washington D.C. loomed across the Potomac and down Pennsylvania Ave. to the Capitol, an inverted white chamber-pot. Outside the Capital, Bloch, after supper began to sweat and bedded down, his fever broke about 4 a.m., he recovered, and at the crack of dawn it was thru the mists to Baltimore. There the car was given a rest an da facial while Bro. Bloch turned green. Baltimore was toured and Bloch turned black. So he was lugged into the presence of a Dr. Johnson.

"Let's see you heave", said the Doc., kindly. He gave Bloch ammonia to drink. "You got low blood pressure and you also got heat-prostration. And fever. Keep out of the sun and drink lots of rye whiskey!"

The fellows went into a Baltimore bar. A 70-year-old bartender with a head like an overripe cantaloup showed Hank a nickel.

"They're gonna call in all these new nickels because there's no flag on the engraving of Jefferson's house!" the guy claimed. Hank squinted dubiously and the bartender said "Here, look thru this microscope!" Hank looked and a big squirt of water hit him in the eye. Hank blinked, looked again, got another squirt. He didn't know what to make of that and took out a cigarette. The bartender supplied the matches. The matches exploded and Hank spilled his drink all over his shirt and the old bird cackled like crazy, slapping the bar with his open palm. That caused the party to leave town.

The sun beat down, Bloch sweat some more, but was felling better. After sleeping in Princeton, lunch came up like thunder out of Newark across the bay. The red car sped in a stream of traffic into Manhattan to the Sloane House YMCA on 34th Street. Vail and Bloch have their shoes shined. It rains. Hank's girl friend, Ted, is in New York at the Taft Hotel and Hank dashes over there.

Julius Schwartz, a literary agent, came by subway to take Bloch and Vail to a tavern and then to supper with Hank in the automat.

Grand Central Station. Penn. Station. Wall Street. Park Avenue. Fifth Avenue. 42nd Street. Broadway. Times Square. Then a subway ride out to the World's Fair to view the symbolic Trylon and Perisphere . . . a real screwball idea. . .

"You ain't goin' in, are ya? cries Hank.

"Naw!" cried Bloch, and they go back to town.

The next day Vail went to a ballgame, Hank Ehr went to Billy Rose' Aquacade. Bloch went to the Weird Tales office where genial Farnsworth W. Wright (sic) was there to greet him. Thence to Standard Magazines where Mort Weisinger waited with outstretched palm. There Bro. Blo. met the fabulous editor off 30 magazines - Leo Margulies, the Pope of Pulpdom.

The next morning was check-out time and the car pounded out past Grant's Tomb, Riverside Drive, thru Central Park, Wall Street, past the Europa and the Bremen at dock, past the Statue of Liberty, into the Bronx, and on through the Catskills.

Rain poured in and the remains of the top were pried out of the back and finally raised. The wind blew it off. They slept just outside Flushing and the next morning did Niagara Falls and by night were in Canada to buy Winchester cigarettes in Ontario Province.

Thence through Michigan to Muskegon at 2 a.m. and in the morning a car ferry across Lake Michigan. Then up the streets of Milwaukee to the Bellview Pharmacy.

Ten days, 2,200 miles, 12 states and the District of Columbia. Bridges, tunnels subways, waterfalls, great lakes, rain storms, heat waves, pocket fuzz. Sixty dollars a piece.

Nice trip.

The Demise of
The Cambridge Library

A Folding

In remote times, early in the dawn of (The) History, the Cambridge Rental Library, located opposite the Knickerbocker Hotel on Milwaukee's east side, distributed books for borrowing at 3 cents per day to drug store stands, hotel lobbies, etc. There was a guy with a truck and some rope to bundle deliveries, and there was someone to mind the store.

After renters had given the volumes a good going over, those roodled speciments, with a big green label ungracefully glued to the inside cover, were offered for sale in the back room at three for a dollar. More expensive or bigger or more popular editions in good shape cost more.

Gradually the boys go to walk right into the back without invitation, as old customers. The library in The Lab festered and swole under that regime.

As the years rolled by, Milt Gelman obtained a job there. It was rumored that a bereft H. Mag also had ambitions to hold that valuable station, but the suspicion was never confirmed. Then a Miss Braun quit and was supplanted by Mary Louise Bell, and Gelman was supplanted by Robert K. Vail, who took over the mop, dust rag and the cover jacket pasting machine.

Bro. Vail took home his $14.85 (15 cents social security deducted) per week, bringing his lunch so he could play tennis at noon, and budgeting his hours so he could get in some golf in the late afternoon, and he twitched with ennui, but something was happening. He became fascinated with books, and with Bros. Bloch and Gauer he waxed bibliophilic. He also tried his hand at writing, listened to the great symphonies. Culture crawled all over and it was extra swell.

But then Mammy Phillipson, owner, sold out. Miss Bell stayed on paid the rent, and remained with the remainders in the basement book bin to operate a retail sales business from there. And Bro. Vail was out on his hinder!

It had been a grand period: Cabell in the Storisende edition, The grapes of Wrath, The Forty Days of Musa Dahg, Hemingway, Dos Pasos, O'Hara, Farrell, Joyce, Waugh, Huxley . . .

Mary Louise Bell and Bro. Vail, employees of the Cambridge Rental Library.

THE BLUE EYE LEAGUE
AT THE ALL-STAR BREAK

HOMBURGS	13	10
FUNGULAS	13	11
MAGS	12	12
HAMMERS	9	14

	T	AB	H	Hr	3b	2b	RBI	Pct.
Studs NOOKY	H	100	39	6	4	9	24	.390
Osw DRIZZLEDRA'S	F	89	34	3	5	4	17	.382
Feckless FURDY	H	103	39	5	6	6	16	.378
Sam LAPIDUS	F	107	40	8	9	5	29	.373
Pos WASSERMANN	F	102	37	6	4	10	19	.362
Count L d'FOTCH	F	92	33	3	4	7	15	.358
Frank FLUMEY	V	101	36	6	9	10	22	.356
F.W.WRIGHT	H	88	31	8	4	4	17	.352
Rookie Joe VET	H	100	35	3	5	7	14	.350
Yad DREEMBUGGER	F	46	16	2	4	2	6	.347
Shorty DOOGE	V	91	31	5	8	3	18	.340
Wally WANGER	H	92	31	8	8	7	32	.336
Barg. SMALLHOUSE	V	90	30	3	4	3	18	.333
LIVERLIPS	V	99	32	5	5	8	17	.323
Milt T BIGSCORE	V	97	31	4	4	5	15	.319
P Gr STAFOONGE	M	97	31	6	5	3	14	.319
Frac W MELEFIGHT	M	91	28	6	2	8	17	.307
Hotfoot O OUCH	M	98	30	3	4	7	12	.306
Joe BUSTAGUT	V	71	21	4	1	1	13	.295
MAHARAJAH	F	106	31	1	6	8	18	.292
Tubal SCROTUS	M	89	26	3	4	4	11	.292
Stab FITSNOODLE	M	105	30	5	6	5	19	.285
Potsy KOOMBACHER	H	89	25	9	2	4	22	.280
Buster BLADDER	V	90	25	3	12	2	19	.277
H L SHAWOWSKY	F	112	31	4	5	5	14	.276
G SPOOLDRIPPER	M	88	24	6	4	4	18	.272
Bishop SHAPIRO	F	103	28	5	4	1	19	.271
Tad ODD	H	96	25	2	4	6	17	.270
GooGoo GOOFSTICH	M	96	26	1	8	1	12	.270
Billy MINSKY	H	98	23	5	4	4	14	.261
Black TOM	V	79	20	5	3	1	17	.253
Fosc RUPTURED	M	95	23	4	2	4	15	.242

Prince of The Finkery

Lawrence LaBorde, long known as Larry Fink the Malted Milk Man, continues to pull the dugs of human kindness at the pharmacy on Bellview & Downer.

He supplies The Mag's aching gut with large vats of melting slush called milk shakes, and Vail's aching soul with hot fudges with butter-pecan ice cream, and Bro. Blochs' passion for double-chocolate malts, and delights to pass the lips of Sister Alice.

In addition to which LaBorde has become an inspired comic with historically significant buffonery.

Example: Upon suffering the arrogant entry of snotty cub scouts dragging a snow-slopped toboggan into the store behind them he did plunge his throwing hand, observers swear, into the vat behind the fountain and pelt them unmercifully with gobs of raspberry fudge ice cream.

It is related that he would grab a double handful of rubber condoms in a fit of windmill jeepers, and throw them into the air behind the cash register with cries of "Whoopee!"

Nor was he loath to furtively secrete into certain soda fountain confections, a pharmaceutical substance that turned the urine an emerald green. He did likewise, they say, mutter mild insults and oaths to deaf old ladies who came in for the service of a postage stamp and the service of a glass of water. Persons overhearing that would fall down and suffer spasms.

BRO ART TOPPEL
A Member of the Supporting Cast
A scoop-artist at the Bellview
And A Friend Of Man

Doctor Doolittle's Circus

(With Apologies To Hugh Lofting)

LIGHTS OUT is a well-known suspense series on radio originating out of Chicago. Bro. Bloch was approached to do a script for it by (ta da ...!!) ...

JAMES DOOLITTLE

He is an uptown boy, WISN-radio announcer, Orchestra leader and zephyr king. He invited Bro. Bloch to write one of the shows. He had connections and would place it.

Bro. Bloch wrote a script for a Lights Out show, on spec.

So what happened? Well, Lights Out FOLDED! That's what happened! O God!

But Bro. Doolittle visited the Brady Street Lab with a cardboard microphone and fonny peetchas were had, plus conversations, and exchange of interesting books, and laffing.

Bro. Doo then spoke in hushed tones about a very secret proposition. Further discussion of it would have to take place at the Milwaukee Athletic Club, where Bro. Doo's father, E.G. Doo, was Manager. Bro. Doo got leader money playing a dance orchestra (under Pap Doo's aegis) on Saturday nights at the Club. (Not to be confused with Colla's Five & Dime Tap, also called The Club). This was some classy layout.

The meeting came to pass, Doolittle Pere and others at the MAC programmed hearty ha-has and hoo-has over the funny peetchas. Bro. Doo confided to Bloch & Gauer that a "deal" for both of them was afoot, details to be announced. They should hold their water. Since they were in no position to quibble about cardboard propositions or speculative ventures into the unknown, they held it.

DOCTOR DOOLITTLE'S ROADSHOW
or
The Wizard of Quiz

UNFORTUNATELY, early in October, 1939, Bro. Jas. Doo blew town. He took a job with WSAU-Radio in Wausau, (Wis.). But not long after that, he had another proposition.

Bro. Doo had spoken to Johnny Olson, who had seen Bloch's *Mr. Zero* script and had spoken to sponsors about it, and they like it! And also, Bro. Doo had been in Wausau only two weeks and already he had four commercial shows. The biggest was the MERRILL HOUR (named after Merrill, Wis) on the stage of the Badger Theater in (ah) Merrill. It was on the air every Tuesday night with Uncle Jim Doolittle as *The Wizard of Quiz!*

Bro. Doo wanted The Authors to bring his car up to Wausau for him. It was in storage in Milwaukee. They were urged to resurrect the vehicle, change the oil grease it, water it, and check the tires. . . "I will pay all expenses!" Bro. Doo quoted himself as saying in a letter marked "Big Score!"

The Authors blithely located the car, a monster Cord Roadster with an enormous snout on it, a two-seater with white tires. H. Mag. Gauer undertook the mechanics himself. Twelve quarts of oil went into the bloated guts of the juggernaut. Pounds of grease. The tank was engorged to its full capacity of 26 gallons of gasoline. It cost $8.37

After stocking the human crankcases with monster Finkery malts late in the evening, it was off in a cloud for Wausau. After driving for about an hour, H. Mag. stopped and got out and stepped to the rear where he blew his lunch, including not only the malt but some other stuff that had been lingering there, over 12 acres in Ozaukee County. Refreshed, he got back in and the journey continued.

* * *

IN WAUSAU, Bro. Doo was home to the number of not. He was already breakfasted and at work at the station. The Authors went there and Bro. Doo found it hard to grab loose of his various duties an the men flattened their podexes as he changed records and announced jazz numbers. After lunch they waited some more and at dinner Doris, Bro. Doo's wife, outdid herself pabulating hearty fare and tasty biscuits. It looked like Bro. Doo would be in Wausau for at least two more months. Right then, however, they had to hustle 20 miles down the pike to make the Merrill Hour in Merrill!

There was a band on stage, and a singer, and Professor Quiz read the advertising messages into the microphone and they were giving away packaged items and canned goods for it was Grocery Nite on the Merrill Hour.

Bro. Doo also scampered out to a squeal of feedback to announce that Mr. Bloch and Mr. Gauer had come all the way from Milwaukee to hear the show! They were the authors of the Light's Out show in Chicago!

Bro. Gauer cringed as the shot skinned past him and splattered against the far proscenium. And having thus excreted thru his vocal chords, the Wizard of Quiz went on toe challenge local yokelry as aides passed out bags of food. It was pretty fierce.

Back to Wausau, and FINALLY, Bro. Doo came out with it. The hinder-weary travelers

The Merrill Hour Quiz Master

were ready to catch a train to the big city and in the privacy of the depot, Bro. Doo revealed that he was on to something important to the futures of all and it was very hush-hush at the moment!

The Authors glanced around conspiratorially and scratched their fundaments, wondering whatinhell The Wizard was talking about.

"I have gone so far as to make an appointment for you boys to see a Very Important Person! Your presence will be very much needed in Milwaukee. When you talk to him you will understand why I made this unexpected move. I'll be there, its at The Club, but I can't stay. You'll be on your own!

"Does this have something to do with writing another script" Bro. Blo quizzed the Question Man.

"No, no, it has nothing to do with that!"

Well, WHAT, then?

The Author's eyes rolled back in their heads so only the whites showed as they awaited the Words of Revelation. And they could hear The Hiawatha rolling into the train shed.

"How would you guys like to create a political campaign and run a guy for Mayor?"

"Gack!" said Gauer

"Urr!" said Bloch

They grabbed their sacks and ran for the train.

"We'll letcha know!" they cried.

Bro. Doo made burping noises on his 8-miles-to-the-gallon Cord Roadster and tooted back home.

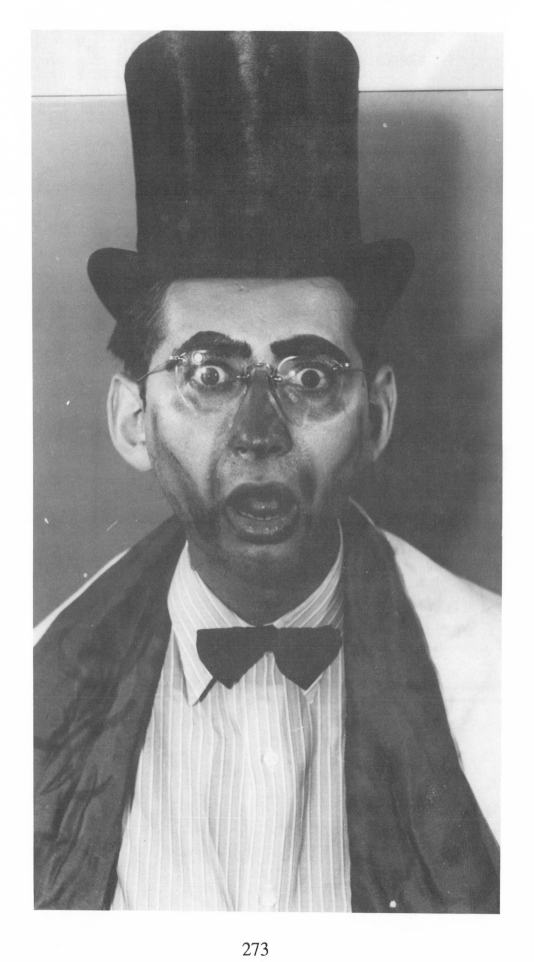

273

Departure From Volume One

WITH THE ADVENT of The Authors into politics, the normal course of life on Brady Street abruptly ceased. The History becomes blended in a larger kind of telling and the old ways are no more.

Nor are the old days the same, either. There are madmen raising hell in Europe, particularly Aloph Hitler and Benito Mussolini, and in their evil aura, the Great Depression may be getting less downcast. And besides, the end of a decade is at hand. That should count for something.

As Oswald Spengler observed in his decline of the West:

"On the surface of history it is the unforeseen that reigns. Every individual event, decision and personality is stamped with its hallmark. No one foresaw the storm of Islam at the coming of Mohammed, nor foresaw Napoleon in the fall of Robespierre. The coming of great men, their doings, their fortune, all are incalculables. No one knows whether a development that is setting in powerfully will accomplish its course in a straight line like that of the Roman patrician order or will go down in doom like that of the Hohenstaufen."

Unquote. An so it was with the coming of Carl Zeidler to be a candidate for the office of Mayor in Milwaukee, with The Authors of THE HISTORY as his speech writers, strategists, and the sole source of his campaign material !

BUT THE TELLING of the unforeseen that reigned and both the coming of a patrician order and the going down in doom of the Hohenstaufen - in the matter of the rise of King Carl and the downfall of Socialism, must be left to
VOLUME TWO
Of This Continuing Saga

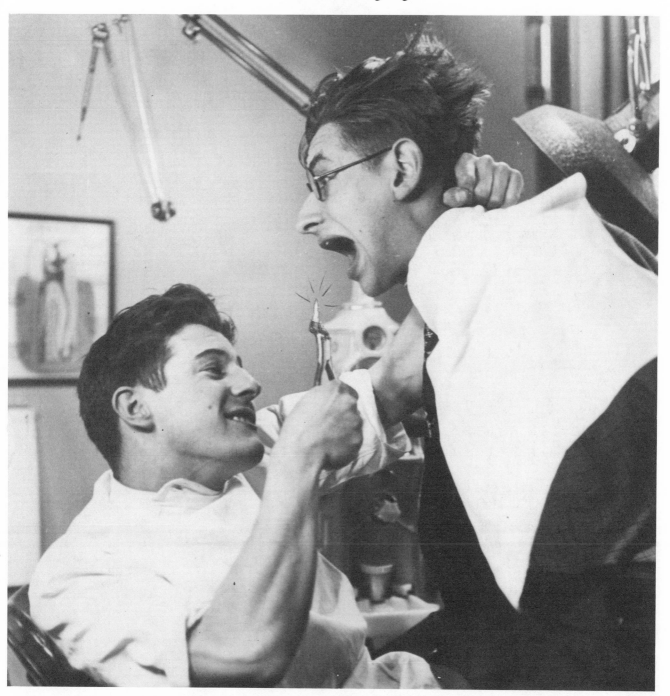

WHICH HAS TO COME OUT SOMETIME!

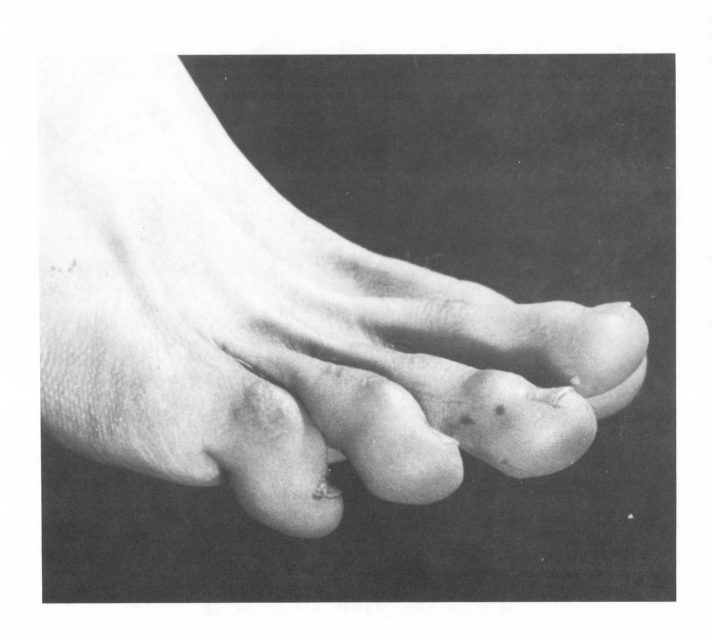

AN AFTERWORD ABOUT
THE HISTORY
(And Its Preservation)

There is more to this thing than just Volume One.

Volume Two is in preparation. It will cover events during the first few years of the 1940s. But The History stretches on = through the '40s, into the '50s and the '60s.

There are at least ten more volumes of this same kind of material waiting to be published.

If they are not published, they will perish. None of us can count on living forever. While there is yet time, a fund should be set up to get them edited and into print.

It would be nice if kind souls would, in spite of its not being tax-deductible, make substantial supporting contributions to the Precision Process Historical Preservation Fund, at the address found at the front of this book.